TRUE CRIME
STORIES

TRUE CRIME
STORIES

50 HEADLINE-GRABBING MURDERS
FROM AROUND THE WORLD

MAX HAINES

BARNES & NOBLE BOOKS
NEW YORK

Contents

Assorted Wives

Throughout the checkered history of crime we often come across gentlemen who favour having more than one wife at a time. Some insist on having two. Then there are those rare birds who positively cannot do without several. Some of these gentlemen have the temperament and indeed the capacity to love all their wives dearly. But, alas, there are those rascals who just don't give a damn one way or the other.

Arthur Goslett was a rascal. Using the name Captain Arthur Godfrey (no connection whatever with the late television personality of the same name) he operated during the First World War in England. Resplendent in the glamorous uniform of a naval officer, the captain carried himself with that arrogant air so common to con artists and bigamists. Despite the uniform, the captain left a lot to be desired in the looks department. His face was marked by a constant scowl, which gave him a mean appearance. This, coupled with a pair of eyes that appeared too small for the rest of his face, produced a sinister impression. But Casanova was not known for his looks either.

By 1918 the dashing captain had gone through so many marriages that, later on, investigating officers gave up counting. It is only necessary for us to realize that, despite all his marriages, Arthur had a bona fide wife alive and well and living in Armitage Mansions, Golders Green, London.

Mrs. Goslett wasn't exactly ignorant of her husband's activities. Some time earlier she had discovered one of Arthur's bigamous alliances and had seen to it that he was thrown into jail for his indiscretion. Arthur had learned his lesson and was now a dutiful husband, or so Mrs. Goslett thought. In fact, the brief jail term only served to revitalize Arthur's amorous tendencies.

In 1918 a lady named Daisy Holt ventured upon the scene. That is to say, she bumped into the captain one day on the street. Apologetic, pleasant, and charming, the captain insisted on accompanying her to her sparsely furnished room. In a few months Daisy, with a decided degree of apprehension, advised the captain, whom she believed to be single, that she was pregnant. Daisy requested one thing and one thing only. Would the dear captain marry her and live happily ever after? Poor Daisy didn't know it, but she was speaking to one of the most married men of all time. Arthur consented without a whimper. What was one marriage more or less, anyway? The phony ceremony was performed in February 1919.

Captain and Mrs. Godfrey took a flat in the Kew District of London. But, alas, the condition of pregnancy did not agree with Daisy. She became so ill she had to spend some time in a nursing home before giving birth to a boy.

Upon being discharged from the nursing home Daisy was chagrined to discover that the captain had given up their flat. There she was, barefoot and no longer pregnant, with no place to live. When faced with this embarrassing situation the captain confessed that his real name was Goslett, not Godfrey, and that there was a Mrs. Goslett and three tiny Gosletts.

The captain had a great idea. Why shouldn't Daisy and the new addition move in with Mrs. Goslett and the three children? It would be simple. Arthur's wife had never met his brother Percy or Percy's wife. Percy had recently died. Daisy could pose as Percy's wife and all six could live happily under one roof.

At first Daisy would have nothing to do with such a wild scheme, but the captain was quick to point out that she didn't have many options. Daisy decided to give it a whirl. Dressed in mourning black, she was accepted by Mrs. Goslett without question.

Daisy at this time refused to have intercourse with the captain, and securely fastened her bedroom door each evening. This annoyed the captain, but things could be worse. For one thing, Mrs. Goslett and Daisy got along famously. In fact, Mrs. Goslett became decidedly fond of her kind, helpful sister-in-law.

Then one day, an old acquaintance recognized Daisy on the street as Captain Godfrey's wife. When she heard her addressed as Mrs. Percy Goslett she smelled a rat. Busybody that she was, she called on the captain's wife and informed her of her suspicions. Mrs. Goslett's reaction was a surprise. She was sympathetic to the plight of Daisy and her baby, but insisted that Daisy find a room elsewhere.

The captain was furious. Now that the truth was known, what would be so terrible if the present arrangements were to continue? You can say what you will about Captain Arthur, but he did have gall. Of course, Mrs. Goslett had the upper hand, for she could always holler bigamy and have Arthur tossed into jail. Besides, Arthur had a bit of a secret. Throwing caution to the wind, he had gone out and acquired a third wife.

He promised his first wife that he would spend some time looking for suitable quarters for Daisy and her baby. Although most of Arthur's waking moments and, we can only assume, some of his sleeping ones as well, were spent on affairs sexual, his mind now turned to murder. It was obvious that his one legitimate wife was spoiling all his fun. Mrs. Goslett had to go.

On the pretense of looking at a new home, Arthur and his wife headed for Hendon at 9:30 on the evening of May 1, 1920. The captain returned home alone about an hour later. Mrs. Goslett didn't come home to sleep that night.

Next day a man and his son were sailing their model boat on the Brent River. They discovered the body of a woman floating face downward in the water. The body was identified as Mrs. Goslett. She had been beaten unconscious and thrown into the water.

When informed of his loss, Arthur took the normally traumatic news with unusual calm. The police became suspicious when he couldn't explain the fact that he had made no attempt to find his wife, although she had never stayed out all night before. Police searched the Goslett home and found the shirt Arthur had worn the previous night. It was blood-spattered. They also found his dead wife's earrings, brooch, and handbag, all of which had been in her possession when she was killed.

Arthur confessed to killing his wife. Nasty man that he was, he endeavoured to incriminate Daisy Holt, as if that unfortunate lady didn't have enough problems. Daisy was able to prove that she had had no idea Arthur intended to kill his wife.

Arthur's confession, which was read in court, follows in part:

I was called a coward by Daisy Holt, and she said that if I didn't kill my wife, then someone would kill me. I kept putting her off, but she dared me and said: "There are plenty of places by the river. I suggest you propose taking her to see a house, stun her, and throw her in."

Down by the river I struck her three or four blows. I took the jewellery, and kissed the hand with the wedding ring on, and said I was sorry, and then slung her overboard. I picked up the things and ran home.

The best Arthur's defence attorneys could do was to try to prove that their client was insane. The jury felt that Arthur wasn't insane, just mean. They quickly found him guilty.

Affairs of the heart sometimes defy explanation. As the amorous captain was led from the Old Bailey, one young lady was seen nearby, sobbing uncontrollably. She was the last person to visit the rascal before he was hanged in Pentonville Prison. She was, of course, his third wife.

Arthur, Beatrice, and Mummie

A rthur Devereux was weird, but he didn't look or act the part. Quite the contrary. Art was a slim, good-looking chemist's assistant who had the ability to turn a young lady's fancy to unladylike actions. Art could charm the birds out of the trees.

One of the birds who came tumbling out was pretty Beatrice Gregory. Beatrice and her Mummie were vacationing in Hastings, England (famous for 1066 and all that) in 1898, when it was Beatrice's dubious fortune to accidentally meet Art. Beatrice fell madly in love and it appears at the outset that Art reciprocated. Despite Mummie's mild objections (for she too thought Art was something of a catch), the couple were married after knowing each other only a few months.

The bloom was soon off the rose. For one thing there was the practical problem of not enough income to provide for anything more than the bare necessities. Then there was Art's attitude. No sooner had the minister blessed the union than Art became a gruff, inattentive companion. To add to the couple's precarious predicament Beatrice found herself, as they used to say, "heavy laden with child."

The arrival of little Stanley only added to the family's financial difficulties. Art tried changing jobs. The Devereux family moved to

London. They moved several times, but nothing seemed to change their bad luck. Art began to hate Beatrice, feeling that she was the focal point of all the ill fortune he was enduring. He heaped abuse and insults upon his wife. At the same time, he was abnormally fond of his son Stanley. Nothing was too good for little Stanley. All Art's future plans revolved around his son.

When Beatrice informed Art that she was again pregnant, he became downright nasty. She gave birth to twins. Just as Art had eyes only for Stanley, so Beatrice's affection was turned towards the twins. This directional split of parental affection did nothing to cement relations between the mother and father.

Art now had three individuals to hate instead of one. The grey matter that he employed at the chemist's shop was now almost exclusively occupied with thoughts of his deep-rooted hatred for his wife and the twins. If there were only himself and Stanley everything would be just fine. His income would take care of the two of them adequately. It wasn't his fault that it couldn't be stretched to handle five.

Art had a solution. The first thing he did was to purchase a large trunk. Of all the things Beatrice needed around her sparsely furnished flat, the last thing was a trunk. She meekly inquired as to the wisdom of the purchase. Art replied that he planned to use it for storage of some things that were getting in the way lately. Beatrice refrained from further questions. She had long since acquired the habit of stopping short of arousing Art's trigger temper.

The following evening Art returned from the chemist shop with a bottle of tonic he had promised Beatrice. Unknown to his family he had spiked the tonic with lethal doses of morphine. Beatrice and the twins took large quantities of the spiked tonic. Before retiring for the night Art placed the three bodies into the new trunk.

The next morning Art awoke bright and early. After making a substantial breakfast for himself and Stanley, Art went to Kensal Rise and

7

made arrangements with a moving and storage company to pick up the trunk. He explained that he would be away for some time and wanted the trunk stored for several months. The same afternoon the trunk was picked up.

Art then moved out of his flat and took new lodgings in another part of London. He quit his job and got another. He enrolled Stanley in a private school. Beatrice and the twins were out of sight and out of mind. Art and Stanley were on the threshold of a new life.

Meanwhile, Beatrice's mother, Mrs. Gregory, couldn't locate her daughter. It appeared to her that the entire family had fallen off the face of the earth. After several weeks she managed to trace Art and was amazed that Beatrice and the twins were not with him. Art gave his mother-in-law a story about Beatrice and the twins being in the country, but he wouldn't give her any address.

Mrs. Gregory left the flat and made discreet inquiries around the old neighbourhood. The only unusual thing that had happened was the removal of a large trunk just before Art had changed addresses. Industrious Mrs. Gregory traced down the moving company, went down to their premises, and demanded that the trunk be opened. She then discovered where Beatrice and the twins had been all the time.

Inspector Pollard of Scotland Yard showed up at Art's flat, but the bird had flown. He knew that it was just a matter of time before his mother-in-law traced the trunk. Art settled in Coventry and once again gained employment as a chemist's assistant. Pollard knew that Art would sooner or later seek employment in order to support himself and Stanley. His men were being informed of all applicants for positions in chemists' shops. In this way Pollard was advised of Art's whereabouts.

The Inspector walked into Art's new place of employment and introduced himself. His quarry's first words were, "I don't know anything about a trunk." Inspector Pollard knew he had his man.

Art was arrested and charged with murder. At his trial at London's

Old Bailey he claimed that his wife had killed the twins and then committed suicide. When he discovered the bodies he claimed that he had placed them in the trunk, knowing that no one would believe that he had not murdered them. Art was right about one thing—no one believed him. The Crown produced telegrams proving that Art had applied for a new job before Beatrice's death. In his telegram he described himself as a widower with one child.

Arthur Devereux was sentenced to be hanged. The day the sentence was passed in the Old Bailey, a middle-aged lady clutched a seven-year-old boy's hand firmly in her own. Mrs. Gregory and her grandson Stanley were all alone.

He Blew Up His Mother

In 1980 John Wayne Gacy was convicted of murdering thirty-three young men and boys, thereby becoming the most prolific mass murderer in U.S. criminal history. Twenty-five years earlier another citizen of the U.S. actually murdered a larger number than Gacy. Only a technicality deprived this earlier day monster from being the all-time champ.

John Gilbert Graham first saw the light of day in 1932 in Denver, Colorado. His father passed away when he was only five years old. Left destitute, Jack's mother Daisy had little choice but to place her son in an orphanage, where he remained for six years. In 1943 Mrs. Graham remarried a wealthy rancher, John Earl King, and brought her eleven-year-old son to his new home. For a while he was joined by his sister, who later moved to Alaska.

Jack was not a contented child. While he got high marks, he never really showed any interest in school work. He is mainly remembered for an explosive temper, which could flare up at the slightest provocation. When Jack didn't get his way he ran away from home. At the age of sixteen he lied about his age to join the Coast Guard. Nine months later his deception was uncovered and he was dismissed from the service.

Jack returned to Denver and found a job, but quickly succeeded in getting into trouble. He stole several of his company's blank cheques, forged the name of one of the company's directors, and cashed $4,200 of the bogus paper. With the proceeds he travelled to Texas, where he became a bootlegger. He was apprehended, and after serving a few months in jail was returned to Colorado to face forgery charges. Daisy King stepped in and made restitution in the amount of $2,500, with the firm promise that her son would pay off the balance of $1,700 in installments.

Jack secured work in a garage, married pretty Gloria Elson, and for a while seemed to settle down. The attractive young couple promptly had two children. Daisy doted over her grandchildren.

In 1954 tragedy once again entered Daisy King's life. Her husband Earl died. This time Daisy was left with a comfortable fortune. She decided that her wayward son would reform if given a proper opportunity. Daisy presented Jack with a new home. She would live with her son and daughter-in-law, but the house was in his name. Daisy had also found a drive-in restaurant, which she purchased for $35,000, and asked Jack to run it. No son could ask more of a mother.

But things just didn't work out. Jack always seemed to be short of cash at the end of the day. Daisy couldn't understand how a twenty-three-year-old intelligent boy could not manage to balance his cash with his cash register tapes. Mother and son began to argue over the operation of the restaurant. To relieve the tension, Daisy decided to visit her daughter in Alaska. During October of 1955 she bought Christmas presents to take North.

On November 1, Jack and Gloria, accompanied by their two children, drove Daisy to the airport. Daisy was catching Flight 629 for the first leg of her trip to Alaska. There was a slight delay at the weigh-in counter when it was discovered that her luggage was in excess of the allowable weight of sixty-six pounds. She was over by thirty-seven pounds. When an attendant was told that one suitcase contained Christmas presents he suggested that those items could be mailed a lot cheaper than the twenty-seven dollars he had to charge. Jack would hear none of it. He talked his mother into paying the twenty-seven dollars.

It is to be remembered that there were no security measures at airports in the 1950s, but insurance was available from vending machines. Jack sauntered over to the machines and popped in quarters. You could buy $6,250 protection for a quarter. Jack bought several policies, totalling $87,500. His mother joked with him as she signed the policies.

Daisy hugged her grandchildren, kissed her daughter-in-law, and clasped her son to her bosom. Flight 629 took off. Before the Graham family was out of the airport word was received that the DC6B had exploded in mid air. There were no survivors. A total of forty-four men, women, and children had perished. Among them was Mrs. Daisy King.

The F.B.I. lab in Washington quickly ascertained that the plane had been blown up by dynamite. Traces of sodium nitrate and sodium carbonate were found in the gaping torn metal believed to be the location of the internal explosion. The huge hole was located in the baggage compartment.

Authorities could not locate the baggage of one Daisy King, leading them to believe that her luggage may have contained the dynamite. They did find Daisy's handbag, which had been carried aboard the ill-fated plane. In it they found newspaper clippings concerning her son, Jack Graham, who four years earlier had been sought by Denver police as a forgery suspect. F.B.I. agents dug into Jack Graham's life and discovered that he had a penchant for getting into trouble with the law.

Nine days after the disaster F.B.I. agents knocked on Jack's door. He denied any knowledge of the crime. A search of his home uncovered a roll of wire used in connecting up dynamite. Agents also discovered gaily wrapped Christmas presents. Had Jack, unknown to his mother, substituted a dynamite bomb in place of the presents?

After three hours of questioning Jack Graham calmly changed his story and confessed to perpetrating the horrendous crime. He told the F.B.I. of actually working as an apprentice electrician for ten days so that he could manufacture the bomb without blowing himself up. He had bought twenty-five sticks of dynamite and all the accessories to construct the bomb. Later clerks in hardware stores identified him as the purchaser of these supplies.

Jack Graham stood trial for the murder of his mother only, thereby escaping the historical notoriety of becoming the greatest convicted mass murderer in U.S. history. After deliberating only an hour and a half, a jury found him guilty of murder in the first degree.

Graham was one of the coolest men ever to be executed. A few days before his date with death he reminded a guard, "If any mail comes for me after next month you can readdress it to hell." On January 11, 1957, he calmly entered Colorado's gas chamber, inhaled deeply, lost consciousness, and was pronounced dead twelve minutes later.

Ronald Killed His Wife

Every country has its celebrated murder case—one that becomes indelibly identified with the country in which it was perpetrated. The United States has contributed the Lindbergh kidnapping. Canada produced Albert Guay, while among its galaxy of infamous cases, England's Jack the Ripper stands above the rest. South Africa has given us more than its fair share of unusual cases, but for sheer intrigue and speculation the one case that rises above all the others is the Cohen case.

Isidore Cohen, like thousands of other refugees, fled from Lithuania to escape the oppressive yoke of Czarist Russia. These young men who left Russia before World War I made new lives for themselves wherever they settled. Many eventually had a great influence on their adopted lands in the fields of culture, the arts, and commerce.

Isidore Cohen landed in South Africa at the age of sixteen. He soon mastered the language and opened a small furniture shop in Cape Town. The store flourished. Isidore correctly deduced that the bulging city would expand along the Atlantic seaboard. The sand-covered bushland was considered almost worthless to everyone but Cohen. He invested heavily in the land, gradually gaining ownership of virtually all of Camps Bay, then almost a desert situated about five miles from Cape Town. When Isidore's property was turned into an entire suburb and resort area, land values soared. Cohen became a multi-millionaire.

Isidore married, and sired one son, Ronald. Because he was a self-made man, he insisted that his son make his own mark in life. His boy would be given every opportunity but he would have to make his own fortune. There would be no handouts.

Ronald attended Rondebosch Boys' High School, one of the best schools in Cape Town. He lived with his mother and father in a large, luxurious home in Kenilworth. After attending the University of Cape Town, Ronald, then twenty-five, took a trip to visit a relative in Paris. There he met Marlit Brand, an attractive Hungarian refugee. Ronald and Marlit were married in September 1954. Four years later the couple were divorced. Marlit left Ronald's life as suddenly as she had entered it.

In 1961 Ronald Cohen met beautiful Susan Jonson. He was thirty-two and Susan was seventeen. The pair fell madly in love and wanted to marry immediately. Susan's parents urged Ronald to wait a year until Susan was eighteen. Then, if the lovers felt the same way about each other, they would receive the Jonsons' blessing.

While Ronald was active in affairs of the heart, so too was he busy in the world of commerce. He started out as a clerk in a hardware store, but quickly rose to become an executive of the firm. He branched out until he owned Fletcher and Cartwrights, one of Cape Town's leading department stores. Soon Ronald Cohen's business empire included over a dozen different profitable enterprises. Like his father before him, Ronald became a multi-millionaire while still a young man.

Ronald and Susan were married, and in 1966 Susan gave birth to a son. Unfortunately this child was the victim of an accident, strangling himself in his crib less than a year later.

The Cohens took the death of their son extremely hard, but little by little the pain of their loss subsided. Ronald threw himself into his various business enterprises, becoming a bona fide workaholic. Eventually the Cohens had two more children, who were adored by their parents.

Ronald built one of the finest homes in Cape Town, if not in all of South Africa. Situated on Monterey Drive, it was a huge, sumptuously furnished Spanish-Moorish showplace, equipped with a swimming pool and Persian rugs. Lush formal gardens surrounded the house. Besides Susan, the home was run by a housekeeper-governess, Miss Yvonne Merry, two servants, and a full-time gardener.

The Cohens, with their lovely home, lovely children, and lovely millions, were a devoted, happy couple until the night of April 5, 1970. Miss Merry had gone to bed early. The other servants were asleep in their quarters. Suddenly, Miss Merry, who was lying in bed reading a book, heard Mr. Cohen shouting, "Yvonne! Yvonne! Come quickly." Ronald Cohen appeared in the doorway of her unlocked bedroom. His shirt was covered with blood. "Come quickly," he urged the startled governess. "Someone has broken in."

Once in the library, Cohen kneeled beside his fallen wife. Miss Merry noticed with horror that Susan Cohen's head had been crushed. Her nose was a pulpy mass and her jaw had been fractured. Susan had taken a blow behind the right ear with such force that it had nearly severed the ear. Miss Merry made a mental note that the door leading from the library to the terrace was open. Rain was falling outside. Cohen instructed the governess to call the police and then gather up the two children, Jonathan and Jacqueline. Under Cohen's direction, Miss Merry ushered the children into a powder room, the only room in the house without windows. Cohen was obviously afraid that the attacker was still prowling about outside.

The police arrived, and after examining the murder scene, questioned the grief stricken husband. Ronald told the investigating officers that he and his wife had been relaxing in the library earlier that evening. He excused himself and left to use the bathroom. When he returned his wife was struggling in the middle of the room with a blond stranger. Ronald described the intruder as being between twenty-seven and thirty years old, with hollow cheeks, blond hair, and dressed in tan sportswear. Beside himself with a mixture of fear and anger, Ronald grabbed a bronze sculpted ram's head and raced towards the struggling pair. Cohen, surprisingly enough, could not say whether or not he had struck his wife's assailant with the bronze statue. In fact, he could only tell the police that the next thing he remembered was regaining consciousness and finding his wife's body behind a couch.

It was a rather unsatisfactory explanation of a life and death struggle. When questioned about the condition of the stranger's hands, Cohen quickly added that he was wearing gloves. Other than a blood-spattered rug and one overturned chair, the library showed little evidence of a struggle having taken place there. Cohen's arms were badly scratched. He claimed that his wife had inflicted the scratches by mistake during the hectic struggle.

The open door leading from the library to the terrace and gardens beyond was the only way the attacker could have gained entrance to the Cohen home. Police thought the grounds should have shown some evidence of an intruder because the area around the terrace was soft mud. Yet no footprint or scuff marks were found. Someone entering the library would surely have muddy feet. No evidence of mud or dirt was found on the library rug.

Police did not believe there had been an intruder. Ronald Cohen was arrested and charged with the murder of his wife.

While out on bail Cohen had an unnerving experience, or at least he claimed he did. After visiting a tailor in downtown Cape Town, he said he spotted his wife's killer on the street. The killer saw Cohen at precisely the same moment and took off. Cohen gave chase, but lost the man in the crowd. Having lost track of his quarry he asked an elderly lady if she had seen a blond man dash past. The lady answered in the

17

affirmative and directed Cohen up Adderley Street. Later, despite advertising for the lady to come forward, Cohen was unable to locate her, and thus lost his one opportunity to prove his story was true.

Cohen later commissioned an artist to paint a picture of the killer from his description. He had the painting widely distributed and offered a substantial reward, but the man in the painting was never located.

On August 24, 1970 Ronald Cohen's murder trial opened in Cape Town. It was one of the most publicized trials ever to take place in South Africa. The entire case boiled down to one question: Was Cohen's story of an intruder to be believed, or did he kill his wife and invent the story to avoid punishment?

The presiding judge stated that, taking all the circumstantial evidence in its totality, he could come to no other conclusion than to find Cohen guilty. He added that in his judgement the crime was not premeditated.

At the time, the punishment for murder in South Africa was death, unless there were extenuating circumstances. The defence lawyers only had a few days to come up with extenuating circumstances in order to save their client's life. This was no easy task, since Cohen still insisted that he was innocent. Despite this, Cohen's lawyers brought forth psychiatrists who had examined Cohen and found him to be a responsible person whose life was predicated by rules and regulations, which he followed to the letter. As the crime wasn't premeditated, they felt that something had happened in the library that night which compelled Cohen to strike out. As one of them put it: "The ferocity of the attack is indicative of a gross disorganization of his personality. It becomes highly probable that this feral behaviour was unleashed by a sudden confrontation with a catastrophic stimulus. All the actions which occurred during this assault emanated from a person in a state of lowered responsibility."

The judge was greatly influenced by the psychiatrists' reports. Had

Cohen wanted to plan his wife's murder he had a gun readily available in his home. Cohen received a sentence of twelve years' imprisonment, which everyone agreed was a far cry from the gallows.

We will never know for sure what happened in the Cohens' library on that rainy night. Only Ronald Cohen knows for sure, and he has never told a living soul.

Nasty Mother

There are some murder cases which from the outset quickly lead police to one suspect. Sometimes it is the evidence, and other times nothing more than an overall impression of guilt that limits the investigation to a lone suspect. After all, why go further if the identity of the killer is obvious? Alice Crimmins was that kind of suspect.

Eddie and Alice had been married seven years. The early bickering had led to shouting matches, which usually culminated in one or the other stomping out of their apartment. You see, Eddie and Alice had a basic difference of opinion. Alice, at twenty-six, thought that life was for living. She loved to go out and have a good time. Eddie figured that a woman's place was in the home. It was quite another thing when he stepped out for a few beers with the boys.

The Crimmins agreed to disagree. Eddie moved out of the comfortable Kew Garden Hills apartment in Queens, New York. He rented a furnished room about a mile from his former home. Alice and the two Crimmins children, Eddie Jr., five, and Missy, four, remained in the apartment, along with the family dog, a half-spitz named Brandy.

The details of the events that took place on the steaming hot morning of July 14, 1965 have been told by Alice Crimmins hundreds of times. It is her story and she has never varied in its telling. She woke up, washed, dressed, and put on makeup in preparation for a custody hearing concerning the two children. Eddie wanted the children, but Alice had no intention of giving them up.

Once in the past Eddie Jr. had jumped out of his bed in the early hours of the morning and raided the fridge. He overate so much that he became violently ill. Alice had put a stop to that. She installed a simple hook and eye on the children's bedroom door. They couldn't get out of their room until Alice flipped the hook. Usually she could hear the kids laughing and carrying on before she liberated them.

On this morning the room was strangely silent. Alice opened the door. Little Eddie and Missy were gone. Alice called her husband, who immediately phoned the police.

Investigating officers answered what appeared to be a routine call. Two children had probably wandered away from home. They quickly changed their minds. A screen covering the children's window had been removed and was found leaning against the wall of the apartment building. The window itself was cranked open to about seventy degrees. Because of a hole in the screen, the window was normally kept closed to keep out insects.

The New York cops, learning of the imminent custody hearing, guessed that one of the parents may have hidden the children. Both parents quickly convinced them that this wasn't the case. It was only a five-foot drop from the window to the ground. Had some demented mind lured the children out of the room, or had they merely wandered away?

The police conducted a massive search. Sound trucks roamed the area, pleading with the children to come out of hiding. Two helicopters scanned open fields for any sign of life. Their task was futile.

Nine-year-old Jay Silverman kicked at some rubbish in a field as he took a shortcut to his home. The rubbish was the body of Missy Crimmins. An autopsy revealed that she had been strangled to death.

The hunt continued for Eddie. Five days later Vernon Warnecke and his son were gathering empty beer bottles beside a path in a field. They stumbled upon Eddie's badly decomposed body. The bodies of Eddie and Missy Crimmins were found about a mile from their apartment, but in opposite directions.

If Alice Crimmins was to be believed, the children had obviously been kidnapped. As their door had been locked from the outside, the only exit route was through the window. This did not sit well with the investigating detectives. The window, cranked partially open, wouldn't allow an adult to enter and leave, particularly with one or both of the children in tow. How could one or even two kidnappers cope with the two children? They would never leave their mother willingly in the middle of the night. What was the motive? The Crimmins were not a wealthy family and could not raise any appreciable amount of ransom money. Above all, why hadn't Brandy, who would bark at the slightest disruption in the house, not made a sound while the children were being spirited away?

Police investigated Alice and Eddie Crimmins, and so uncovered the swinging lifestyle Alice was leading. While working as a cocktail waitress Alice, a beautiful woman, had come in contact with high-rolling businessmen and politicians. Investigation revealed that she had several lovers. Under intense and often confidential questioning, the men in Alice's life all had one specific comment to make: Alice was fabulous in bed, quite unlike other women these men had known. Under questioning Alice admitted that she had a full and varied sex life.

Alice's estranged husband knew of her wild ways and tortured himself in this knowledge. Once he hooked up a listening device in his wife's bedroom where he could hear every noise from his listening post in the basement. The squeaking of his wife's bed drove him crazy.

Police thought that Alice had murdered her children, probably with the help of a friend. Eddie Crimmins, who cooperated with the police, had an alibi for the night of the killing and was eventually eliminated as a suspect. That left Alice. Had she killed her own children in order to rid herself of the last ties that held her to a life of domesticity? She stuck to her story, but the police looked no further. They couldn't prove Alice was a killer, but they didn't give up trying. Every room in her home was bugged. The phone was tapped and manned by police twenty-four hours a day for two years. Her friends were trailed. Several were harassed into becoming agents for the police.

Two years after the double murder police felt they had enough evidence to bring Alice to trial. She was arrested and charged with the murder of her daughter. Mrs. Sophie Earomirski, who lived in the same apartment complex as the Crimmins, wrote to the police about staring out of her window on the night of the murder. She didn't sign her name to the letter, but police traced her through her handwriting. Mrs. Earomirski was to become the prosecution's star witness.

She swore that on the night of the children's disappearance she couldn't sleep, due to the heat. She went to an open window and saw a man and woman on the street below. The woman had a bundle under one arm and was holding onto a walking child with the other. A dog was trailing the group. The man took the bundle from the woman and tossed it into the trunk of a parked car. Mrs. Earomirski heard the woman say, "My God, don't do that to her." Then they entered the car and drove away. After giving her evidence Sophie Earomirski pointed to Alice Crimmins and positively identified her as the woman on the street that night. Nothing could change her mind.

Thirteen days later the Crimmins jury returned a verdict of guilty of manslaughter in the first degree. Alice received a sentence of from five to twenty years imprisonment. Her attorneys launched a successful appeal, based on the wanderings of three jurors who, contrary to instructions, had taken it upon themselves to visit the murder scene. The trial that followed in 1971 resulted in a verdict of guilty of manslaughter in the death of Missy. In addition, Alice was found guilty of first degree murder in the death of her son. During this trial a former lover stated that Alice had told him she would rather kill the children than give them up to her husband.

Alice was carried, kicking and screaming from the courtroom. Her accomplice in the murder of her children has never been identified.

Murder Down Under

Folks down under in Melbourne, Australia, were becoming down-right apprehensive. In 1942 they had every reason to believe the seemingly invincible Japanese army would invade their country. Hordes of Allied servicemen were stationed in Australia. Life had taken on a nervous, superficially carefree attitude.

On May 9, 1942, Mrs. Pauline Thompson, the estranged wife of a Melbourne police officer, was found strangled in front of her rooming house on Spring Street. A post mortem indicated that tremendous pressure had been applied to Mrs. Thompson's neck by someone with unusually strong hands. Although the victim had not been sexually interfered with, her clothing had been torn to shreds. Mrs. Thompson's handbag was found a short distance away. Her attacker had obviously taken the few pounds the bag contained before tossing it away.

What caused the police concern was the similarity between Mrs. Thompson's murder and that of Ivy Violet McLeod, which had taken place six days previously. Mrs. McLeod, a forty-year-old domestic, was found in a doorway about three miles from her home. Her neck had the same grotesque indentations as those later found on Mrs. Thompson. Although she hadn't been raped, she too had had her clothes ripped into shreds. Both women had been killed where their bodies were found.

Despite the imminent threat of a Japanese invasion, the citizens of Melbourne were well aware that a monster was in their midst. Police could come up with no concrete clues. Nine days later the maniac struck again.

Miss Gladys Lillian Hosking, forty-one, was a secretary employed at Melbourne University. Her body was discovered by a gardener in Royal Park on the morning of May 19, 1942. As in the case of the two previous victims, Miss Hosking's neck had been viciously mangled by someone intent on something beyond cutting off her air supply.

Because of the threat of invasion, an air raid trench had been dug in the park. Distinctive yellow mud had been excavated from the trench. Miss Hosking's body lay face down in this mud. She hadn't been sexually attacked, but her clothing was torn into tiny strips. Miss Hosking's gloves, shoes, handbag, and umbrella were scattered within a ten-yard radius of her body.

Three women had been murdered in strikingly similar circumstances within fifteen days. All were accosted relatively close to their homes. It was obvious that they were not well acquainted with their attacker. He killed on the streets with little regard for his own safety. In the case of Miss Hosking, police surmised that she too had been initially attacked on the street and had been dragged into the park.

Royal Park was located near Camp Pell, at the time an American army installation. Investigating officers, who at this point had come up with little to lead them to the killer, decided that it was possible that the murderer could be an American soldier. Sure enough, they found a guard who remembered a soldier returning to the camp late on the night of Miss Hosking's death. The guard remembered him because he was covered with yellow mud. When casually questioned by the guard, the soldier said he had fallen over a mound of mud while taking a shortcut through the park.

Homicide officers W. Mooney and F. Adam visited Camp Pell. They slowly walked down rows of canvas tents. When they came to tent number 29 they stopped. There on the ground at the entrance to the tent was evidence of yellow mud. Inside the tent the officers found more of the telltale mud adhering to a metal bed. The officers left the camp, taking mud samples with them. Later their suspicions were verified when laboratory analysis proved that the mud taken from in front of the tent and the bed matched perfectly with mud samples from the freshly dug trench in Royal Park.

The two detectives returned to Camp Pell to interrogate the occupants of tent 29. Before doing so they required clearance from the company commander. He surprised the officers by telling them that he had already received a complaint concerning one of the men in tent 29.

Private First Class Edward Joseph Leonski was continually returning to the camp intoxicated. He caused a disturbance in the tent, babbling incoherently, sleeping fitfully, and waking up in the middle of the night screaming. Once he had inquired of his buddies whether they had ever heard of Dr. Jekyll and Mr. Hyde. During the day he pored over details of the murders that appeared in the newspapers.

The detectives were incredulous that Leonski's tentmates hadn't complained sooner. The soldiers explained that Leonski was such a likeable big guy when sober it was very difficult to suspect him of hurting a fly, let alone of being a vicious murderer.

When Mooney and Adam finally came face to face with their quarry, they knew what the soldiers had meant. Private First Class Eddie Leonski was a well built, tall, blond, twenty-four-year-old with a cherubic face. He was a pleasant good-natured guy, well liked by everyone. He did, however, have the reputation of turning into a real trouble maker when under the influence of alcohol. The guard who had stopped the soldier covered with yellow mud on the night of Miss Hosking's murder picked Eddie out of a line-up of twelve uniformed men.

The police investigated Leonski's background. Born in New York, Eddie had taken up weight lifting while still a teenager. He had a reputation for having extremely strong hands. Eddie was an honours student who played the piano and sang in the choir. The more police delved into his history the more he resembled an enlistment poster. Eddie exemplified the all-American boy.

Eddie's father had died while he was still a youngster, but his mother had managed to make ends meet and brought Eddie up to be a fine upstanding citizen. Or so she thought. In reality Eddie was overly devoted to his mother. His accomplishments were for her only. His setbacks affected him because he had let his mother down. When Eddie was called into the army he cried at the thought of being separated from his mother.

Once in Australia, Eddie began to drink heavily. While under the influence he would become belligerent and, according to his army buddies, he would undergo a strange transformation. His voice would change dramatically, becoming soft and high pitched, very much resembling a female voice.

Eddie began by picking up girls in Australia. He didn't do anything to them. He just liked to drink with them and listen to them talk. He drank at every opportunity, was often absent without leave and, in general, was a poor soldier. His army record was in direct contrast to his exemplary behaviour in civilian life.

Eddie himself knew something terrible was happening to him. Once he pleaded with a guard, "Please put me in the guardhouse and keep me there. I'm too dangerous to run around loose!"

Slowly Eddie gravitated from just talking to girls to trying to strangle them. He would release his grip before they lost consciousness. Eddie later explained that he really didn't want to kill the girls. Their voices reminded him of his mother. He only wanted to remove their voices. These girls had reported his attacks to the police, but in each case the attack had taken place in the dark and they were not able to provide useful descriptions.

Eddie couldn't explain why he became a murderer. He didn't know any of his victims, but he had struck up a conversation with each of them before clasping his hands around their throats. After killing Mrs. McLeod he knew he had to kill in order to possess the voices of his victims. Eddie couldn't explain his compulsion to rip his victims' clothing. He did say that when he read about his crimes in the newspapers he would cry. Yet, knowing what would happen when he drank, he never hesitated to go on a bender whenever the opportunity presented itself.

Eddie told the authorities of meeting Miss Hosking on the street. He asked her for directions back to camp. She was obliging and walked a way with him. As the hapless woman talked, Eddie knew he had to possess her voice. Without warning, he clutched her throat and, as his victim went limp, he dragged her into Royal Park. It was here that he stumbled and fell on the excavated mounds of yellow mud.

Eddie was examined by psychiatrists. They all agreed that he was full of unnatural feelings for his mother and was undoubtedly a fetishist. However, in the strict legal sense he was found to be sane.

Eddie was tried by a U.S. Military Court, found guilty, and sentenced to death. Just prior to his execution Eddie sang a song in his cell. He sang in a soft, clear female voice.

Edward Joseph Leonski was hanged for his crimes on November 9, 1942.

Scotch Rocks

The Isle of Arran is the largest and most scenic of the Clyde Islands. Situated in the estuary of the River Clyde in Scotland, it has often been referred to as one of the most picturesque locations in the world. Certainly an unlikely spot for murder, but wouldn't you know it—one of Scotland's most notorious murders took place on the side of Goatfell Mountain, Arran's most outstanding feature. Goatfell is a grey cone rising 2,866 feet above sea level.

At the turn of the 20th century the steamer *Ivanhoe* made its way down the Clyde each day, stopping at various ports in Arran. On Friday, July 12, 1889, two young men boarded the *Ivanhoe* at Rothesay. Both were planning to vacation in Arran.

Edwin Robert Rose was a thirty-two-year-old Englishman who was looking forward to two weeks' vacation from his job with a building firm in London. He boarded the *Ivanhoe* in the best of spirits. Edwin wasn't long aboard the steamer when he met a fellow traveller with the same destination. John Annandale and Edwin became friends.

When they reached the port of Brodick, the two men disembarked for the afternoon. The steamer would return for them that same evening. The pair separated in Brodick. Annandale found it difficult to obtain rooms because a local fair was taking place that week. Finally, he located lodgings at a Mrs. Walker's, who could only provide facilities, such as they were, in a lean-to beside her house. Annandale took the lean-to for a week, informing Mrs. Walker that he and a friend would occupy the premises the following day, Saturday. He would be staying a full week. However, his friend would only be staying until the following Wednesday.

Later that day the men met, boarded the *Ivanhoe*, and returned to Rothesay. Here Rose introduced Annandale to two men he had met during the previous few days, Mr. Thom and Mr. Mickel. All four planned to take the *Ivanhoe* back to Brodick the following day. Rose was delighted that Annandale was able to procure accommodations for them both. The best the two newcomers, Thom and Mickel, could do was to secure lodgings on a boat anchored in the bay.

On Sunday, the men went sightseeing in pairs. That evening all four met and spent the evening together. Over the weekend Thom and Mickel formed an unfavourable opinion of Annandale. They couldn't put their finger on it, but he seemed evasive and uncommunicative about his past. On Monday, when Rose mentioned that he and Annandale would be climbing Goatfell Mountain together, Mickel advised Rose of his intuitive feeling regarding Annandale. Rose shrugged off the warning.

Next day, when Thom and Mickel boarded the *Ivanhoe* to return to Rothesay, Rose and Annandale waved goodbye to them from the pier. The two men then set off to climb Goatfell.

The following morning Mrs. Walker noticed that there was no sign of her two lodgers. She waited until 11 a.m. before entering the lean-to. The skimpy room gave evidence of having been slept in, but the two men were missing. Mrs. Walker assumed that her roomers had skipped without paying the rent.

Rose had been due back in London at his place of employment on Thursday, July 18. He never showed up. Within a few days, relatives of the missing man arrived in Brodick, and after hearing Mrs. Walker's story, contacted the police.

The disappearance became the chief topic of conversation in the area. Soon police, in conjunction with volunteers, formed a search party. In a deep gully covered with granite boulders the search party found the body of Edwin Rose. The dead man had suffered fearful blows to the head, probably caused by a rock. His trousers pockets had been stripped of their contents. Later it was ascertained that Rose had probably been pushed over a precipice. His attacker, realizing the fall had not been fatal, leaned over the fallen man and rained blows upon his head. The missing persons' inquiry had turned into a brutal murder.

Where was the man who had hiked up Goatfell Mountain with Rose? Where was John Annandale?

Police traced Annandale's activities before his meeting with Rose. They found out that before travelling to Arran, he had taken rooms under a fictitious name from a Mrs. Currie of Port Bannatyne. He left wearing a straw hat. When he returned he sported a white yachting cap and brown tennis jacket. During the balance of his stay with Mrs. Currie, the wanted man had mentioned that he had climbed Goatfell Mountain. Abruptly one morning he went for a walk and never returned. He stuck Mrs. Currie with his bill, but left two pieces of clothing in his room. The yachting cap and tennis jacket were turned over to the police. They had belonged to Edwin Rose.

Two weeks after the murder, reporters from the North British *Daily Mail* managed to get a handle on John Annandale. His real name was John Watson Laurie of Glasgow. The twenty-five-year-old man was from a well-to-do, respectable family, but had been in and out of minor scrapes all his life. The industrious reporters located a James Aitken, who knew the wanted man as Laurie, and who had been on the *Ivanhoe* with Laurie and Rose. When Aitken first met the two men travelling to Brodick, Rose was wearing a white yachting cap. When he met Laurie after the visit to Brodick he thought it strange that Laurie was now wearing his former companion's cap.

Strangely enough, Aitken met Laurie for a third time in Glasgow after Rose's body was found. He asked Laurie about the case, now referred to by the newspapers as the Arran Mystery. Laurie became flustered and swore the man he had been with was not the same man who was found murdered. Then he dashed away and disappeared into a crowd.

Laurie left his job in Glasgow, walked out on his landlady without paying the rent, sold his pattern maker's tools, and went into hiding. Now actively being sought as a murder suspect under his real name, Laurie wrote his first of several letters. The most wanted man in Scotland wrote his landlady, enclosing his back rent. Suspected murderers usually don't do that. Then again, most murderers don't wear their victim's cap and jacket after the foul deed has been done.

Laurie made his way to Liverpool, where he left several of Rose's shirts in a rooming house that he hastily vacated. He then took the amazing step of writing to the British public by sending a letter to the North British *Daily Mail*. In it Laurie explained that he had left Rose alive and well with two strangers on top of Goatfell.

Laurie's literary talents received wide acclaim throughout Britain. This was better than Robin Hood. No doubt encouraged by the excitement caused by his first letter, Laurie again took pen in hand and dashed off greetings to the Glasgow *Herald*. The letter, published on August 29, filled several pages in an endeavour to convince the public that Laurie was a cross between an angel and a martyr.

On Wednesday, September 3, over a month after the murder, Laurie was apprehended. A station master became suspicious of a man loitering near the depot. It was Laurie's bad luck that at precisely that moment a constable strolled into the station. Laurie realized what was about to happen. He dashed out, but was tackled in some nearby woods.

Laurie stood trial in Edinburgh for the murder of Edwin Rose. He pleaded not guilty, claiming that Rose had fallen to his death. He admitted to robbing and then concealing the body. His clean-cut appearance at the trial weighed heavily in his favour. The public had expected a monster, but instead were presented with an articulate young man. Despite this, Laurie was found guilty and sentenced to hang.

Surprisingly, the public didn't want their dashing letter-writing Robin Hood to die. A petition was circulated, pleading for the convicted man's life. Copies were placed in offices, banks, and churches throughout Scotland. The mass petition with 138,140 signatures affixed to it was presented to the Secretary of Scotland. As a result, an order was issued to have Laurie undergo a mental examination. He was found to be of "unsound mind," and the death sentence was commuted to life imprisonment. The convicted murderer was sent to Peterhead Prison to serve his sentence.

Four years later the Arran murderer climbed an eight-foot wall and escaped. He managed to get to a wooded area before guards surrounded him and brought him back. He had been outside the prison compound for only half an hour. It was his last taste of freedom.

John Watson Laurie died in prison on October 6, 1930, at the age of sixty-nine, after serving forty-nine years behind bars.

The crime is still occasionally a topic of conversation in the area. Today there is a cairn marking the spot where Rose's body lay concealed beneath the boulder. A few miles away, in the picturesque village of Sannox, in an ancient graveyard, lies the body of Edwin Rose. The huge granite boulder that serves as a headstone gives no hint of how Rose met his death. The inscription merely states "In loving memory of Edwin R. Rose who died on Goatfell, July 15, 1889."

Who Killed Mr. Little?

Mr. Little was a creature of habit. In the years previous to 1858 traces of grey were discernible about his temples. The reliable Mr. Little had slipped gracefully into what the young charitably refer to as the middle years.

As a trusted employee of the Midland and Great Western Railway Company of Dublin, Ireland for years, Little had worked his way up the ladder to the lofty position of chief cashier. Along the way Mr. Little never found time to marry. His work was his life.

Each morning Mr. Little (no one ever called him by anything as familiar as a Christian name) arrived at the three-story director's building of the Dublin Railway Terminus at precisely 10 a.m. While the rest of his staff left promptly at five, Mr. Little would often work well into the night. Even back in 1857 that was considered steady and conscientious.

The afternoon of November 14 was no different from the thousands of afternoons that had preceded it. The female staff left at five, followed by a clerk, Mr. Chamberlain. As was his custom, Mr. Little stayed on to enter the cash receipts for the day into his accounts. Mr. Little was never to leave his office again.

At home, waiting patiently, was his unwed sister. Naturally enough, Miss Little was deeply concerned. Her reliable brother had never been one for nocturnal dalliances of any kind. In fact, he had never stayed out overnight before. Miss Little hardly slept a wink. Next morning she went down to the terminus building to see what had happened to her brother.

Stalking back and forth in front of her brother's office was none other than clerk Chamberlain. He, too, was concerned. It was 10:15 a.m. and Mr. Little had never been late before. Mr. Chamberlain turned decidedly pale when Miss Little informed him that her dear brother had not been home all night. Dear me, thought Chamberlain, could Mr. Little have spent the night in his office?

A carpenter was summoned and easily gained entrance to the office through a glass roof. He opened the door from the inside. Mr. Chamberlain and Miss Little dashed inside. Mr. Little was lying beside his desk in a pool of blood. A neat but gaping incision was evident across his neck, and had served to nearly decapitate the poor fellow. Other wounds, any one of which could have been fatal, were visible about the head. The murder weapon or weapons had been carried away by the killer, who had obviously made his way out of the office through the roof. Mr. Little's key was still in the door. A bloodstained towel had been used to wipe blood from the killer's hands and to clean the blade of a razor and knife that had been used on the hapless Little.

No further clues were uncovered at the murder scene. Of course, at the time, fingerprints had not yet been developed as a means of identification. Investigating authorities at first believed that robbery was not the motive for the murder. There was over a thousand pounds in gold and silver on Mr. Little's accounting table, but upon examining the chief cashier's accounting books, they changed their minds. Over six hundred pounds was missing.

Everyone around the terminus instantly became suspect. One must keep in mind that in those days many railway employees lived in and near the station yard. There was Mr. Hanbury, the stationmaster, and his wife, who made their home on railway property. Another railway employee, Mr. Gunning and his wife, lived with the Hanburys. The Hanburys' servant, Catherine Campbell, was in close proximity to the murder scene on the night Little was killed. This galaxy of suspects served to keep the Dublin police hopping, but did little to identify the killer. In desperation police decided to drain a canal that ran adjacent to the station, under the theory that the killer may have tossed the murder weapon into the canal. It wasn't a bad theory. They came up with a hammer covered with red lead paint. Had the killer used the paint to obliterate bloodstains?

Slowly all the prime suspects were exonerated, and the investigation wound down. The police then decided to wander further afield, and began by questioning all railroad employees, even if it had been established earlier that they had not been in or near the directors' building on the evening of the murder.

The expanded investigation involved the questioning of a man named Spollen. Mr. Spollen had been questioned earlier and dismissed as a suspect. He was employed with the railway as a painter, but had been home with his wife shortly after five on the evening of the murder and could not have been the killer. Detectives couldn't help but notice that Mrs. Spollen had recently undergone a change from being a bright, cheerful woman before the tragedy to her present sullen, nervous state. The transformation was interesting, but had been explained as depression, no doubt caused by the tragic murder of Mr. Little, with whom she had been acquainted.

Despite a large reward offered by the railway for the apprehension of the murderer, nothing further developed for a full six months. Then all hell broke loose. On June 20, 1858, Mrs. Spollen walked into the police station. She stated that she had become a nervous wreck because she knew her husband was the murderer. He had not come home soon after five on the evening of the tragedy. She and her children had lied to the authorities in order to provide her husband with an alibi. In reality Mr. Spollen had arrived home at 7:30 p.m. with a paint bucket full of money taken from Mr. Little's office. Spollen had hidden the money in various caches around the neighbourhood, planning to use it as the occasion arose. He had threatened both his wife and children with death if they breathed a word about his guilt. Mrs. Spollen told the police she knew the various hiding places in which her husband had stashed the money. She led detectives to the locations and, sure enough, the robbery loot was found.

Mrs. Spollen swore that on the evening of the murder her husband had come home with blood on his clothing. He dabbed red lead paint over the bloodstains. She pointed to a section of the canal that hadn't been drained. Mrs. Spollen told police that it was here that her husband had thrown away the murder weapon, his straight razor. When this section of the canal was drained, a razor was found with the name Spollen scratched into the handle. Mrs. Spollen's story had checked out in every detail.

Spollen was arrested and charged with murder. With such strong evidence against him, one would think that Spollen's trial would be routine, but such was not the case. There were complications. The prosecution was hampered by the fact that Mrs. Spollen, by law, could not be a witness against her husband. Corroboration of her evidence by other witnesses was admissible. This law prevented Mrs. Spollen from actually taking the witness stand.

Spollen's four children testified against their father. The children, three boys and a girl, ranging in age from six to seventeen, actually saw their father hide some of the stolen money. They had also been warned by Spollen to remain silent about the whole affair.

You would think that such strong evidence would serve to convince the jury that Spollen was guilty. Not so. The children related their tale as if they had been rehearsed. This may have been the case, but should not have been confused with the truth of what they were saying. It also doesn't sit well with juries to see children giving evidence against a parent.

Despite all the evidence against him, Spollen was acquitted and walked out of court an obviously guilty, but free man. Neither Mrs. Spollen nor her children ever spoke or had anything to do with him again. He was fired from his job at the railway. On the streets of Dublin, Spollen was pointed at as an object of derision. Practically driven out of Ireland, he made his way to England and oblivion.

Back in Dublin, a sympathetic public raised enough money to enable Mrs. Spollen and her children to emigrate to the United States.

The Bermuda Terror

Bermuda is an unlikely locale for murder but, as we all know, the ultimate of crimes knows no boundaries nor class distinction. The semi-tropical paradise, with its bright blue skies and crystal clear water, conjures up images of easy going natives, retired British officers, and playboy millionaires. Homicidal maniacs rarely run amuck in Bermuda. In July of 1958 all this changed.

Mrs. Florence Flood lived outside Hamilton with her taxi driver husband. The attractive thirty-four-year-old was attacked outside her home. She was sexually assaulted and horribly beaten by her attacker. Left for dead, Florence recovered, but was unable to describe her assailant, other than to state that he was young, dark, and thin, which in Bermuda was tantamount to no description at all. The brutal assault was considered by police to be an isolated incident until the following March. This time the victim wasn't as fortunate as Florence Flood.

Mrs. Gertrude Robinson lived alone in a little cottage about a mile from the Flood residence. Gertrude was seventy-two. On the morning of March 7 her naked body was found close by her home. She had been so mercilessly bludgeoned and clawed that witnesses had difficulty identifying the body. No weapon had been used. After raping his hapless victim, the attacker had used his bare fists to beat the life from the frail elderly widow.

This second brutal attack crystallized the fact that a madman was loose on the island. The sale of every conceivable type of lock soared. Citizens purchased watchdogs and revolvers, but most realized that if a cunning, depraved sex maniac was at large, he would sooner or later find a woman alone. Police seemed helpless as the attacker had left no clues, no footprints, no fingerprints, and had used no weapon other than his hands.

Nine weeks passed. On May 11, the Bermuda rapist struck again. Dorothy Pearce was the divorced wife of a Royal Navy officer. She lived alone in a cottage facing the sea. Her immediate neighbour thought it strange that he hadn't seen the elderly woman for over two days. When he strolled next door to investigate he found two full milk bottles outside Dorothy's locked door. He called the police.

The police broke down the door and entered the cottage. Mrs. Pearce's body was found in a pool of blood in her bedroom. The brutality of the attack was evident from the swollen and beaten condition of the nude corpse. Again the maniac had used nothing but his bare hands, nails, and teeth to kill the victim. As in the previous cases, cash and jewellery had been ignored.

Six weeks later, the Bermuda Terror, as he was now called by the press, struck again. Rosaleen Kenny lived in the same general area as the three previous victims. One night she woke up and, to her horror, spotted the figure of a man ready to pounce upon her bed. Paralyzed with fear, Rosaleen screamed. A young couple who occupied the second floor of the two-story home heard her screams and rushed downstairs. The intruder heard them coming and loosened his grip on his victim. Then he let go altogether and ran out the open front door into the night. Rosaleen's description of the madman was understandably vague.

Dorothy Barbara Rawlinson was twenty-nine, an attractive English woman who had first visited Bermuda for a vacation. Dorothy loved the island so much she never left. Because she was a fully trained secretary she had no difficulty finding employment. Dorothy lived with Anne and Thomas Sayres in Pembroke, near Hamilton. On her two days off, Thursday and Sunday, she loved to sunbathe. Dorothy had received permission from a retired army officer to sunbathe on Southlands Beach, which he owned.

On Sunday, September 27, Dorothy cycled down to Southlands Beach as usual. She never returned. As the hour grew late the Sayres discussed calling the police. They decided to wait until morning. Next morning Thomas Sayres, accompanied by police officers, went down to Southlands Beach looking for Dorothy. The windswept beach was deserted. The wind had smoothed out any tracks that may have been there the night before. Dorothy's bicycle was found lying in the sand.

Police found some blood splattered rocks. That was enough. They returned with twelve officers, equipped with shovels. Soon the beach was criss-crossed with trenches. The officers uncovered Dorothy's wristwatch, green shorts, and white blouse.

Next day frogmen searched the shoreline, but still found no trace of Dorothy. A half mile away, seventy-year-old Frederick Astwood was fishing from his rowboat in a sheltered cove. He found what was left of the battered, half-eaten body. Doctors were able to distinguish which wounds had been inflicted by sharks and which had been inflicted by Dorothy's killer.

All the Bermuda Terror victims had met their deaths in Warwick Parish, a one-square mile of Bermuda that was now practically deserted after dark. Yet it was believed that the latest victim had been killed during daylight hours. Why was no one seen coming to the beach or leaving? The entire Bermuda police force of 150 men were now working on little else.

Police Superintendent Lodge asked Scotland Yard for help. The Yard responded by sending Detective Superintendent Richard Lewis and Detective Sergeant Fred Taylor to Bermuda.

The Scotland Yard detectives were successful in locating witnesses who remembered seeing Dorothy sunbathing just before five o'clock on Sunday. Others swore that she wasn't there at 5:45. Someone had committed the crime during that three quarters of an hour span. The detectives felt that after the killer had raped and murdered, he had carried the body into the sea, hoping the sharks would obliterate all traces of his crime. They thought it reasonable to search for anyone who had been seen with wet clothing around the time of the murder.

The two detectives re-enacted the crime. They figured the killer had followed the shoreline after depositing the body in the sea. Lewis and Taylor followed the beach until they came to an area overgrown with brush. Upon examining this wooded area they uncovered a trail. The trail led to a road, which took them to a golf course. Here the detectives questioned a shopkeeper whose store had been open on the day of the murder. Sure enough, he remembered one particular customer that day—because the man's clothing was wet. The young man often bought cigarettes from the shopkeeper and sometimes caddied at the golf course.

Within an hour the two Scotland Yard detectives were in front of the dilapidated shack of nineteen-year-old Wendell Willis Lightbourne. At first Lightbourne denied any knowledge of the crime. Then he admitted to having been near the beach fishing, and finally he confessed to talking to the girl, but swore he left her unharmed, sunbathing on the beach.

Lightbourne was arrested and charged with the murder of Dorothy Rawlinson. As his trial unfolded he emerged as a rather pathetic figure, who could neither read nor write. Sometimes he caddied to make a little money. At other times he did whatever menial tasks he could find. He told of an uncontrollable urge to inflict pain on the opposite sex. He did not know the women he had attacked and had no personal reasons for harming those particular women. They just happened to be in the wrong place when his uncontrollable urge came over him.

Lightbourne was found guilty of murder, with a recommendation for mercy. Despite the rider on his sentence, he was condemned to death. In January 1960, this sentence was commuted to life imprisonment. As there were no prisons in Bermuda capable of housing a convicted killer, Lightbourne was transported to England to serve his sentence.

The French Connection

In the hot and humid climes of South America, tempers sometimes flare with little provocation, resulting in murder most foul. In the United States, violent sick rampages by violent sick men have been the rule rather than the exception. England has always produced its intriguing, weird murders.

Ah, but for crimes of passion and affairs of the heart, we must turn to the French. Innovative triangles and other strange permutations too risqué to even whisper about have always been identified with the passionate inhabitants of France.

Mademoiselle Gabrielle Bompard was not a classic French beauty. Her countenance had a stern hardness to it that detracted from her even, chiselled features. But Gaby had an hourglass figure: an ample bosom and a waist so tiny as to be sinful; well-proportioned hips that tapered down to a perfect pair of long lean legs.

Gaby was a prostitute in Lille. Finding the pickings too slim for her liking, she looked for greener pastures and, like many others, she headed for Paris. The year was 1890, and Gaby found, much to her dismay, that her chosen profession was overcrowded with women who were as well stacked as she.

Times were tough, but a ray of sunshine was just around the corner. The ray's name was Michael Eyraud, whose main occupation was a never-ending search for the ways and means of avoiding work. A tall, thin man with a full beard, Michael was a small-time punk and petty thief. He took one look at the voluptuous Gaby and thought to himself, that's for me. The twenty-two-year-old pro and the small-time punk became—first things first—lovers, and then partners in crime.

Gaby hung out in the better class bars. Balding, middle-aged men, with wallets bulging like their tummies, were enticed to the apartment, where Michael relieved them of their overstuffed wallets. Most were in a position where they could ill afford to report the robbery to police. Gaby and Michael made their precarious living in this way for months.

Just when the villainous pair turned their thoughts to murder we do not know. What we do know is that they picked as their first victim a solicitor named Gouffe. This unfortunate gentleman made pursuing the opposite sex his main activity in life. Gaby lured him to her apartment many times. Michael resisted the urge to take his money and call it a day. He and Gaby knew that Gouffe was supposed to have a large amount of cash in his office safe. He always carried the keys to his office and safe on his person.

Michael set the scene for their rather original plan. He rented a posh room in the Rue Tronson-Ducoudry. Gaby informed Gouffe that she had procured new lodgings. Soon he would be invited over to enjoy the new digs. Gouffe could hardly wait.

Meanwhile, back at the new room, Michael had set up a quaint little pulley system. The room had a rather large alcove, enclosed by a curtain. Gaby's bed was just outside this curtain. A pulley with a rope threaded through it had been fastened to the ceiling. One end of the rope was hidden behind the curtain, while the other end hung innocently down the outside of the curtain, falling beside the bed. This end was equipped with a small hook.

Before inviting Gouffe up to the room, Gaby and Michael took a trip to London, England, where they purchased a large trunk. Then the big night arrived. Gouffe, his mind full of things sexual, took the steps leading to Gaby's apartment two at a time. Gaby greeted him at the door, clad in a nightgown. Holding a bottle of wine in her right hand, she waved the anxious Gouffe into the room.

It is difficult to say whether Gouffe died happy, or whether he realized at the very end that something was amiss. As they sipped their wine, the lovers sat down on the bed. Gaby untied the cord of her nightgown. Teasing her lover, she drew it around his neck and fastened it securely. In a flash, Michael tiptoed from behind the curtain, attached the hook to the nightgown cord, and gave a mighty pull on his end of the rope. Voilà, Gouffe rose as if by magic, and without a sound was hanged.

Next morning the body was placed in the waiting trunk and taken to a wooded area near the village of Irigny, near Lyons. Once back in Paris Michael dashed to Gouffe's office to gather up the loot. He had no trouble gaining entry to the office, but try as he might, he couldn't open the safe. In disgust he left empty-handed. Ironically he missed a large sum of money in a box sitting on the victim's desk. Michael and Gaby had gained nothing by becoming murderers. The whole thing was a terrible mistake. They panicked and fled to the United States.

Denis Coffy was working repairing the road near Lyons. After his noon-day lunch, he stumbled upon the decomposed body of the unfortunate Gouffe.

Because he had already been reported missing to the Paris police, it wasn't long before Gouffe was identified. A photograph and description of the trunk was widely published throughout Europe. A clerk in Schwartiger's shop in Euston Road spotted the picture and immediately recognized the trunk he had sold. The transaction was clear in his mind because the couple who had bought the trunk were French. He gave the police a perfect description of Gaby and Michael. Soon the pair were being sought as prime suspects in the murder case.

Gaby couldn't stand the good old U.S.A. For one thing, no one spoke French. She returned to face the music. Michael had made his way to Cuba, where a Frenchman stood out like an elephant at a flea circus. Michael was taken into custody and returned to France.

During the early winter of 1890, France and, indeed, much of Europe discussed little else than the sensational trial of Gaby and Michael. To make matters more dramatic, the partners in crime blamed each other for the unique murder.

In the end both were found guilty. Gaby received twenty years' imprisonment, but was released after having spent less than half that time behind bars. Michael lost his head to the guillotine.

The Justice Minister
Was a Killer

Thomas John Ley was not your typical murderer. Then, John McMain Mudie was not your average victim, either. You see, Mr. Ley was the wealthy former Minister for Justice of New South Wales, Australia; Mudie was an English bartender. The tale of these two men, and how one killed the other, without ever exchanging a word of conversation, has been described by the Lord Chief Justice of England as one of the strangest cases ever presented to an English jury.

Ley was born in England but moved to Australia when he was eight years old. While still in his twenties he became deeply involved in politics. In 1922, at age forty-one, after a gradual climb up the political ladder, he became Minister of Justice. For years the Honourable Thomas Ley was one of the most influential men in Australia. With power came wealth. Ley was the director of several large companies, but left Australia for England in 1928, hurt because he hadn't been chosen Deputy Premier when the Prime Minister visited Europe.

Thomas Ley's wife was unaware that he supported a mistress for over twenty years. Mrs. Brooks was a widow, whose daughter was married to an Englishman named Barron. When Ley went to England he took Mrs. Brooks with him, leaving his wife behind in Australia.

Strangely enough, Ley ceased having intercourse with Mrs. Brooks after returning to England. In fact she acted as Ley's housekeeper and companion in the twelve years prior to the Mudie murder.

Mrs. Brooks' daughter required an operation. Ley suggested that Mrs. Brooks move in with her son-in-law while her daughter was convalescing in hospital. The Barrons lived on Homefield Road in London in a house of flats operated by a Mrs. Evans.

One of the roomers at Homefield Road was John Mudie, a bartender who, as the saying goes, never did anyone any harm. From all reports Mudie was a decent, hardworking, quiet man. Mrs. Evans spoke highly of Mudie and doted upon the only bachelor residing in her establishment. Sometimes she tidied up his rooms. In return Mudie was most obliging in running errands for his landlady. Occasionally John Ley dropped over to the Evans' establishment to have tea with Mrs. Brooks. In this way he met Mrs. Evans.

It is not our function to analyze people's minds, but certainly the obsession which was to overtake, envelop, and eventually ruin John Ley defies explanation. Later, psychiatrists would conveniently decide the successful businessman and politician was suffering from paranoia. Whatever the reason, Ley became obsessed with the idea that John Mudie was carrying on a torrid love affair with the sixty-six-year-old Mrs. Brooks. He became insanely jealous of the entire fictitious relationship. Mrs. Evans was to state that Mudie met Mrs. Brooks only once, and that was in her company, on a stairway where the three passed the time of day for a moment or two.

The seed of insane jealousy firmly planted, Ley proceeded to hatch a diabolical plot to murder Mudie, who was in all probability the most innocent victim of any premeditated murder ever committed.

Ley approached a hotel porter named Minden at the Royal Hotel in Woburn Place. Minden knew Ley as a solicitor and a former guest of the hotel who in the past had visited with his wife from Australia. Ley inquired of Minden if he knew of a man with a motor car who could be trusted, letting the porter know that such a man could earn as much for one piece of work as he normally would in an entire year. Minden, assuming that the vehicle was to be used by the solicitor for legitimate purposes, put Ley in contact with an acquaintance, William Buckingham. Minden received ten pounds from Ley for the favour.

Ley and Buckingham met and for the first time Ley told someone else of his intentions. He alleged that a young man had seduced a mother and daughter and was now blackmailing the two women. It was Ley's plan to kidnap the young man and give him a good scare. Then he would provide him with a sum of money and force the culprit to leave the country. Ley promised he would pay Buckingham well for his assistance. He told Buckingham that another accomplice in the scheme, Lawrence John Smith, a carpenter, would eventually meet with them to iron out the details.

The following evening the former Minister of Justice, the man with the car for hire, and the carpenter met at the Royal Hotel to finalize their plans. Buckingham suggested bringing a friend of his, Mrs. Lillian Bruce, into the plot in order to lure the victim into a car on his way to Ley's residence at 5 Beaufort Gardens. Buckingham was so enthused with the promise of easy money that he brought his son into the scheme as well.

In fairness to all the conspirators, it is quite possible that at this time, they believed Ley's story. When Minden suggested that Buckingham had a car for hire he asked if it would be used for legal purposes. Mrs. Bruce also inquired if anything asked of her was illegal. All received assurances from Ley that as a solicitor he was operating well within the law.

And so all the characters of the diabolical plot are now in position—Ley, Buckingham, his son, Mrs. Bruce, and, of course, the bartender at the Reigate Hill Hotel, the unsuspecting John Mudie.

Mrs. Bruce, posing as a well-to-do customer, made it a point to become acquainted with the pleasant, unassuming Mudie. It wasn't difficult. Young Buckingham posed as her chauffeur. Eventually Mrs. Bruce asked Mudie if he would care to earn some extra money working as a bartender at a cocktail party she was giving on the evening of November 28, 1946. Mudie jumped at the opportunity.

On the appointed night young Buckingham and Mrs. Bruce picked up Mudie at the Reigate Hill Hotel for the ride into London. Young Buckingham drove his father's Wosley. Unknown to Mudie, another vehicle, a Ford, licence number 101, which had been rented a week earlier by Smith, preceded the Wosley to 5 Beaufort Gardens. Smith and his passenger, Buckingham Sr., entered Ley's residence.

Mrs. Bruce, young Buckingham, and Mudie entered 5 Beaufort Gardens. Young Buckingham merely opened the door and returned to the car. Once the victim was delivered, Mrs. Bruce's work was done. She excused herself, saying she had to consult with her chauffeur. As the door closed behind her, the senior Buckingham and Smith threw a carpet over poor Mudie's head. He was gagged and firmly tied with rope.

Exactly what went on behind the closed door will never be known for sure. Young Buckingham and Mrs. Bruce drove to the Crown and Sceptre for a few drinks. Buckingham and Smith were supposed to join them. Only the elder Buckingham showed up.

Meanwhile the terrified Mudie sat with a carpet tied firmly over his head with no idea of what was happening to him. Smith remained in the room. Ley, his brain racing in ecstacy, had managed to pull it off. After all the scheming and plotting, his supposed antagonist was trussed up and helpless before him.

◆ ◆ ◆

On Nov. 29, 1946, Walter Coombs of Woldingham, Surrey, was walking home after finishing work. It was he who discovered the body of John Mudie in a chalk pit. Death was the result of strangulation with a rope, which was tied around the neck. John Mudie's body was identified immediately. His killers had overlooked his personal card in his pocket.

Buckingham and Mrs. Bruce read about the terrible conclusion to the kidnapping plot in the newspapers. The chalk pit murder, as it became known, received wide publicity. Buckingham and Mrs. Bruce went directly to the police and told the whole story, but insisted that when they left Mudie he was definitely alive. A gag and pick axe found at the scene of the crime were later traced to 5 Beaufort Gardens.

When the entire plot unfolded Smith and Ley were charged with murder. All the other participants turned King's evidence and were never tried.

As the architect of the murder there was little doubt as to Ley's guilt. Smith claimed that the last time he saw Mudie he was alive. The evidence of two alert citizens proved that, unlike his fellow conspirators, Smith knew that Mudie was to be murdered, not merely kidnapped.

Clifford Tamplin and Fred Smith, two landscape gardeners, were cycling past the chalk pit on November 27, the day before the murder. They were startled to notice a car parked in the desolate area. As they came upon the scene a man appeared some distance inside the pit. When the man spotted the cyclists he dashed wildly to his car and quickly drove away. The two men noted the licence plate number— 101—and the make of the vehicle, a Ford.

Later, when they heard a body had been found at that exact spot on November 29, they went to the police with their story. As the killing was definitely committed on the 28th, using a Ford car with licence plate number 101, their story proved that Smith, who had rented the car earlier in the week, was reconnoitering the location to dump the body the day before the murder took place. This proved he had prior knowledge that murder was to take place.

Both Ley and Smith were found guilty of murder and sentenced to death, although it was never established which one actually strangled John Mudie. Later their sentences were commuted. Smith was given a sentence of life imprisonment, while Ley was judged insane and sent to Broadmoor, where he was one of the wealthiest men ever to be incarcerated in that institution. Three months later the Honourable Thomas John Ley, former Minister of Justice of New South Wales, suffered a stroke and died.

Not with My Sister

It is a source of amazement to me that in recent times there has been a drought of honest-to-goodness bigamists. Has this art form gone the way of hula hoops, stained glass windows, and chimney sweeps? Where are those dapper gentlemen who led double lives, not for weeks or months, but for years?

Indeed, to resurrect one such rogue for your reading pleasure, it is necessary to turn back the calendar to 1892 and visit with James Canham Read, who lived in assorted towns and villages close by London, England. Jimmy was tall, dark, and handsome. He was also a real rascal when it came to his relationships with the opposite sex. Jimmy didn't just lead a double life. Our boy Jimmy had four on the string at one time.

Let's see now, there was the original Mrs. Read, a loyal homebody who tended to the washing and cleaning. Mrs. Read didn't have that much choice. As the mother of eight little Reads she rarely had time to enjoy herself. It is disheartening to relate that Mrs. Read, despite her more than adequate domestic contribution to the care and comfort of the main character in our little drama, had absolutely nothing else to do with the entire affair. I understand she cried a lot.

In August 1892, Jimmy just happened to bump into Mrs. John Ayriss, a tiny but well-endowed mother of four healthy strapping children. It wasn't long after their initial chance encounter that Jimmy was having encounters of a sexual kind with Mrs. Ayriss.

One can't help but wonder how Jimmy financed his affairs, being all the while employed as a clerk at the Royal Albert Docks at a salary of £140 per annum. Even at that time this sum was not a fortune.

One fine day in September, handsome Jimmy and Mrs. Ayriss were taking a leisurely stroll on Clapham Common, when who should they bump into but Mrs. Ayriss' younger sister Florrie. As any dutiful sister would, Mrs. Ayriss introduced Florrie to her friend Jimmy Read. You guessed it; Jimmy took one look at Florrie, who was a knockout, and decided then and there that two sisters were better than one.

It was only a matter of weeks before Jimmy initiated Florrie into his stable of willing lovers. From the last half of 1893, well into May of 1894, Jimmy bedded down with his wife, Mrs. Ayriss, and Florrie at every opportunity, but not necessarily in that order. It appears that Florrie, who lived in Sheerness, may have been his favourite.

Although Jimmy and Florrie were careful to keep their relationship secret, Mrs. Ayriss found out about the unfaithful Jimmy and her own sweet sister Florrie. She smouldered from within, but there was little she could do. When you are unfaithful to your own husband it is difficult, if not impossible, to blow the whistle on your lover for rolling in the hay with your sister.

In the midst of all this intrigue, Jimmy found himself one day innocently partaking of some sweets in a confectionary store. He sampled a Turkish delight and found it to his taste. Jimmy, who never stopped hustling, also found the sweet young woman who served him to his liking. Miss Kemper soon became Jimmy's fourth partner in sex. The innocent purveyor of sweets knew Jimmy as Edgar Benson, a commercial traveller. She was soon ensconced in an apartment which she shared with Jimmy, never knowing that she was only one of four.

Tending to the sexual desires of all four ladies was tiring, time-consuming, yet enjoyable. Then Jimmy received a decidedly distressing piece of information from Florrie. "I am going to have a baby and it's yours," she said.

This unsettling bit of news did not go over well with Jimmy. For one thing, if Mrs. Ayriss found out, as she undoubtedly would, there would be the devil to pay. Besides, Jimmy felt he had enough children already. No, definitely no. Florrie had to go.

Jimmy then proceeded to swing into action. On June 24, 1893, he met with Florrie to talk over their embarrassing predicament. The couple went for a stroll hand in hand near the village of Prittlewell, just north of Southend. Jimmy simply produced a revolver and shot Florrie in the head. He then threw her body over a hedge and returned via a well-used footpath. In order to obscure his trail Jimmy walked all night toward London. At 8 a.m. Monday morning he called on a friend at Leyton, washed, shaved, and had breakfast. By 10 a.m. he was at his office at the Royal Albert Docks.

Whatever else Jimmy was, he was not a dunce. He realized that at some point he would be questioned about Florrie's death. He needed to disappear. With this thought in mind, Jimmy opened his employer's safe and took £160, more than his salary for an entire year, and left his office. He went to Rose Cottage at Mitcham, where the lovely Miss Kemper waited with open arms. Jimmy planned on permanently becoming Mr. Edgar Benson, commercial traveller.

Elsewhere the universe was unfolding. Florrie's body was found that same Monday. A medical examination revealed that the murder victim was in an advanced state of pregnancy. Her identity was immediately established as Florrie Dennis. Mrs. Ayriss had reported her sister missing when she was unable to locate her on Monday morning.

Jimmy spent the next four days at Rose Cottage, but it was no use. Now a robbery suspect, as well as a possible murderer, Jimmy was traced to his love nest. On June 29, Scotland Yard detectives showed up at Rose Cottage and arrested Jimmy Read.

On November 13, 1894, Jimmy Read stood trial for murder. The Crown presented a formidable circumstantial case. Jimmy had sent Florrie a wire setting up their last meeting. He was identified by a Mrs. Kirley as being near the scene of the murder on the fateful Sunday. Another witness, a Mr. Douthwaite, testified that he saw the accused man walking with Florrie close to the hedge where the body was later found. Several witnesses, including a constable, identified Read as the man who inquired about directions to London during the early hours of the morning of Monday, June 25. Even Miss Kemper revealed the facts surrounding Jimmy's appearance at Rose Cottage on the Monday following the crime. He urged her to fetch papers featuring the murder, was nervous, and hardly left the tiny cottage for four full days.

In an attempt to counteract this testimony, the defence pointed out that there was no real evidence that Jimmy was the father of Florrie's unborn child. The prosecution had been unable to come up with a murder weapon and had failed to prove that Jimmy had ever owned one.

Despite this, the Read jury deliberated only a half hour before finding Jimmy guilty of murder. All appeals failed. James Canham Read professed his innocence right up to the time he was hanged on December 4, 1894 in Springfield Prison, Chelmsford.

Wholesale Slaughter

We are all familiar with that nasty gentleman known as Jack the Ripper, who held London, England in a state of terror during the autumn of 1888. Jack passed his time murdering and mutilating prostitutes. His true identity remains a mystery to this day. Earlier in the nineteenth century, another man terrorized London, keeping its inhabitants in much the same state of fear as the Ripper, but his murders are not nearly as well known. This may be because his identity was established at the time, removing the element of mystery from his dastardly deeds.

Mr. and Mrs. Marr had worked hard to build up their dry goods store in London's rough, tough east end. Sailors from around the world wandered the street in 1811 looking for hard drink and loose women. Seagoing voyages lasted months, and who was to blame a man for letting off a little steam when he hit port? Mr. Marr had been a sailor for years before deciding to save his money, marry, and settle down to the life of a shopkeeper. His shop, located at 29 Ratcliff Highway, prospered.

The Marrs had an infant daughter, a fourteen-year-old apprentice, and a servant, seventeen-year-old Margaret Jewell, on the premises. Mrs. Marr was pregnant. On this particular day, Saturday, December 7, she had a craving for something unusual to eat. She asked Margaret to fetch some oysters at a nearby fish shop. Margaret left on her errand at closing time, 11 p.m.

It was a dark, foggy night. The streets were full of carousing drunken sailors. Margaret tried two different fish shops, but the hour was late and they were closed. Giving up, she returned to the Marr's shop, which she found locked and in darkness. This was strange, as Mr. Marr had promised to leave the door ajar for her. Margaret, somewhat apprehensive, pounded on the door. Finally, a neighbour, Mr. Murray, came to her rescue. He told the frightened girl that he would go to the back of the shop and try to gain entrance from the rear. When he got there, he was surprised to find the back door wide open. A lone candle cast an eerie shadow across the back room of the shop. Murray cautiously entered the building.

He found Mr. Marr lying in a pool of blood behind the shop counter. His head had been smashed in with one vicious blow. Someone had then leaned over the fallen man and cut his throat from ear to ear. Murray came across the bodies of Mrs. Marr and the apprentice in the same room. They too had had their throats slit in the same manner. The hysterical man made his way through the carnage to the front door and let in Margaret Jewell and the small crowd that had gathered. The baby was found in her room. Her throat had also been slashed.

Margaret promptly fainted and had to be carried from the shop.

The only clues to the madman's identity was a heavy bloodied mallet found at the scene, which bore the initials J. P. The inhabitants of the east end were accustomed to brawls and beatings, but this was different. An entire family, including an innocent infant, had been wiped out in twenty minutes. Could such a madman strike again?

Twelve days passed. Mr. Williamson, the proprietor of a public house, The King's Arms, was no longer a young man, but he was tough and hard. The King's Arms was located in the same general neighbour-hood as Mr. Marr's dry goods shop.

This Thursday evening was no different than the thousands that had preceded it. At closing time, 11 p.m., Williamson's customers began drifting off into the foggy night. Mrs. Williamson and a waitress helped clean up. A granddaughter was peacefully asleep in a bed upstairs. A young carpenter named Turner, who lived at The King's Arms, strolled in and continued on straight up to his room.

At precisely 11:25 p.m., Turner sat bolt upright in his bed. A blood-curdling scream rang through the building. Turner immediately thought of the recent murders in the neighbourhood. He slowly got out of bed and quietly walked to the landing, which afforded him a view of the scene below through an open door. He perceived a tall man bending over Mr. Williamson's body. When the man straightened up to rifle the cash drawer, Turner heard the stranger's boots give a distinctive creak.

He waited no longer. Quaking with fear, for Turner was sure the assailant would search the bedrooms and kill him, he decided to escape. Fastening his bedclothes into a rope, he lowered himself out of his bed-room window. The rope was too short. Poor Turner was found dangling there with no place to go by passersby.

He told his terrifying story, and in a few minutes several neighbours entered The King's Arms. Mr. and Mrs. Williamson and their servant were dead. They had each received a solitary blow to the head, after which the murderer had slit their throats, with one vicious well-practised slash. The group of neighbours apprehensively walked up the stairs to the granddaughter's bedroom, not daring to think what might await them. The eleven-year-old child was unharmed. She had slept through the entire slaughter.

Thousands of handbills describing the tall man with the creaking boots were distributed throughout London. The handbills also men-tioned the mallet with the initials J. P. One of these handbills came to the attention of a lodging house proprietor named Virmiloe. He recognized the mallet as belonging to a lodger of his named John Peterson. His lodger's tool chest was examined and the mallet was missing, but Peterson had been at sea for weeks and could not have been the killer.

Another lodger, John Williams, immediately came under suspicion. Fellow lodgers remembered that on the night of both murders Williams had come in late. He always had plenty of money, but never worked. Recently he had purchased a new pair of boots, which squeaked loudly whenever he walked. Williams was a good-looking, pale man with bright yellow curly hair. He was blunt with fellow roomers, and not at all well liked.

There was little doubt that Williams was the earlier day Ripper. Once taken into custody and well aware of the fate awaiting him, Williams made a noose of his bedclothes and hanged himself in his cell. In keeping with the barbaric customs of the times, his body was placed on view to the public before a stake was driven through his heart.

Six weeks after his death a blood-encrusted dagger was found in Williams' room at his lodging house. He had stuffed it into a mousehole in the wall just before he was taken into custody.

Was He Guilty?

The trap door springs open and the convicted killer plunges to eternity. Later it is distressing to learn that the executed man may not have been a killer at all. In hindsight a reasonable doubt has crept in. Could the prisoner's protestations of innocence have been sincere? Did an innocent man hang?

Jane and Henry Dobson owned a farm about a quarter of a mile from the tiny village of Wolviston, England. The farm, known as High Grange, afforded the Dobsons a comfortable living. Besides the main house on the farm, another dwelling was usually occupied by a farm labourer and his family.

On January 18, 1938, Jane Dobson left High Grange heading for Wolviston. She never made it. When she failed to return that evening Henry Dobson rationalized that his wife may have continued on to Newcastle to visit their married daughter. That night he made three trips down from the farmhouse to the road to meet the bus, but each time there was no sign of his wife.

The next morning at 9:35 a.m. he decided to walk into the village. Taking a shortcut across a farm track, he noticed a crumpled object lying just off the path, partly in some grass and partly in a plowed field.

He found his wife's body. Stunned, he circled the body for a few moments and then took off for the village to summon the police.

An autopsy was performed by pathologists at Sunderland Royal Infirmary. Mrs. Dobson had been viciously raped. She had been stabbed directly into the chest and neck. Either of the two stab wounds would have resulted in death. The victim had also been beaten about the head before expiring.

Who would do such a thing? The presence of strangers in the isolated farming district would be conspicuous. The victim was a hard-working honest farmer's wife. She had no bad habits, didn't drink, nor had she any male friends outside her own family.

Police questioned Mr. Dobson, who at first could not recollect one single enemy. Searching his memory he recalled that several years before he and his wife had had a rather bitter argument with the hired hand who lived on his farm at the time. The man's name was Hoolhouse. Dobson had ordered the family off his property. They had left, but still lived nearby in Haverton Hill, about four miles from High Grange. At the time of the incident the Hoolhouses had a son, Robert, who was now a strapping twenty-year-old.

In the meantime police were endeavouring to trace Mrs. Dobson's last walk. According to Mr. Dobson's statement, his wife left the farm between 4:30 and 5:00. At about 5:30, Percy Swales and Thomas Nelson drove their cattle truck off the road onto the farm track. It was dusk. Their headlights picked up a man standing beside the road. The man quickly dropped to the plowed field. The stranger's obvious mode of travel was a bicycle, which was lying beside the road.

Swales drove up to the man and shouted, "Hullo, what's the game here?"

The man replied in an easily distinguishable local accent, "I'm all right. I have had one over the nine. Drive on." Loosely translated: "I've had one too many. I'm drunk."

Swales and Nelson drove on. They didn't know it at the time, but they had interrupted the killer in the act of raping and murdering Jane Dobson. Later, under questioning, the men were able to describe the appearance of the man they had seen for only an instant. They told the police that the killer wore a cap and leggings. His bicycle had the appearance of a racing bike with dropped handlebars.

Swales and Nelson drove on to the Dobson farm, unloaded some pigs, and returned past the area where they had seen the bicycle. It was now 5:45 p.m. The bicycle was gone and the men drove on, never giving the incident another thought.

Because the Hoolhouse family had been mentioned as the only ones Mr. Dobson could think of as enemies, police called on Robert Hoolhouse. They observed that he was pale, nervous, and had scratches on the right side of his face. Hoolhouse explained away the scratches and nervousness by telling the police that he had taken a rather bad spill off his bicycle. The police exchanged knowing glances when the bicycle proved to have dropped handlebars. Hoolhouse was taken to Haverton Hill police station where he gave a statement.

In essence he claimed that he had visited the home of William Husband on the day of Mrs. Dobson's murder. He called on Husband's daughter and a Miss Lax, remaining there until about 3:30 p.m. He stated that he left the Husband residence, which is located close to the Dobson farm, and cycled home, arriving at about four o'clock. It was on the trip home that he fell off his bike. That evening he returned by bus and accompanied Miss Lax to the movies at Billingham.

The story seemed plausible enough, and neatly removed Hoolhouse from the scene of the crime at 5:30, the most probable time of Mrs. Dobson's murder. Police hurried over to interview Miss Husband and Miss Lax. They corroborated Hoolhouse's story in every detail except one. They said that Hoolhouse didn't arrive until 3:45 p.m. and stayed for an hour and a half. That placed him squarely on the road at the crucial time with the opportunity to rape and kill Mrs. Dobson some-time after 5:15. Remember Swales and Nelson actually spoke to the killer at 5:30.

When the police returned to Hoolhouse and advised him that Miss Husband and Miss Lax differed with his story as to times, he said that he must be mistaken. They were right. Poor Hoolhouse gave another state-ment, suggesting that he had made a terrible mistake the first time around.

Hoolhouse was arrested and charged with Mrs. Dobson's murder. The prosecution made much of the fact that Hoolhouse had fabricated ficti-tious times in order to place himself at his home at the time of Mrs. Dobson's murder. The scratches on his face weighed heavily against him. Hoolhouse's trial lasted three days. He was found guilty and sentenced to hang. All appeals failed, and he was duly executed at Durham Gaol.

Since Hoolhouse's execution there have been grave doubts expressed as to his guilt. Hoolhouse would not be the first innocent man to concoct a false story out of fear of being wrongly convicted.

Knowing that he was near the scene of the murder at the time it was committed, did Hoolhouse stupidly lie about the time to remove him-self from the scene of the crime? The fact that he was in the vicinity at the time of the crime is not proof of guilt. Miss Lax swore that she hadn't noticed any scratches on Hoolhouse's face on their date at the movies. Did Hoolhouse have a legitimate fall off his bike the day after the murder when police noted the scratches? Knowing how incriminat-ing they were, did Hoolhouse move his bicycle mishap up a day so that it would appear that he had the scratches before the murder?

We will never be certain of the answers to these questions. Hoolhouse never had the advantage of the real killer coming forward to confess all, as often happens in fiction. The truth of the Dobson case will forever remain a mystery.

The Butchered Bride

James Greenacre was a nasty man. He didn't go around killing people in wholesale lots, however. He was much more selective. James was a prosperous grocer who dabbled in local politics. He also manufactured and sold a terrific remedy, guaranteed to cure you of any ailment.

In 1835 he was a man who had almost everything. He lived comfortably in a large home in London, and had a wide circle of business and political acquaintances. The one thing he didn't have was a wife. There were plenty of young women around London at the time who would have been more than pleased to become Mrs. Greenacre. Unfortunately James insisted that they be well-endowed with cash, or property, or both.

In the meantime James did not live alone. His housekeeper, Sarah Gale, saw to it that his sex life was both active and stimulating. She even became pregnant and blessed James with a baby boy. The lad was a chunky four-year-old when James, continuing in his search for a rich wife, met Hannah Brown.

Hannah, who was fully aware of James' quest for a rich girl, let it drop that she had several parcels of choice property just waiting to be shared with the right man. James, at long last, thought his search was over. Hannah, however, was as poor as a church mouse. And Sarah did not take kindly to the idea of her man marrying Miss Brown.

As Christmas approached, Hannah told James that she thought the festive season was a good time to get married. She had one fear; that James would find out she was penniless and drop her. On the other hand, if she could get him to the altar in a hurry, she would reveal her destitute financial situation to him after the marriage. Hannah felt confident that all would be forgiven.

Hannah managed to get James to set the date of their marriage. It was to be on the last Wednesday of the year. They would have their very own intimate Christmas dinner at his house to seal the engagement.

Things were going along famously, but wouldn't you know it, some spoilsport told James that Hannah didn't have a penny to her name. She had actually been borrowing from her brother, based on the assumption that she would land Greenacre. James was fit to be tied. To think that he had come within an ace of being tied down to a woman whom he would have to support for the rest of her days.

It had been a close call for Sarah too. She knew that if James had gone through with the marriage her son would almost certainly be disinherited by his father. Now, she rubbed salt into James' wounds by telling him that if he declined to marry Hannah she would probably sue him for breach of promise. He would be held up to ridicule in front of his business and political acquaintances.

Sarah planted the seed of murder in James' mind. There was no alternative. The lying, deceiving Hannah wouldn't go away without raising an embarrassing fuss.

Christmas Eve came. Sarah answered the knock on the door. Radiant Hannah walked in and probably complimented Sarah on the beautiful banquet table. Greenacre entered the room. He couldn't restrain his anger. He verbally blasted Hannah, who admitted her lies and insinuated that now they were about to be married Greenacre was help-less to do anything about it. In a fit of anger, he picked up a rolling pin and with one vicious blow caved in his fiancée's skull. Hannah lay dead at his feet.

Sarah came up with a rather novel approach: "Let's cut her up into three pieces and deliver each one to a different district." If the three individual parts of Hannah were ever found, the authorities would think they had three mysteries on their hands and never connect the parts to one crime.

With his Sarah taking an active part, Greenacre managed to dissect the body. He delivered the head to Stepney and flung it into Regents Canal. The legs were disposed of in Coldharbour Lane, while the trunk, wrapped in a portion of a child's blue cotton dress, was dropped off in Kilburn.

Greenacre had a morbid Christmas, but things were looking up for a happy new year. He and Sarah were now indelibly bound together by the act of murder. They probably realized they were stuck with each other for the rest of their lives.

In the meantime, on December 28, 1835, Hannah's torso was found in Kilburn. No one came forward to identify the torso, so it was pre-served. Ten days later a lock keeper discovered the head in the Regents Canal. Despite Sarah and Greenacre's theory that no connection would be made between the two parts of the body, the Stepney police imme-diately contacted the Kilburn police. It was ascertained that the two parts were from the same body.

Hundreds of people viewed the body but it remained unidentified for a further two months. A basket maker found the parcel containing the legs in a ditch. The police now had the complete body.

Poor Hannah had only one living relative, her brother. He viewed the body and identified his sister. When questioned he said his last contact with his sister had been just before Christmas. She mentioned she was going to have Christmas dinner with James Greenacre. At that time he had inquired about his missing sister and had been told by Greenacre that the pair had quarrelled. Hannah had not shown up for dinner, and Greenacre said he never wanted to see her again.

The police turned their efforts towards our hero, James Greenacre. Neighbours told of hearing wild noises from the house on Christmas Eve. They all thought it strange that Sarah was cleaning and fumigating the house for days after Christmas. Most people clean up before the holiday, not after.

Greenacre heard of the questions being asked, and booked passage to the U.S. He was arrested only hours before he was to sail. A search of the Greenacre house produced the matching portion of the child's dress that had been used to wrap the torso.

Greenacre at first denied any knowledge of the murder. Then he said it was the result of an accident during the course of a practical joke. Finally, he confessed to murder.

Both Greenacre and Sarah stood trial for murder in London's Old Bailey. Both were found guilty. Greenacre was publicly hanged before a jeering crowd of thousands on May 2, 1837. Sarah was sentenced to "transportation beyond the seas for life."

Sarah Gale eventually made a new life for herself in Australia. Fifty-one years later, in 1888, she died of natural causes.

He Came, He Saw, He Buried

The efficiency and cleanliness of the British, especially in the matter of murder, has never ceased to amaze me. The citizens of that tight little island are often careless and sloppy in other affairs, but absolutely never when it comes to murder.

At the turn of the 20th century, young Edgar Edwards resided in Leyton. He was unemployed, with no prospects of changing that status. One day, while scanning the newspapers, he noticed a business for sale. We will never know whether it was at this moment that he decided to become a killer, or if he was studying the paper with the thought of murder already firm in his mind.

The business for sale was a grocery store owned by a Mr. Darby on Wyndham Road, Camberwell. Edwards wrapped a heavy iron sash weight in newspapers and dashed over to Camberwell to take a look at the store. He arrived after business hours, and was let in by Mrs. Darby.

The grocery was a highly profitable venture for the Darbys. They explained that the only reason it was up for sale was because they had decided to move on to bigger and better things. In fact, because of the heavy trade during the Christmas season, they had to purchase a larger cashbox, and happened to have an unusual amount of cash on hand.

The Darbys, in their late twenties, appeared to have everything to live for, including a baby son. Edwards explained that he realized he was inconveniencing them, but he was a busy man himself and would appreciate taking a look at the books. Mrs. Darby led Edwards into the living area, while Mr. Darby continued to work in the store proper. Edwards courteously held out a chair for Mrs. Darby, who sat down with her child on her lap. Then Edwards took out his sash weight and struck Mrs. Darby on the head with such force that the chair she was sitting on crumbled to the floor. The baby screamed. Edwards snuffed out the child's life with two quick blows of the sash weight. Mr. Darby, hearing the commotion, rushed into the room. The sash weight came down on his head again and again. The three Darbys lay still in death on their living room floor.

Edwards didn't grab the cashbox and run. He had other plans. He coolly and callously dismembered his three victims and placed their bodies in three separate packing cases. He packed the contents tight with the addition of straw. He was in a grocery store, so there was an abundance of packing material available. Into a fourth crate Edwards tossed the sash weight, chair, and rug from the murder room. All four boxes were secured with nails and cord. Edwards, using the Darbys' typewriter, typed a note to the effect that they had sold their business, which would soon reopen under new management. He tacked the note on the front door. Edgar Edwards washed up and went home.

The next morning Edwards, using the Darby's money he had taken from the cashbox, rented an attractive house on Church Street, Leyton. The rest of his rather hectic day was spent systematically removing everything of value from the Darbys' living quarters. Edwards had rented a truck and hired two local lads to help him with the heavier pieces. He took particular care of four securely wrapped packing cases.

Many of the Darbys' regular customers who came to shop at the store were shocked to read the notice on the front door. Edwards met them and was quick to point out that while the sale of the business appeared to be very hasty, it really wasn't so. He had been negotiating with the Darbys for weeks. They had come to terms only the evening before. The Darbys had dashed away that very same evening in order to close a deal they had been working on in Northern England. The story had the ring of truth to it. The Darbys had mentioned to many of their customers that they were trying to purchase a larger business. No one was even mildly suspicious.

Edwards spent one whole night digging in his back yard. He dug a large hole and placed the three Darbys and the box of incriminating furniture inside. Out of sight, out of mind. He had apparently succeeded in getting away with murder.

For a time all went well. Edwards spent most of his evenings at home, reading. His daylight hours were often spent in the library. Edwards neither drank nor smoked. He made the acquaintance of a young, respectable woman, who soon became infatuated with her polite, mild-mannered suitor. The pair became engaged. The only worry that Edwards had during these months was the ever-diminishing number of pound notes in the Darbys' cashbox.

Back at the Darbys' store the police had run into a blank wall. They deduced that the Darbys had absconded with all their belongings and cash in order to avoid paying suppliers. The man who had moved the furniture no doubt was in league with the Darbys. They had no idea murder had taken place.

Edwards needed to refill his cashbox and logically decided that since everything had worked out so well the first time, he would try it all again. He picked a grocery shop that was up for sale. Edwards invited Mr. Garland, the owner of the shop, over to Church Street to discuss the deal. He had taken the precaution of purchasing a new sash weight to assist in the negotiations.

When Garland arrived, Edwards hit him over the head with the sash weight. Instead of caving in, Garland screamed and fought his attacker. His screams brought the assistance of neighbours, and the struggle came to an end.

When the police arrived, Edwards was in bed, claiming that Garland must be crazy. He stated that Garland had attacked him for no apparent reason. Edwards said that he was sorry if Garland had his head split open in the struggle, but he was only acting in self-defence. The sham didn't work.

During the fight a desk had overturned. Stationery bearing the Darbys' name had scattered across the floor. Once the police found something connecting Edwards with the missing Darbys, they hung on like bulldogs. Friends and former customers of the Darbys were brought over to Church Street. They recognized pieces of furniture as belonging to the missing couple. The police then came up with the two lads who had helped move the four sealed crates. They identified Edwards as the man who had hired them. The police discovered newly turned earth in the back yard. They dug up the bodies of the three Darbys.

Edwards stood trial for murder. He never confessed and, in fact, refused to discuss any relevant aspects of his case. During the proceedings he often confided to his lawyer that the whole thing was a lot of nonsense and was an utter bore.

He was found guilty and sentenced to be put to death. As his execution date approached he became more cheerful and talkative. Edwards joked and laughed on the scaffold before the trap door was sprung.

A Grisly Find

It is one thing to want to live in a certain city. It is quite another thing to lose one's head over it. Santosh Kumari Bali did just that. This tale of terror begins in New Delhi, India, and ends in Toronto, where Mrs. Bali did, in fact, lose her head.

Mrs. Bali, a forty-two-year-old divorcée, made her living in New Delhi in the real estate game. When Harbhajan Singh Math, thirty-six, told her of the opportunities that existed in Canada, she could hardly wait to leave India. There were a few minor problems, but nothing seemed to be too difficult for Harbhajan to handle. He arranged for airline tickets, passports, and took care of other immigration red tape. Mrs. Bali travelled to the promised land in July 1974.

After her arrival things just didn't work out. As soon as her thirty-day visitors' permit ran out she was told by Harbhajan that she was now an illegal immigrant, which was true enough. She could obtain employment only where details such as social security numbers and unemployment insurance deductions could be passed over. Leave it to Harbhajan to fix things. It so happened his brother Harmohinder Singh Math, thirty-four, and the latter's wife, Paranjit Kaur Math, twenty-eight, would be only too glad to assist Santosh in getting a job as a domestic. With Paranjit's assistance, Santosh was employed as a domestic in the home of Mr. and Mrs. André Allain of Weatherstone Crescent in North York, a suburb of Toronto.

Later evidence indicated that Harbhajan threatened to reveal Santosh's illegal status unless she turned money over to him. Terrified of being exposed as an illegal immigrant, Santosh paid off Harbhajan each month. Finally, after being blackmailed for almost a year, she informed Harbhajan that she would pay no longer.

That's where things stood with Santosh and the Math clan until September 1975. On September 15, two garbage collectors in Etobicoke were startled to discover that the trash can at the corner of Bloor Street W. and Eagle Avenue contained more than trash. They uncovered a female torso wrapped in burlap. On the very same day the Allains reported Santosh Kumari Bali missing. Two days later a woman's left leg was found sticking out of a pail beside a North York factory.

After questioning the Allains, police suspected that the torso and leg might be those of the missing woman. Upon searching Santosh's room, they found the addresses and telephone numbers of the Maths. As a result, Staff Sergeant Murray Crawford ended up at the Math residence on Burnett Avenue.

Harbhajan admitted knowing Santosh slightly. He claimed that she was away on a trip to Montreal. A search of the Math residence revealed pails, plastic bags, and burlap sacks that matched material used to wrap the torso and leg. At Harmohinder's home on Steeles Aveune, police found Santosh's coat, which Mrs. Math claimed belonged to her.

All three Maths were arrested and charged with murder. Because of the illegal status of the victim, and the lack of identification due to the missing head, it became imperative to legally identify the body as that of Santosh Bali. Two Toronto detectives, Staff Sergeant Gerald Stevenson and Sergeant Winston Weatherbee, flew to New Delhi to verify Mrs. Bali's identity. They brought with them X-rays and descriptions of operational scars found on the torso.

Weatherbee describes the trip as a strange but necessary one. "Mrs. Bali had a Caesarean section and a gall bladder operation some time before coming to Canada. We were able to confirm these facts with medical authorities and obtained other verification by interviewing members of Mrs. Bali's family."

In May 1976 the Maths stood trial for murder in a Toronto court. For thirteen days Crown Prosecutor Robert McGee built a formidable case against Harbhajan Singh Math. Math's brother and his wife remained silent, never admitting to any involvement in the case. There was very little connecting evidence McGee could bring forward against the couple, but Harbhajan was quite another kettle of fish.

Harbhajan claimed that Santosh had had a drinking bout in the basement of his home the previous September 12. He said she had fallen on the concrete floor before passing out on a bed. Next morning when he attempted to wake her, she didn't stir. Santosh was dead. Harbhajan was in a fix. He knew that he would be in big trouble for assisting an illegal immigrant. Who knows, he might even be suspected of murdering Santosh. There was only one thing to do and that was to dispose of the body. Unfortunately, the rigid, unyielding corpse would not fit into his Volkswagen. Harbhajan thought for a moment, and then it all became clear. He would dismember the body and distribute the parts hither and yon.

In court, Math described his grisly task. "I started with a sickle, but it only got so far. It didn't work right, so I threw it away and picked up a saw. I cut the head off first." Calmly and unemotionally he described how some limbs were difficult and had to be twisted and pulled in order to be detached. He then took several trips in the Volkswagen to distribute the various parts of the body throughout the city. Above all, Math insisted that he did not murder Santosh.

Crown Prosecutor McGee remembers the Math case as "certainly my most gruesome case in fourteen years as a Crown Prosecutor." He recalls Math using a Bible to illustrate how he wrapped portions of the body. McGee felt certain that Santosh had been strangled, but without the head it was difficult to prove. The defence maintained that Santosh had met her death by falling several times on the concrete floor of his basement.

Defence attorney David Humphrey startled the court to stunned silence when he indicated that his client would reveal the location of the victim's head to the court. McGee describes the unusual manoeuvre as "the most amazing opening address I ever heard when the defence attorney suggested driving out to find the head."

It was obvious that the defence was trying to refute the Crown's contention that the victim had been strangled. And so the entourage of lawyers, doctors, and police found themselves being directed by the defendant to a field behind Holy Cross Cemetery north of Toronto. There, in the eerie darkness, in a plastic tote bag, the head of Santosh Kumari Bali was recovered.

Examination of the severed head proved that the defence was right all along. Santosh had not been strangled. However, this did the defendant little good, for he had made one fatal mistake. After cutting off Santosh's head he had thrown it in a pail containing engine oil. This coating of oil, along with the fact that the bag containing the head had lodged in nine inches of ice cold water all winter, combined to maintain the head in an excellent state of preservation.

Dr. John Ferris, a pathologist, indicated that the cause of death was asphyxiation. The victim's jaw was fractured in two places. Santosh had been beaten to death. Her nose was broken, her eyes blackened, and her head badly bruised and lacerated.

One minor mystery remains unsolved to this day. No blood was ever found on the pails, saw, and sickle Harbhajan professed were used during the dismemberment at his residence. It is the belief of investigating officers that Santosh was killed elsewhere. Her movements during her last hours on earth may never be known.

Due to the lack of evidence connecting Harmohinder Math and his wife, Paranjit, to the murder, the jury saw fit to find the pair not guilty. Harbhajan was not as fortunate. He was found guilty and received the severest sentence possible at that time—life imprisonment with no possibility of parole for twenty years.

Goodnight, Irene

It takes no special talent to be a murderer. Ladies and gentlemen of a murderous bent come from all walks of life. They range from bungling morons to college professors. A select few take extraordinary steps to cover their tracks. As we have already seen, sometimes these steps include attempts to dispose of their victims' bodies.

Chester Stanton Jordan shifted his 225 pounds from foot to foot as the clerk inquired if the hacksaw felt comfortable in his hand.

"Very fine," Chester replied. "It will do the job nicely." The job Chester's nimble mind alluded to was the systematic dismemberment of his wife's body, but of course at the time only he knew that.

"I would appreciate it if you would sharpen the butcher knife."

"No problem at all," the obliging clerk responded.

Thus equipped with new cutting tools, the six-foot three-inch Chester ambled out of the hardware store to address himself to the task at hand.

As Chester smartly walked through the streets of Boston that day in 1908, the good citizens of Beantown had no way of knowing that Chester Jordan would soon be the best-known name in the city. Chester's cutting and hacking would provide the main news story for the Boston press for the following year.

Chester was born twenty-eight years earlier in Indianapolis. As a youngster he displayed a natural affinity for the stage, which prompted him to leave school to become an actor. To keep the wolf from the door, Chester supported himself by working between engagements in a furniture store. When he was twenty-one, his family moved to Boston. Chester developed an act and appeared on the stage whenever the opportunity presented itself.

In 1904 Chester met a stripper who disrobed under the name of Irene Shannon. It was considered politic for anyone appearing on the stage in Boston to have an Irish name.

On September 25, 1904, Chester and Irene got married. They tried to combine their acting abilities by forming an act together, but their attempts were fruitless. Instead, Chester got a job as a collector for a finance company, while Irene was able to continue to make a living stripping.

It is difficult to say just when Irene began to accuse the hulking Chester of being impotent. Irene had the audacity to insinuate that Chester preferred male company to her own. Later, Chester claimed the whole topic of his impotence exploded into violence during an argument. He growled at his wife, "You're a dirty, evil-minded bitch"—to which Irene replied, "I'll show you whether I'm a bitch or not." Then the five-foot, two-inch Irene advanced on her huge husband with a butcher's knife. Chester, acting strictly in self-defence, you understand, struck his wife, sending her crashing down the stairs. Irene lay dead on the floor.

The next thing Chester remembers is waking up the following morning and finding his wife's nude body on the floor. Inexplicably, her throat was cut from ear to ear, but little details like that didn't seem to bother Chester.

What to do? Chester thought the whole thing over. If he went to the police he felt sure he would be accused of murdering his wife. Like many a murderer who went before him, Chester decided to dispose of the body.

He found a straight razor and a butcher knife in his home and began his gruesome task. While the work wasn't easy, Chester managed to remove both arms and legs. He then lifted the armless and legless body and placed it in one of a pair of stationary stone washtubs. The arms and legs fitted nicely into the second tub.

Chester washed up and went to a neighbourhood bar, where he had a quick shot of whiskey to steady his nerves. He then visited the hardware store and purchased the hacksaw. At the same time he had the clerk sharpen his new butcher knife.

That evening Chester cut off Irene's head with his hacksaw. No one ever thought to ask so we will never know why Chester took the trouble to scalp his wife. We do know that he threw the scalp into the stove. The draft carried the scalp to the back of the stove, away from the flames. It was later recovered in almost mint condition.

Chester spent the entire evening cutting and carving until Irene was in a total of twelve individual sections. Exhausted and hungry, he paused to eat two cold pork chops. Ironically, they had been cooked by Irene the day before. Then Chester placed all twelve parts back into the two washtubs, cleaned up his tools, and left his residence to take a brief stroll.

Is a murderer's work ever done? When he returned from his walk, Chester placed Irene's head and thighs in the furnace. He lit the furnace and figured that was that.

Next day Chester bought a trunk and a spool of good strong cord. What remained of Irene he placed in the trunk. Chester went looking for a horse and wagon in which to transport his macabre cargo.

George W. Collins followed the honourable profession of what was then called a hackman. He was hailed by Chester and for the rest of his life was able to tell cronies the story of how he lugged Irene Shannon's body through the streets of Boston.

Earlier in the day Chester had rented a room at #7 Hancock Street from a Mrs. Mary Haley. He gave the landlady four dollars for the first week's rent.

Collins, who wasn't a big man, had some difficulty placing the trunk on his hack, but his obliging fare gave him a hand. Collins couldn't help but notice that his passenger drew the shades of the hack even though it was broad daylight.

Finally the horse-drawn vehicle pulled up in front of #7 Hancock. Again Collins' passenger helped carry the heavy trunk. The men lugged the trunk up the stairs and placed it in what was obviously Chester's room. Collins received a dollar for his trouble and took his leave, but he couldn't get the big man and the strange trunk out of his mind. He went to the police and told his story.

The police didn't think the incident was extraordinary, but they promised to look into the matter. That evening two police officers intercepted Chester as he was returning to his room. They asked him what was in the trunk. Chester hedged. Under further probing, Chester opened the trunk and began to lift clothing from a tray inset in the top of the trunk. One of the policemen became impatient. He lifted the tray and peered inside. Sure as shooting, Irene was in the trunk.

Chester was hustled down to the police station, where he confessed to dismembering his wife in an attempt to dispose of the body. He certainly hadn't murdered dear Irene. It had all been a horrible accident.

It took the Boston cops exactly one hour to formally charge Chester with murder. It took only three more hours for those same cops to find out that Chester had a well-heeled brother-in-law, none other than Jesse Livermore.

In 1908 Livermore's name was synonymous with American success stories. Jesse had left school at fifteen to work for a brokerage house in Boston. Starting with $3.12, he netted $140 on his first deal in the stockmarket. On the way up Jesse married a secretary who worked at another brokerage office. The secretary, Nettie Jordan, was none other than our boy Chester's sister. Within a year Nettie and Jesse Livermore had made their first fortune trading in copper stocks. Moving on to Wall Street, they cleaned up over $3 million in cotton. No question about it, Chester had wealthy champions in his sister and brother-in-law. They publicly stated they would stand behind Chester, no matter what.

Chester stood trial for murder on April 20, 1909, in East Cambridge, Massachusetts. He stuck to his story throughout, but the prosecution's evidence proved positively embarrassing. An efficient medical expert testified that Irene had not met her end by falling downstairs. She had died from manual strangulation.

The police had found a flatiron in Chester's residence. A medical expert, displaying poor Irene's skull in court, neatly fitted the flatiron into depressions in the skull. From the evidence it appeared impossible for Irene to have met her death by falling down the stairs.

Twenty hours after retiring to deliberate, the jury found Chester guilty as charged. With Livermore's bankroll behind him, Chester was able to exhaust every possible legal avenue in order to stay out of Massachusetts' dreaded electric chair.

It was all for naught. On September 24, 1912, Chester was firmly strapped into the electric chair. One minute and eight seconds later Chester was pronounced dead.

Patrick Was a Charmer

Whatever else I might say about Patrick Mahon, I have to admit he was a handsome devil. Not only was Pat's countenance pleasing to the eye, he also had a charming manner and was fastidious about his personal appearance. All in all, a fine cut of a man.

In 1923 Pat had already been married for thirteen years, having wed a remarkable young woman who was to stand by him through good times and bad. There were a few rough spots in Pat's past, but nothing compared to those that were to come.

For example, there was the time shortly after his marriage when Pat forged a cheque and took off to the Isle of Man with another woman. This little escapade landed him in jail for twelve months. Of a more serious nature, in 1916 he broke into a bank. During this robbery he struck a female employee over the head with a hammer. Pat spent five years in prison for that caper.

Throughout these exploits Mrs. Mahon stuck by her man. She gave birth to two children, a son and a daughter. The son died while Pat was serving his prison term.

To support her family while Pat was in prison, Mrs. Mahon took a job in London with the Consols Automatic Aerators Company as a clerk. Ambitious and hard-working, she received several promotions, and advanced to a responsible secretarial position.

Through her influence she secured a job for Pat with her firm when he was released from prison. He too, proved to be somewhat of a success, and climbed quickly from salesman to sales manager.

All things considered, the Mahons were making something of their lives. Except for one thing. Pat couldn't stay away from women. With his charm and good looks he could have the pick of the crop.

By 1923 Pat was entwined in a prolonged affair with shorthand typist Emily Kaye. Emily worked for a firm of chartered accountants who had business dealings with Pat's company. Emily, who was thirty-seven, was completely enamoured of her handsome boyfriend, who was four years her junior. As the affair wore on, Pat vaguely hinted that someday he would leave his wife and be free to marry his very willing mistress.

Emily became disenchanted with vague promises. She sported an engagement ring and told acquaintances that she and Pat were planning to marry and move to South Africa, where Pat had an executive position waiting for him. Emily, who had been working steadily for twenty years, had a tidy nest egg of several hundred pounds stashed away.

In anticipation of Pat's divorce and her own marriage, she quit her job. Her income was now being augmented by the investments Pat made with her money. Every so often he borrowed a hundred pounds, with the promise of substantial profits in the future.

At this time Pat was going along with the tide, delaying love-struck Emily with plausible excuses—difficulty in obtaining passports, trouble with his wife. He hoped to keep Emily on the string forever. Meanwhile, he was blowing her hard-earned savings at the racetrack.

This idyllic situation received an abrupt jolt one day when Emily informed Pat that she was pregnant. Pat gulped. To alleviate any fears Pat might have about their future together, Emily suggested they go away for a few days as a sort of love experiment. Not to a sleazy room, but to a real home. It would prove that they were meant for each other and could live happily ever after. Pat, who was always game for anything, thought it was a great idea.

Emily had another firm hold on Pat. One day, quite by coincidence, Emily was cleaning out a drawer which was lined with old newspapers. There, staring up at her, was an account of Pat's trial concerning the bank holdup and his five-year prison term. Emily knew that Pat dearly loved his position as sales manager. If exposed as an ex-convict to his employer he would most certainly be dismissed. In her subtle way Emily let Pat know that she wouldn't be above such a ploy if deserted. No wonder Pat opted for the love experiment.

Pat chose for his romantic interlude a desolate stretch of beach situated between Eastbourne and Wallsend on Pevensey Bay. This two-mile strip of Sussex beach is commonly referred to as the Crumbles. Located on the Crumbles were some cottages, which were once part of the Langley Coast Guard Station. Early in April 1924 Pat rented one of the isolated cottages, using the fictitious names of Mr. and Mrs. Waller. He paid for the first week's rent in advance.

The month of April proved to be a very busy one for Pat. Let's follow his movements step by step. On Monday, April 7, Emily travelled to Eastbourne and checked into a hotel. On Thursday, April 10, Pat, still in London, met young, attractive Ethel Duncan on the street. It was raining. Pat offered to share his umbrella and walked Miss Duncan home. Charming, attentive, and polite, Pat had no difficulty obtaining a dinner date with Miss Duncan for the following Wednesday.

On Friday, April 11, Pat joined Emily in Eastbourne and took possession of their cottage on the Crumbles. Pat didn't stay the night, but returned to London.

On Saturday, April 12, Pat returned to Emily at the cottage for the weekend. On Tuesday, April 15, Pat murdered Emily Kaye. On

Wednesday, April 16, Pat travelled to London, purchased a butcher knife, then kept his dinner date with Miss Duncan.

During their dinner date, Pat invited the thoroughly enthralled Miss Duncan to spend the following weekend at his cottage by the sea. Miss Duncan was lonely. She had recently lost her job. Her handsome companion, who quoted Latin phrases and spoke French fluently, was very debonair. She accepted the invitation. Later, the thoughtful Pat sent her four pounds to cover the expenses for her trip.

And so Miss Duncan travelled to the lonely Crumbles to spend her weekend of love with her charming stranger. The cottage may have been thought by some to be drab. Others might have called it rustic. Miss Duncan loved the location. She loved the cottage and, above all, she loved Pat Mahon.

The attractive couple made love whenever the mood came upon them. Sometimes, spent from their efforts, they cuddled in silence, staring into the fireplace. Who knows, thought Miss Duncan, someday Pat might be divorced from his horrible wife and be free to marry me. He was so kind, so gentle. It was perfect with him, like being married. She had the run of the cottage. All except one room, which was always locked.

Miss Duncan had no way of knowing she was making love to a monster, while the body of Emily Kaye lay in the locked room awaiting the very special machinations of Patrick Herman Mahon.

Ethel Duncan left the Crumbles with a kiss and a promise of future love trysts. Later Pat was to state that he needed to have someone around for company after Emily's death. Unfortunately for Miss Duncan, she happened to be that someone.

While Pat had been busy spending time with his two lady friends, back in London, his wife became suspicious of his long absences.

It was true his occupation as sales manager necessitated a certain amount of travel, but lately he had spent every weekend, as well as several weekdays, on the road. When questioned, Pat always seemed to have an answer. However, when a friend mentioned that he had seen Pat at Plumpton Races Easter Monday, it was just too much. Mrs. Mahon felt Pat had slipped back to heavy gambling. She decided to search his suits for any evidence that he had been attending the races.

As she was looking through his pockets, Mrs. Mahon came across a cloakroom ticket from Waterloo Station. She was puzzled. What would her husband leave on deposit in a cloakroom? She decided to ask a friend, who by coincidence had once worked as a railroad policeman, to investigate the matter for her.

This gentleman presented the ticket at Waterloo and withdrew a Gladstone bag. He peeked inside and immediately called Scotland Yard.

Detectives put a guard on the cloakroom and returned the ticket to Mrs. Mahon with instructions to put it back in Pat's suit. The distraught woman asked what was going on, but could only find out that the ticket had nothing to do with bookmaking, which up to this point was Mrs. Mahon's greatest fear.

Next day, Pat Mahon strolled up to the cloakroom and claimed his Gladstone bag. Detectives picked him up without any fuss. He was taken to Kennington Road Police Station and asked to explain the contents of the Gladstone.

It had contained a large butcher knife, bloodstained clothing, and a tennis racquet case monogrammed E.B.K. All of these items had been liberally sprinkled with disinfectant.

Initially, Pat attempted to dream up some story about transporting dog meat, but this tale quickly crumbled when he was informed by the police that tests had already been done on the bloodstained clothing. The blood was human.

Pat then confessed, but his confession was riddled with lies in an effort to cover up one of the most ruthless premeditated murders ever committed. According to Pat, he and Emily had an argument that ended up in a struggle. They fell to the floor with him on top. Emily struck her head on a coal scuttle, which killed her instantly. He then moved her body to a spare room, locked the door, and proceeded to have his new guest, Miss Duncan, down to the Crumbles for a pleasant weekend interlude.

When Miss Duncan left, Pat told police he cut the body into small pieces in an attempt to rid himself of the ghastly thing.

Detectives, accompanied by a pathologist, proceeded to the cottage on the Crumbles. They opened the front door and walked into hell. Throughout the cottage was the grim evidence that a human being had been methodically sliced and carved into small pieces. There was no doubt that the unfortunate victim was Emily Kaye.

Bloodied articles of female clothing were found in a trunk with the initials E.B.K. painted on its top. Four large portions of a human body were in the trunk. Greasy saucepans were scattered throughout the cottage. Upon examination the grease proved to be human fat. One two-gallon pot contained a piece of boiled human flesh.

Other human remains were found. Thirty-seven small pieces of human flesh were taken from a hat box, while a biscuit tin concealed human organs. Detectives also uncovered a bloodied rusty saw. Ashes from a fireplace contained bits of charred bone. A broken axe was believed to be the murder weapon.

Detectives and the pathologist gathered up the bits and pieces of what had once been Emily Kaye and returned to London. Little by little they reconstructed the body as best they could. The head and one leg were never found.

Pat Mahon was arrested and stood trial for the murder of Emily Kaye. Pat tried to turn on the charm that he had used to his advantage all his life. This time it didn't work.

He took the stand in his own defence and explained that Emily had struck her head on the coal scuttle, causing instant death. He also claimed that he had purchased the butcher knife after Emily's death, indicating that the dismemberment was not planned.

However, the prosecution was quick to point out that the quality of the coal scuttle was so poor that falling on it would scarcely cause a fatality. The prosecution also proved by receipts that Pat had purchased the butcher knife on the morning of April 12, when Emily was still alive. It was obvious to the jury that he knew what he was about to do and knew exactly how he would do it.

Pat readily admitted dismembering the body. His main hope was to attempt to discredit premeditation and attribute the death to an accident.

The courtroom was silent as Pat related how, on a stormy day, he built a roaring fire in the fireplace and positioned his victim's severed head on a log. As the flames leaped about the grisly object, Emily's eyes suddenly popped open. At that exact moment there was a flash of lightning and a clap of thunder. Pat, frightened out of his boots, ran out the door. It was some time before he could re-enter the cottage of death. Doctors explained that exposure to heat could cause the eyelids of a severed head to open.

Three days later Pat was still on the witness stand going through his gory tale step by step. Again he approached the part of the story that concerned the burning of the head. Suddenly, a thunderclap shook the courtroom. Many spectators gasped. Pat, visibly shaken, steadied himself on the witness railing.

Pat claimed that he had completely burned the head, but no trace of any part of it was found in the ashes of the fireplace. Scotland Yard believed that he burned what he could and possibly pulverized the balance into powder, which he threw into the sea.

Patrick Mahon was found guilty and sentenced to be hanged. All appeals failed to save his life. He was hanged on September 9, 1924, at Wandsworth Prison.

Death on Centre Island

Bill Newell was a ladies' man. Good-looking, muscular, oozing confidence. Born in Toronto on May 20, 1914, Bill led an ordinary early life. His most outstanding accomplishment appears to have been in athletics. He was pole vault champion of Scarborough Collegiate Institute.

Bill married Winnifred Moores in 1934. He and Winnifred had a daughter, Doreen, but the marriage didn't last. A year before his divorce he was living with attractive Aune Paavola, the daughter of strict Finnish immigrants. Three weeks after his divorce from Winnifred became final, Bill married Aune, who had given birth to his son, Bill Jr., some six months previously.

Aune Paavola accepted Bill at face value. It was true his charming manner was often interspersed with impulsive temper tantrums, but she tried to overlook such minor faults.

However, Aune eventually became disenchanted with Bill's uncontrollable temper and his wandering ways. The couple separated. Bill rebounded without missing a bounce. Within a year he was living with another Finnish Canadian girl, Elna Lehto.

It was 1940. Russia had invaded Finland. In a grandiose gesture, Bill joined a Canadian force going to Finland's aid. Two months later, on April 5, he was back in Toronto. It was an embarrassingly short tour of duty, but Bill came up with a plausible explanation. He claimed that he had received serious wounds around one eye, forcing him to return to Canada.

As usual, Bill was lying. It was later learned that he had refused to sign an agreement to serve with the Finnish forces. As a result, he was deported to Canada. So much for Bill Newell's distinguished two-month war record in defence of Finland.

On August 26 Bill joined the R.C.A.F. and was sent to Brandon, Manitoba for training. For the first time in years Bill had a steady income. It was the distribution of his Air Force dependents' allowance cheques that gave rise to his problems.

Aune was still Bill's legal wife. She and her son Billy were certainly entitled to some kind of living allowance. Then there was Winnifred, who had the full responsibility of raising Doreen. Also squarely in the picture was Bill's current companion, Elna, who, according to the Canadian Armed Forces, could not claim common-law status as she and Bill had not been living together for a full year. The only way Elna could share Bill's income would be if Aune signed an agreement to that effect or consented to a divorce.

Using his muddled affairs as an excuse, Bill obtained a transfer from Brandon to St. Thomas, Ontario. On September 20, 1940 he returned to Toronto on leave and spent almost every evening with Aune.

Bill made arrangements. On Saturday, September 28, he spent the night with Aune. He planned to take her and her roommate, Orvokki Hakamies, to a concert at the Active Service Canteen. At 8 a.m. he left Aune and returned to Elna, but stayed only a few hours. At noon he took Aune out to lunch, telling Orvokki that they would return in an hour or so.

When they left Aune's home at 15 Grange Street at 1:30 that Sunday afternoon, there is little doubt that Bill Newell was leading his wife to her death.

Mrs. Toini Ranpors, the girls' landlady, thought Bill looked gallant in his crisp new Air Force uniform. She watched the good-looking couple as they walked east on Grange and turned south on Beverley. They had a bite to eat at the Active Service Canteen about 2 p.m., walked down to the ferry docks and caught the 2:50 boat, the Sam McBride, to Centre Island.

They strolled hand in hand down Manitou and Iroquois Avenues onto a footpath to the northeast section of a filtration plant located there. They were within a stone's throw of St. Andrew's Cut, one of several lagoons intersecting the island's coast. It was an isolated, lonely place.

Aune had believed that there was still hope for a reconciliation with her husband, but now she knew it was no use. Bill was pressing for a divorce or, failing that, was attempting to have her sign off her rights to his family allowance cheques. Aune would have none of it.

Suddenly Bill pounced on his wife. Aune struggled. A rope was twisted around the hapless girl's neck and pulled until she lay dead. All was quiet in that isolated, overgrown section of Centre Island. Bill's mind raced with the details of what still had to be done.

Without warning, unexpected intruders came upon the scene. Charles and Marion Maynes, who lived on the island, were canoeing through St. Andrew's Cut. Bill saw them first. He propped Aune's body up to a sitting position, tied a string on a stick and pretended to be fishing. Mrs. Maynes later testified that she thought it strange that the woman sitting so erect seemed to be staring straight ahead. She noticed the airman fishing and looked away.

Slowly the Maynes disappeared from view. Bill carried his wife's body off the path and stripped it of everything that might identify her. He covered Aune's body with her black coat. Then he gathered as much brush as he could find and dumped it over her inert form. With luck, Bill thought, the body might not be found until spring.

Bill caught the 4:30 ferry back to the mainland. At 8:45 he met Orvokki Hakamies and inquired if Aune was at home. When Orvokki replied that she didn't know where Aune was, Bill continued on to his living quarters with Elna at 172 Howland Avenue.

Aune Newell was immediately reported missing. Next day Bill returned to St. Thomas. On Tuesday, in an attempt to allay suspicion, he wrote a pleasant letter to Aune.

Bill managed a 48-hour leave. This time Elna met him with the disconcerting news that there were radio reports of his wife's disappearance. She suggested that he contact police. Bill took the advice and told Detective Sergeant Fred Skinner that, in his opinion, his wife was not missing, but hiding somewhere to avoid being served with divorce papers. He also told Skinner that he had last seen his wife the previous Sunday at 7 p.m., when he had bumped into her at the corner of Yonge and Adelaide Streets.

On Sunday, October 6, Harry Lemon, a parks department employee, whose job it was to make a circuit of Centre Island every Sunday, spotted a woman's shoe. It captured his attention because it appeared new. Harry looked further and found a garter, a purse, a stocking, and finally the body of Aune Newell. Exactly one week had elapsed since she had been strangled to death.

Bill was immediately picked up and held as a material witness while detectives gathered evidence. Bill's letters to Aune indicated that his main concern was to obtain a divorce and custody of his son Billy so that his service cheques could be diverted to Elna. A piece of rope was found at the scene. It matched rope found at 172 Howland Avenue, where Bill lived with Elna.

Bill stood trial three times for the murder of his wife. The first two resulted in hung juries. He was an obstreperous prisoner, continually fighting with guards. During court proceedings he shouted at the presiding judge and witnesses.

New evidence was presented at the handsome airman's third trial. A torn Y.M.C.A. envelope with an R.C.A.F. crest had been found near Aune's body. The reassembled envelope revealed a sketch of the remote death site. Elna identified the map and notes as being in the handwriting of Bill Newell. He had written to her many times using similar envelopes. One was found among his belongings. Elna also testified that Bill had written her suggesting that the murder of his wife was the solution to his problems.

Bill Newell was found guilty and sentenced to hang. All appeals failed. On February 12, 1942, Bill had a breakfast of bacon, eggs, toast, and coffee. He refused a sedative and, proclaiming his innocence to the end, walked erectly to the Don Jail scaffold, where he was executed.

Buried on the Farm

"There was no direct evidence that murder had been committed, not even a body. Yet I knew that Viola had been murdered, and I had a pretty good idea who killed her. The case was bizarre in many ways," said Inspector Bill Perrin of the Ontario Provincial Police. Sitting in his office at the O.P.P. Headquarters talking about the apprehension of murderers, I got the distinct impression that once Bill Perrin becomes convinced of something he doesn't let go until he either proves or disproves his beliefs.

For years Inspector Perrin was attached to the Criminal Investigation Branch, where he was in charge of many of Ontario's strange murder cases. None was stranger than that of Viola Leahy.

The Leahy farm is situated along R.R. #4, Lakefield, Ontario, and has been in the Leahy family for as long as anyone can remember; certainly four or five generations. Jim Leahy worked hard on the farm, and supplemented his income by operating heavy excavation equipment. Everyone agrees that Jim is one of the best operators in the Peterborough area. Viola, his wife of over twenty-five years, also had interests that drew her away from the farm. Before her marriage she had received formal training as a Registered Nursing Aide, a vocation she continued to follow after she became Mrs. Leahy. Both Jim and Viola had independent natures, and this independent bent, combined with their physical absence from each other, drove a wedge into an otherwise normal relationship.

Viola in particular craved some sort of social life. She enjoyed taking in the local dances, and sometimes visited a tavern with a woman friend, Emgard Woodzack, although she never drank anything stronger than a soft drink.

The long-standing marriage deteriorated until, finally, in 1972, Jim and Viola had an argument that turned into a fight. Viola charged her husband with assault. He was forced to appear in Family Court in Peterborough, where the charge was dropped. Viola then separated from Jim for a while and took legal action to obtain a half share of the family farm. For some reason known only to herself, she changed her mind and returned to live with Jim. Things were never the same after that. The Leahys settled down to a strange and unusual lifestyle. Viola supported herself. Jim did likewise. They conversed only when necessary. Viola continued to cook and wash Jim's clothing. They slept in separate rooms.

Every Friday, Viola would leave the farm and visit with Emgard. She always returned on Monday. And so, month after month, year after year, the strained lives of Viola and Jim Leahy continued.

Jim's brother Emmett worked a farm directly south of the Leahy farm. Actually, Jim had sold the house to Emmett some years before. Besides farming, Emmett had been steadily employed at the Westclox plant in Peterborough for the past twenty-five years. Emmett was raising four sons; the oldest, Ralph, was nineteen.

Although all was not well with the Leahy marriage, there was really nothing to distinguish them from hundreds of other farmers throughout the country: two brothers with adjoining farms, supplementing their incomes by working away from the soil. Hardly the scene for a bizarre and unusual murder.

In 1975 Jim suffered a fractured skull in a farm accident. From that time on, Emmett and his sons gave Jim a helping hand with the chores. Viola, too, was not well. She suffered from arteriosclerosis (hardening of the arteries), which resulted in serious memory losses.

Because of the coolness between husband and wife, Viola came to depend a great deal on her brother and sister-in-law, Jack and Zetta Leeson. She phoned them every day. If she wanted to go anywhere, it was the Leesons who picked her up and brought her back to the farm.

On Friday, September 17, 1976, Viola was picked up by Jack Leeson and taken to Peterborough, where she stayed with her friend Emgard. Two days later, on Sunday, Jim was admitted to Sunnybrook Hospital in Toronto to have bone chips removed from his skull. This confinement was the result of the fracture he had suffered two years previously. Thus, Jim was away from the farm from September 19 until his return from Sunnybrook on October 3. He was never to see his wife again.

Meanwhile, Viola's movements are well documented. On Monday, September 20, she paid a visit to her doctor in Peterborough. The Leesons picked her up at her friend Emgard's, and gave her a lift to Dr. Flak's office. He prescribed pills and rest. Jack and Zetta Leeson then drove Viola back to the farm. They helped the sixty-five-year-old woman into the house with her luggage. They left the farm at about 7 p.m. It was the last time they ever saw Viola.

A half hour later Emgard received a phone call from her friend. The conversation was normal in every way. Viola gave no indication of unusual stress or anxiety. Emgard assumed that everything was fine.

Next day Zetta Leeson tried to reach Viola on the phone all day, with no success. On Wednesday Zetta and Jack drove over to the farm. They found Viola's luggage exactly where they had placed it the previous Monday. There were several cigarette butts in an ashtray. This bothered the Leesons because they knew that neither Viola nor Jim smoked.

On Thursday they notified Emmett Leahy that Viola could not be located. Together with Emmett, they searched the farmhouse but found nothing that could lead them to the missing woman. On Saturday, five days after she made the phone call to Emgard, Viola was reported missing by Jack and Zetta Leeson. The report was turned in to E. D. Martin of the Peterborough detachment of the O.P.P.

During the preliminary investigation into the missing persons' case the O.P.P. turned up three pieces of information that were later to prove of the utmost significance. David Ramsay had cleaned the furnace of the Leahy home on September 22. The only person he had come in contact with on the property was young Ralph Leahy. Ramsay stated the boy seemed to be lurking near an open barn door when he spotted him. Ramsay was interested in getting someone to sign his bill that the work on the furnace had been completed. He thought it odd that when he approached Ralph with the bill the boy said, "I'm not supposed to be here." Ralph signed the bill.

Another bit of information that gave the investigators food for thought was Emmett Leahy's statement that although he was taking care of his missing sister-in-law's mail, it had disappeared from his house. Jack, Zetta, and Emmett remembered that when they searched the house on the 23rd of September, Ralph had mentioned that he had seen Viola at about 8 a.m. on September 21. He thought she was heading for the bus.

The investigation continued. Jim Leahy came home on October 3, into the midst of an investigation into his wife's disappearance. All of Viola's personal effects were found in the house. More and more it became apparent that she had met with foul play.

Two weeks went by. The Lakefield postmaster received an unusual piece of mail. It was a "Change of Address Notice," apparently signed by Viola Leahy, directing her mail to the Sudbury post office, General Delivery. The card was turned over to the O.P.P. They quickly established that the signature on the card was a forgery.

In the meantime Ralph left his father's farm to seek employment in Edmonton, Alberta. The police checked his handwriting against the signature on the Change of Address card and established that the signature had been forged by Ralph.

Detective Inspector A. D. R. Smith and Constable G. Katz thought that Viola Leahy had been murdered. Despite snide insinuations that she had taken off with a man, neither policeman believed it to be true. They flew to Edmonton to interrogate Ralph. At first he denied forging the signature. Then he admitted it, stating that a friend of Viola's had given him $50 to do it. Ralph was returned to Peterborough, and charged with uttering a forged document. On June 9, 1977, he received three months imprisonment, to be followed by a two-year probationary period.

On June 13, the then Detective Inspector Bill Perrin was assigned to the case. "I believed that Viola Leahy was dead," the Inspector says, "and that the case could only be solved through her nephew, Ralph Leahy." Perrin made the decision to place Constable Bill Campbell of the Intelligence Branch of the O.P.P. into jail with the suspect. Within a day Campbell was playing cards with Ralph in the Quinte Regional Detention Centre in Napanee. Other prisoners were preparing for a transfer to Kingston Penitentiary. Ralph told his new friend that he too would probably be transferred before he finished his current sentence. He bragged that he and a friend had killed someone during the course of a robbery. Campbell didn't press the matter, but made a date to get in touch with Ralph when both men were released.

On August 9 Ralph Leahy was released. Unknown to him, he was under constant surveillance by the O.P.P. The following night Campbell met with Ralph at the Jolly Roger Lounge of the Holiday Inn in Peterborough. During their conversation, Ralph boasted to the undercover agent that he had killed his aunt the evening after his Uncle Jim had gone to hospital in Toronto. Once Ralph began talking he wouldn't stop. He confessed to seventeen or eighteen robberies, and bragged about serving two years in jail. Ralph thought he was impressing Campbell, who had posed as a member of an auto theft gang working between Montreal and Ontario. He wanted a job with the gang.

Campbell didn't believe any of Ralph's bragging, with one exception. He firmly believed he had a murderer on the line. They made a date to meet again on August 13. This time Campbell brought along Constable Terry Hall, posing as his brother and fellow member of the auto theft gang.

Ralph was duly impressed. He talked incessantly of having killed his aunt. Late into the night the three men talked. In the end Ralph promised to show them where he had hidden Viola's body.

The following Friday the two officers and Ralph left the Holiday Inn at 1:30 a.m. for the Leahy farm. In deep bush beside a swamp, the three men dug for a body. Later, the officers were to relate that while Ralph dug he made derogatory remarks about his aunt. "You old bitch, where are you? You've given me enough trouble."

Throughout the early morning the men dug by flashlight, but Ralph couldn't find his victim's body. He promised his two friends that if they returned with him at some future date, he would produce the missing woman.

On August 25, at 11:05 p.m., Inspector Perrin decided to pull the plug on the investigation. He arrested Ralph and, at the same time, picked up his girlfriend, Barbara Hartwick, for questioning. At the time Ralph remarked, "You'll never find her in a million years." When questioned, Barbara revealed that Ralph had admitted to her back in November 1976 that he had killed his aunt. He said he had shot her three times.

Perrin interrogated the suspect. Ralph claimed he had nothing to say. Then he informed Perrin, "You made a mistake picking me up today, you should have waited a day and you would have had the body."

In the wee hours of Friday, August 26, Ralph indicated that he wanted to see Perrin. Perrin questioned and informed the suspect of his rights: "Are you prepared to show us where Viola is buried? You know you don't have to show us or do anything that may be used as evidence, Ralph."

At the ungodly hour of 3:30 a.m., Ralph Leahy led the officers to the area beside the swamp where he and the two undercover agents had dug previously. He stated that he had marched his aunt down to the edge of the swamp, and had shot her three times with her husband's .22 calibre rifle. The murder weapon was turned over to Perrin.

Digging began later the same day, but try as they might, they couldn't find the body. Finally, Perrin brought in some heavy earth-moving equipment, and on Tuesday, August 30, the shovel uncovered the body of Viola Leahy. She had been shot three times in the area of the chest and abdomen. Ballistic tests confirmed that two of the bullets had been fired from the Leahy's .22 rifle.

Later, Ralph told doctors that he hated his aunt. The killing had not been a spur of the moment sort of thing. He had mulled over the possibility of killing her for several weeks. After murdering his aunt at the edge of the swamp, he left her where she fell, but returned the next day with a shovel and buried her. He told the doctors that his aunt was not worth the time he was going to spend in prison. He had no remorse for what he had done and was only sorry that he would have to go to jail.

The rather smallish five-foot-six-inch farm boy had killed his aunt because he didn't like her. All indications are that she was kind and considerate to her nephew.

Viola Leahy had spent eleven months and ten days buried on her farm. On February 4, 1977, her nephew, Ralph Leahy, was sentenced to life imprisonment.

Murder for Profit

Times were tough. The country was in the throes of the most disastrous depression this nation has ever known. None found it tougher than the isolated Canadian farmers who had no market for their produce. That's why William J. Larocque and Emmanuel Lavictoire decided to go into the murder business.

Both men owned scrub farms about a mile apart near L'Orignal, Ontario. No matter the amount of toil they expended, nothing seemed to lift them from the poverty they endured day by day. Both men were approaching sixty and had been close friends for years.

During the severe winter months, huddled beside their Quebec heater puffing away on their pipes, they plotted to insure the lives of acquaintances, murder them, and make the deaths appear to be terrible accidents. It is doubtful if Larocque and Lavictoire ever considered the possibility of being caught. They acted openly, with little regard for concealing their actions.

Athanase Lamarche was to be the diabolical pair's first victim. Athanase's father, Felix, was an elderly gentleman who resided in the township of Cumberland. Speaking as a friend of the family, Larocque approached Harvey Cameron, an agent for Manufacturer's Life Assurance

Company about insuring young Athanase. Cameron, ever on the lookout for prospects, was pleased to set it up. Accompanied by Felix and Larocque, Athanase was issued a policy for $5,000, with double indemnity (providing for payment of twice the face value) in case of accidental death. Father Felix handed over the first premium of $62.50, a princely sum during the depression, and was promptly named beneficiary.

Athanase, who apparently was not all that swift, was then boarded out with a Mrs. Desjardins. This kind soul ran a home specializing in the care of the mentally afflicted. Not satisfied with the sum of $10,000 on Athanase's life, Larocque was successful in obtaining another $10,000 policy through Northern Life Assurance Company. Again Felix was named the beneficiary.

Athanase wasn't long for this world. On April 4, 1930, he accidentally fell off the ferry dock at Masson, Quebec, and promptly drowned. Chief witnesses to the unfortunate accident were none other than our friends Larocque and Lavictoire.

Daddy Felix collected from the insurance companies, but never seemed to be able to hold onto the loot. Larocque and Lavictoire only had to ask and Felix would cough up the amount requested. Lavictoire bought a new truck. Larocque picked up a sleek new Ford. It has been suggested that Felix was in on the plot to murder his own son, but in light of future events, this avenue of inquiry was never fully investigated. However, there seems little doubt that the two men were blackmailing Felix.

Everything had come up roses for the two friends now turned murderers. They looked around for additional victims. Insuring their prey proved to be more difficult than it had been with the unfortunate Athanase. Many applications were refused. For some reason, when they applied to La Société des Artisans Canadien Francais Insurance Company for a $5,000 policy on Leo Bergeron's life, the application was accepted. When the policy was issued, it, of course, contained the double indemnity clause in case of accidental death. This time Larocque was named as beneficiary.

Leo Bergeron was a poverty stricken young farm labourer. It had been his misfortune to desperately need ten dollars, and to have asked Larocque for some help. Larocque, never one to overlook an opportunity, hustled Leo down to the Bank of Nova Scotia in Rockland. The manager loaned Leo the ten spot and had Larocque sign a promissory note. In this way Leo was indebted to the cunning Larocque.

Leo, who laboured long and hard on the farm of Eugene Morin, began to smell a rat, or I should say rats. He had a premonition that Larocque and Lavictoire were planning to kill him.

During the harsh January of 1932, both Larocque and Lavictoire took turns trying to lure Leo over to Larocque's farm. Leo stubbornly refused to budge. He told Morin he knew that he would meet with foul play if he ever ventured onto Larocque's property. The two schemers persisted. They offered the young lad more money in one month than he could make in a full year working for Morin. Leo finally consented to visit Larocque at his farm. Lavictoire accompanied him.

Once there, Leo saw Larocque waiting for him beside a barn. A team of horses stood harnessed to a small portable thrashing mill. Leo walked into the barn. Larocque nonchalantly asked him to close a cowshed door. Leo complied.

When he turned around, the two men rushed him, jabbing him in the groin, hands, and arms with pitchforks. Leo ducked and weaved, screaming for mercy, but the men showed none. Using the handle of the pitchforks they rained blows upon Leo's head with such ferocity that one of the pitchforks snapped as the young man sank to the ground, his head a bloody mass. Larocque and Lavictoire then rushed the horses into the enclosed barn. Being whipped with no place to go, the team bucked and thrashed about, inflicting terrible blows with their hooves to Leo's prostrate form.

Larocque hid the pitchfork handle on top of a dusty old beam. According to a prearranged plan, Lavictoire dashed across a field to seek help in quieting the horses from a neighbouring farmer, Alcide Deschamps. As Deschamps approached the barn he could hear the bucking horses and Larocque's obvious attempts to quiet them. With Deschamps' help, the men moved the portable threshing mill out of the barn and settled down the horses. There lay Leo Bergeron, with half his skull crushed away. Within an hour doctors and police were at the scene.

Police examined the horses' hooves. They were splattered with blood. It looked like a pure and simple farm accident. Before the body was removed, a police officer made a strange discovery. He found a broken pitchfork handle on a dusty beam. It was obvious that the handle had been recently placed there. Neither Larocque nor Lavictoire could explain the presence of the pitchfork handle. The handle wasn't perfectly clean. There were stains on it that were later identified as human blood. Blood stains were also evident on the walls, indicating that Bergeron must have received several blows that had bled profusely before he had fallen. Police wondered if any man could stand after being kicked repeatedly by two horses.

When the story of the two men's insurance schemes came to light, both men were arrested and charged with murder. Before going to trial, the Crown had Leo Bergeron's body exhumed. Although an original post mortem had been conducted, indicating that Leo's injuries were consistent with being kicked to death by horses, this closer examination sealed the fate of the two accused men. Small puncture wounds were found in Leo's groin, arms, and hands. These were the wounds inflicted by the pitchforks, proving that Leo had been struck many times before the horses did their work.

Both men were found guilty of murder. On March 15, 1932, William Larocque and Emmanuel Lavictoire walked briskly to the scaffold built especially for the occasion in L'Orignal, and were hanged for their crimes.

Who Was He?

If you drive along picturesque Highway #3 from Simcoe to Dunnville in southern Ontario, you will pass through the tiny hamlet of Nelles Corners. Just a few miles north of Lake Erie's shores, Nelles Corners is off the beaten track. In 1854 a crime took place in this community that gave rise to a series of events that made it one of the strangest murder cases in Canada's history.

John Nelles operated a general store. He and his wife lived together with his brother, Augustus, and his wife's sister, Lucy Humphreys. On the night of October 18, the family had finished supper. The early evening was no different from hundreds that had preceded it. A chill wind whistled outside as one by one the family retired for the night. John, left alone at the kitchen table, took a long last pull on his pipe before knocking the ashes against the grate of the kitchen stove. He was about to go to bed when it happened.

Five men burst through the front door. Their intent was never in doubt. Their faces were blackened with burnt cork. The desperate men demanded money. Nelles rose from the kitchen chair, but made no attempt to comply with the robbers' wishes.

A shot echoed through the once peaceful home, and John Nelles sank to the floor. The badly wounded man moved slightly, eliciting a further shot from the pistol carried by one of the men. Mrs. Nelles and her sister Lucy rushed into the room and ran to John's aid. The five bandits tore a watch from the wounded man. Ignoring the women, they continued to search the house for anything of value.

Augustus Nelles woke up with the first shot. Wisely, he remained in bed; not the most heroic action, but one that most certainly saved his life. As quickly as the wanton killing had taken place, the five men opened the door and disappeared into the darkness.

A few miles down the road the killers bumped into two farmers, who were relieved of the few dollars they had in their possession. Within hours the unknown assailants had boarded a train bound for Buffalo. Once in the U.S. the men separated, having left heartache and tragedy in their wake.

Despite the fact that their faces had been blackened with burnt cork, a good description of the wanted men was given by the two women, as well as the two farmers who had been robbed. Three of the men, King, Blowes, and Bryson, were quickly apprehended. They were placed in prison in Cayuga, Ontario. All three men were tried, found guilty, and sentenced to death. King and Blowes were hanged, but Bryson's sentence was commuted to life imprisonment. He probably saved his skin by confessing to being one of the men in the house at the time of the murder. All three men claimed that they hadn't fired the fatal shot. They stated that the trigger had actually been pulled by one William Townsend.

Meanwhile, an event took place that had a direct bearing on the shooting at Nelles Corners. Approximately a month after the murder of John Nelles, two men entered a hotel operated by a Mrs. Jordan at Port Robinson, Ontario. While the two men were eating, other men in the hotel swore that one of the strangers looked like William Townsend, the wanted killer of John Nelles. They notified the authorities.

Several police rushed to the hotel to apprehend the wanted man. One of the policemen, Constable Charles Richards, faced the stranger, who immediately pulled a gun and shot him. The constable died a few hours later. The man known as Townsend got away.

Over two years went by, and again Townsend was recognized. This time he was taken into custody without incident by the Cleveland, Ohio authorities. The government of Canada immediately proceeded to have the wanted man extradited to Canada. In May 1857, he was delivered to the Canadian authorities and placed in jail in Cayuga to await his trial for the murder of John Nelles.

From the moment he was taken into custody, William Townsend captured the imagination of the country. Townsend remained hostile toward the authorities, but despite this hostility, well-placed powerful men took an interest in his case. Throughout his stay in custody and his ensuing trial, Townsend claimed that he wasn't Townsend at all. He swore he was Robert J. McHenry, a Scotsman who worked as a mariner out of Cleveland, Ohio. He further swore that he had been in California searching for gold at the time of John Nelles' murder.

Townsend's unusual trial began on September 27, 1857. The Cayuga courthouse had never seen such an array of legal talent. The Crown was represented by Henry Smith, the Solicitor General of Canada. S. B. Freeman, Q.C., one of the finest orators of his time, represented Townsend. The accused pleaded not guilty. From the beginning the trial boiled down to the question of whether the accused man was Townsend or McHenry.

Lucy Humphreys identified the prisoner as the robber who had fired the shots that killed her brother-in-law. William Bryson was brought from Kingston Penitentiary to testify and identified the accused as the murderer Townsend. Sometime previous to the murder of Nelles, Townsend had been employed as a cooper in the neighbouring community of Dunnville. A number of former neighbours of the man in the dock took the stand, and all identified him as being William Townsend.

Surely this was enough to convict the prisoner, but such was not to be the case. Freeman paraded close to a hundred witnesses to the stand, all of whom swore that they knew Townsend well, and that the prisoner was not William Townsend. Townsend's brother-in-law, Ezra Smith, said the man in the dock was a stranger to him. Benjamin Diffin, who worked with Townsend one whole winter, said the accused was unknown to him. No expense was spared to place witnesses in the stand who swore the accused was not William Townsend.

After six hours of deliberation, the jury returned and informed the court that they were undecided. They were dismissed. The accused man was about to be returned to his cell when the deputy sheriff of Welland County read a warrant charging the prisoner with the murder of Constable Charles Richards of Port Robinson.

William Townsend, or whoever he was, was taken from Cayuga and lodged in the Welland (then called Merrittsville) Jail.

On March 26, 1858, he again stood trial for murder. Again his case rested on his claim that a terrible mistake had been made. He was not the murderer William Townsend. All the same witnesses were heard again. This time the foreman of the jury spoke out loud and clear, "The prisoner is McHenry, and is not guilty." That night the taverns of old Merrittsville rocked with celebrations held by McHenry's friends.

Townsend-McHenry was returned to Cayuga, for he still was in custody for the Nelles murder. But within a few days he heard that the Crown had no intention of trying him again. He was released on bail with the understanding that he would make himself available if the Crown ever decided to place him on trial again. This never happened. The strange, silent, hostile prisoner walked out of the Cayuga jail a free man.

For some time after, Robert McHenry was in great demand as a speaker at clubs and fairs throughout the country. Later, he dropped from sight and was never heard of again.

To some he was a killer named Townsend, who got away with murder. To others he was a harassed, innocent man named McHenry. Who was he? This question remains unanswered.

Canada's First Murder

Thomas D'Arcy McGee was born in 1825 in Carlingford, Ireland. At seventeen he heeded the adventurous call of the New World, making his way to Boston, where he obtained employment with a Catholic Irish newspaper, the Boston *Pilot*. By the time he was nineteen, he was editor of the paper.

The following year McGee returned to his homeland, and became an avid foe of Great Britain's union with Ireland. He was a leading figure in the Fenian Movement, an organization devoted to achieving Irish independence from England.

In 1848 McGee had to flee the country; some say he left disguised as a priest. He made his way once more to the U.S., but moved to Canada in 1857. A year later he was elected to the Legislative Assembly of Canada, representing Montreal West.

Once in Canada, it was assumed by Irish patriots that McGee would continue to expound his Fenian sympathies, but such was not the case. McGee split with the Fenians, believing their policy of violence too extreme. In fact, he became an adversary of the Fenian Brotherhood and was considered a traitor by many sympathizers of that movement.

On the evening of April 6, 1868, exactly nine months and six days after our country officially became the Dominion of Canada, the Honourable D'Arcy McGee, one of the finest orators ever to address the House of Commons, was at his eloquent best. A little after 2 a.m., the House adjourned. McGee, accompanied by Robert MacFarlane, a fellow Member of Parliament representing Perth, Ontario, left Parliament Hill. MacFarlane and McGee parted company at the corner of Metcalfe and Sparks. McGee walked towards his boarding house on the south side of Sparks between Metcalfe and O'Connor.

He reached his destination, the Toronto House at 71 Sparks Street, owned and operated by Mary Ann Trotter. Mrs. Trotter, as was her custom, lay asleep on the cot in the dining room. She thought she heard a noise at the door. Believing it to be her son, thirteen-year-old Willie, a parliamentary page boy, she rose to open the door. Just as she did so, she witnessed the flash of a discharging revolver and saw the form of a man fall at her doorstep.

The Honourable Thomas D'Arcy McGee, one of the thirty-three Fathers of Confederation, was Canada's first murder victim. As he had bent over to insert his key into the lock of the boarding house door, his assailant silently pointed a revolver at the back of his neck. The Smith and Wesson revolver roared as the bullet entered McGee's neck and exited through his mouth. He died instantly.

In the days immediately following the assassination, several men were arrested as co-conspirators in the young country's most infamous single violent act. All would eventually be exonerated and released. All except one—James Whelan.

The bewhiskered Whelan had been employed in Ottawa as a tailor since November. He had previously followed his trade in Quebec City and Montreal.

When questioned within twenty-four hours of the assassination, he had a fully loaded revolver in his coat pocket. One chamber appeared to have been recently fired. Whelan was taken into custody. After a lengthy preliminary hearing, he was held over for trial.

On September 7, 1868, Whelan stood trial for the murder of the Honourable D'Arcy McGee. News of the trial dwarfed all other events in the young Dominion. One of the founders of the country lay dead. His suspected killer came under microscopic examination.

The prosecution attorney, James O'Reilly, contended that Whelan had attended the House of Commons on the night of the murder, leaving before McGee. He had lain in wait for his victim in a gateway and had shot McGee in front of the door of his rooming house. O'Reilly claimed that the plot to kill McGee had been hatched in Montreal.

He asserted that Whelan had once visited McGee's home in Montreal. On that occasion he was met by John McGee, the victim's brother, and told him of a plot to set fire to the McGee residence. The threat was taken seriously and reported to police, although no attempt was ever made to set McGee's home on fire.

Most damaging of all, O'Reilly stated that someone, Jean Baptiste Lacroix, had actually witnessed the shooting. To back up his contentions, O'Reilly presented strong witnesses. John McGee confirmed Whelan's early morning visit to the McGee residence in Montreal.

Detective Edward O'Neill of Ottawa testified that he had found the .32 calibre revolver in the right-hand side pocket of Whelan's coat. In the opposite pocket he recovered a box of cartridges. Although the revolver was fully loaded when confiscated, O'Neill stated that upon examination it was clear to him that it had been recently fired.

"I looked in the cylinder and the six chambers, and I found six cartridges. Five of these cartridges looked like they'd been in there for some days. But one seemed to be put in recently." O'Neill went on to explain that one cartridge was bright, while the other five were dark and dull.

Jean Baptiste Lacroix told of walking home at the time of the murder. He saw a man at the door of the Toronto House and saw another man sneak up behind him. A shot rang out. The moon was full. Lacroix, from a distance of fifteen yards, saw the whole thing. When he heard the shot he stepped into the shadows. The assassin walked quickly past his place of concealment and Lacroix was able to identify him. It was James Whelan. Other witnesses took the stand, claiming that at various times they had overheard Whelan threaten to kill McGee.

Whelan was defended by the Honourable John Hillyard Cameron, believed by many to be the ablest lawyer in the country. The courtroom was silent. Shy, black-haired Euphemie Lafrance, a servant at Storr's Hotel on Clarence Street, took the stand. When in Ottawa Whelan lived at the hotel.

Miss Lafrance stated that she knew Whelan, and that one of her duties was making up his bed. One morning she found a revolver under his mattress. She picked it up and it accidentally discharged, wounding her in the area of the left elbow. She displayed her scar to the court. Miss Lafrance claimed the accident occurred shortly before the McGee murder. This evidence effectively explained the reason for the one shiny bullet in Whelan's revolver.

Prosecution witness Lacroix's reputation was vigorously attacked. An array of tough lumberjacks who had known Lacroix for years took the stand and swore that the Crown's chief witness was a notorious liar. Their testimony had a forceful effect on the court, particularly when it was learned that Lacroix did not reveal his eyewitness account of the crime until he knew that a $20,000 reward had been offered for the apprehension and conviction of the killer.

The trial, attended by Prime Minister John A. MacDonald and his wife, lasted seven days. Whelan was found guilty. When asked if he had anything to say before sentence was passed, Whelan gave a long dissertation covering his history and the events of the night of the murder, all the while professing his innocence. He even absolved the jury for their wrong verdict, stating that based on the erroneous circumstantial evidence placed before them he too would have reached a guilty verdict.

On Thursday, Feburay 11, 1869, accompanied by Father John O'Connor, James Whelan walked directly to the scaffold built for his public execution. His last words were, "God save Ireland and God save my soul." Father O'Connor pressed a crucifix to the condemned man's lips. The trap door sprung open, the crowd gasped, and James Whelan was no more. His was the last public execution to take place in Canada.

A plaque commemorating D'Arcy McGee's assassination can still be seen opposite 143 Sparks Street in Ottawa.

Twilight Years

Has the perfect murder ever been committed? I am alluding to those rare and mysterious cases of murder where all clues lead to a dead end. We have to go back in time to another day and another world to find such a pure murder mystery. Come along to the tranquility and pastoral beauty of rural England. You'll be presented with all the circumstances and clues left at the scene of the crime. You can even pass judgement on the one suspect in the case, much as Scotland Yard did so many years ago.

Major General Charles Edward Luard had served in the British Army for thirty years with the Royal Engineers. His distinguished military career concluded when he retired to lead the life of a country squire. His devoted wife was thrilled when the old warrior purchased a large brick manor house, Ightham Knoll, in beautiful Kent county. Situated on Maidstone Road, between the quaint villages of Seal and Ightham, their home held nothing but promise for their twilight years.

Mrs. Luard, the daughter of a prosperous property owner, was quite accustomed to such a lifestyle. After so many years of leading the comfortable but unsettling life of an army officer's wife, she enjoyed every minute of retirement.

By 1908 the general was firmly entrenched as a country gentleman. He took an interest in local affairs, and sat on the Kent County Council. But it was strolling through the woods hand in hand with Mrs. Luard that the old gentleman loved most.

On August 2, everything abruptly changed. Luard later gave a clear, concise statement of the events that unfolded that day.

At 2:30 p.m. Mr. and Mrs. Luard left their manor house to take a walk through the woods. Both had definite plans for the balance of the day. Accompanied by their Irish terrier, they crossed Fish Pond Woods, which was located on the property of their closest neighbour, Horace Wilkenson. They then took a footpath they had used many times before.

The general planned to continue to the Wildernesse Golf Course at Godden Green, which was about three miles from Ightham Knoll. Mrs. Luard planned to accompany her husband part way. She had told him that she expected an acquaintance, Mrs. Stewart, back at the manor house for tea, and would leave him around three o'clock for the return stroll home.

As they walked hand in hand through Fish Pond Woods they came upon Mr. Wilkenson's summer house. The couple had often had tea there that summer. They had just passed the empty summer house when Mrs. Luard felt it was time to return home to meet Mrs. Stewart. It was about three o'clock.

Luard reached the golf course at 3:25. He spoke to a member of the golf course staff at that time. Five minutes later the club house steward, Harry Kent, gave the general his golf clubs. The general practised a short while and then decided to walk home, using the road rather than the footpath through the woods. Rev. A. B. Cotton picked up Luard and the Irish terrier in his car and gave them a lift back to Ightham Knoll. They arrived home at precisely 4:30 p.m.

General Luard was shocked when he found his wife's guest, Mrs. Stewart, waiting at the house. Mrs. Luard had not returned home. She had left him at three o'clock and shouldn't have taken more than a half hour to return. The general had tea with Mrs. Stewart, feeling that his wife must have inexplicably been detained.

Finally, he could wait no longer. He went down to the footpath and started out once again on the route he had taken earlier that day. As he approached the Wilkenson's summer home he saw his wife's form stretched out on the veranda of the summer house. Thinking she had suffered a fall or had fainted, he rushed to her side. Mrs. Luard had not met with an accident. She had been brutally murdered.

Mrs. Luard's head lay in a pool of blood. Her left glove had been removed. The killer had obviously wrenched three valuable rings from her fingers. The glove was found inside out not far from the body. The glove on her right hand was in place and undisturbed. Strangely, some-one had cut her entire pocket from her dress in order to remove her purse. General Luard ran to the Wilkensons'. He arrived there at 5:25 p.m. and gave the alarm.

Doctors examined the body at the scene. They noted that Mrs. Luard had been beaten about the head with some kind of stick or club. There were bruises and abrasions on the fingers of her left hand where some-one had violently ripped away her rings. She had been shot twice with a small calibre revolver, once behind the right ear and once over the left temple. Powder burns were evident, indicating that she had been shot at close range. From the position of the body it was ascertained that the second bullet probably entered her head as she spun around in the act of falling. No club or revolver was found.

General Luard was genuinely distraught by the brutal murder of his wife. He was interrogated by the police and wrote out a statement that included all the facts as I have outlined them here. Every fact was verified by witnesses involved.

The crime was an unusually vicious one for peaceful Kent County. Scotland Yard uncovered two separate witnesses, who proved they had nothing whatever to do with the crime, but who were in the woods at the time of the murder. Both independently heard two shots at precisely 3:15 p.m. Detectives felt certain these were the shots that had killed Mrs. Luard.

Another witness, Thomas Durrant, a respected citizen of the area, had seen General Luard at 3:20 p.m., walking in the direction of the golf course. He was well over five minutes walking or running distance from the Wilkensons' summer home.

Who had killed Mrs. Luard and why?

Detectives walked and even ran the distances involved between manor house and summer home, and from summer home to golf course. The general and all the witnesses were telling the truth. It was impossible for him to have been at the summer home at 3:15, the time of the murder. He was just about at the golf course, having arrived there at 3:25. The general, the last known person to see his wife alive, was eliminated as a suspect.

Mrs. Luard had only been a couple of minutes beyond the summer house when she left her husband at three o'clock, yet she wasn't killed until 3:15. Police felt that, unknown to her husband, she may have been waiting for someone on the veranda of the summer house.

Police conducted an extensive search into the backgrounds of both the general and his wife. They were what they appeared to be—a retired, devoted couple with no known enemies.

Why did the murderer cut away a pocket containing the victim's purse? The purse could easily have been extracted from the pocket without cutting it. Scotland Yard had a theory. They felt it may have been an attempt to promote the murder for robbery motive. On the surface the cut-away pocket and the missing rings indicated robbery, but police thought that the killing was a cool calculated one made to look as if it had been committed during the commission of a robbery.

There were those who felt that a tramp may have just happened upon Mrs. Luard. Do tramps carry revolvers? Would a tramp cut away the pocket of a dead woman? Everyone seems to have seen General Luard that day. Surely someone would have spotted a stranger. All the surrounding villages were canvassed without uncovering anyone unusual.

Weeks went by and no progress was made in solving the case. The murder weapons were never found. Mrs. Luard's jewellery was never located.

Despite the evidence to the contrary, many believed that General Luard had murdered his wife. A steady stream of hate letters poured in to Ightham Knoll. The general read each one. He became so depressed that close friends feared for his health. One such friend, Colonel Warde, invited the general to get away from it all and visit with him at his home near Maidstone. The general accepted the invitation, but the change didn't help.

On September 17, the old gentleman could stand the harassment no longer. He threw himself into the path of an oncoming train. Luard left a suicide note to his friend Warde. In it he told of his unhappiness since the death of his wife, and how he now chose to join her rather than live without her. It was hardly the letter of a murderer.

Who killed Mrs. Luard? Why did they do it? The brutal murder that took place in Kent County in 1908 is as much a mystery today as it was the day after it was committed.

Did Grace Do It?

Unfortunately, factual murder mysteries do not always have the satisfactory conclusions associated with fiction. Case in point: the Croydon murders. I'll lay out the salient details of the murders and you can attempt to pick the murderer. Good luck, but I should warn you no one has conclusively solved this one despite the many years that have passed.

Our whodunnit took place during an eleven-month period beginning in April 1928 and concluding in March 1929. The locale was a respectable district of London known as Croydon, and involves two interrelated families, the Duffs and the Sidneys.

Edmund Duff had been employed as a civil servant in Nigeria for eighteen years before returning to England and settling down in a large comfortable home at 16 South Park Hill Road, Croydon. His pension was not large, but allowed him and his wife Grace to enjoy a quiet, if frugal, lifestyle.

In 1928 Edmund was fifty-nine. The Duffs had three children, John, fourteen, Mary, twelve, and an infant. Maid Amy Clark completed the household.

On Monday, April 23, Edmund left to spend a short fishing vacation with an old crony in Fordingbridge, Hampshire. On Tuesday he phoned Grace and told her he would be returning home on Thursday. Edmund was met by Grace at the South Croydon Station at 6:40 p.m. They arrived home within minutes.

Edmund complained of feeling feverish. The family physician, Dr. Robert Elwell, was phoned at 7:00 p.m. Meanwhile, the maid brought Edmund a hot meal and a bottle of beer. Edmund picked at the meal, but consumed the beer.

At 8:00 p.m. Dr. Elwell arrived, gave Edmund a cursory examination, but could find nothing wrong. Edmund mentioned that he had a slight headache and an extremely dry throat. Dr. Elwell prescribed aspirin and quinine. He left the Duff residence at 8:20 p.m.

About two hours later, Edmund and Grace went to bed. The Duffs slept in separate bedrooms. Throughout the night Grace thought she heard her husband vomit on several occasions.

Next morning Grace gave Edmund a cup of tea. He threw up immediately. Dr. Elwell was called, but was not available. His partner, Dr. John Binning, arrived at the Duff home around 12 p.m. Dr. Binning did not feel that Edmund's illness was serious. He stayed only five minutes.

After the doctor left, Edmund's condition worsened. He perspired and complained of stomach cramps. Dr. Binning looked in on his patient that afternoon and found that Edmund's condition had deteriorated. His hands and feet were ice cold. Binning left, but called Dr. Elwell to let him know that Edmund was very ill and could possibly be dying.

Binning then received a call from Grace. She was extremely agitated, stating that Edmund could hardly breathe. Binning headed for the Duff residence. When he arrived, Dr. Elwell was already there. Despite the actions of the two doctors, at 11 p.m. Edmund Duff breathed his last.

Both doctors agreed that they had no idea of the actual cause of death. An autopsy was performed, which indicated that no toxic substances were present in the body. Death was attributed to natural causes. Edmund was buried.

Grace Duff's single sister, Vera, and her widowed mother, Violet Sidney, lived only moments away at 29 Birdhurst Rise. They employed a maid-cook, Mrs. Kathleen Noakes. Because they lived so close to Grace, it was natural that they visited often, especially after Grace lost her husband.

About nine months after Edmund's death, Vera felt ill. Her diary notations dated January 1929, indicate that she was tired and generally unwell most of the month. Everyone liked Vera. She, in turn, at forty, devoted most of her time to her family. Grace and Vera had one brother, Tom Sidney, who was married and also lived close by.

On Monday, February 11, Vera had supper with her mother. The meal consisted of warmed over vegetable soup, fish, potatoes, and pudding. Mrs. Sidney never took soup, but Vera had some, as did the cook, Mrs. Noakes. Both became ill and vomited throughout the night.

By Wednesday Vera and Mrs. Noakes appeared to have recovered. On Thursday Vera was again ill after taking a small quantity of soup. Dr. Elwell was called in by Grace Duff to attend to her sister. Grace was understandably worried and was continually popping in and out of 29 Birdhurst Rise.

Vera's condition deteriorated. On Friday, February 15, she died. Dr. Elwell attributed the death to natural causes.

Mrs. Sidney now faced life in the large old home without the company of her daughter. It was small consolation to her that her daughter Grace and son Tom visited her every day.

On March 5, not quite three weeks after Vera's death, Mrs. Sidney took ill. She vomited violently, attributing her illness to Metatone, a medicine prescribed for her by Dr. Elwell. Mrs. Sidney had finished the bottle of Metatone that day and had commented on its bitter taste. Grace called Dr. Binning.

Tom Sidney dropped in and was startled to find his mother so ill. When he heard of his mother's suspicions concerning the Metatone, he suggested that Dr. Binning take charge of the empty bottle along with the wine glass from which the medication had been taken. That night at 7:25, Violet Sidney died.

An inquest was held into the untimely death. Rumours now ran rampant throughout the community. Poor Grace Duff. She had lost her husband, sister, and mother, all within eleven months.

An autopsy on the body of Mrs. Sidney revealed traces of arsenic. Arsenic was also found in the Metatone bottle and the wine glass. Scotland Yard was called into the case. Vera's body was exhumed. Arsenic was found in her vital organs. Edmund Duff's body underwent a second post mortem. This time all organs tested were found to contain arsenic.

Clearly, someone had murdered three people in less than a year. But who? Bottles, jars, and tins were confiscated from the two homes. Weed killer containing arsenic was found in several containers, but this was not considered an unusual circumstance for homes with lawns.

Most important was the Metatone bottle. Obviously, someone had slipped poison into Mrs. Sidney's medicine. We may also conclude that one individual was responsible for all three murders.

Let's eliminate Amy Clark, the Duffs' maid. She was never in the Sidney home. The same goes for the Sidneys' maid, Mrs. Noakes, who was never in the Duff home. The Duffs' two children, John and Mary, were not present during their grandmother's illness. That leaves Dr. Elwell, Dr. Binning, Grace Duff, and Tom Sidney with the means and the opportunity to administer poison to all three victims.

Dr. Elwell was a fine, upstanding doctor with no possible motive for harming any of the three victims. The same cannot be said for Dr.

Binning who, although married, was something of a ladies' man. It was felt that he had designs on Grace Duff, and some slight suspicion has been cast his way.

Tom Sidney came under serious suspicion. He was not a great fan of Edmund Duff's and stood to gain financially from the deaths of his sister and his mother, as did Grace Duff.

Pick whoever you fancy, but for my money Grace Duff was the culprit. Her husband Edmund, from all reports, was not an easy man to live with. She may have tired of her life with him and seized the opportunity to murder him when he arrived home from his fishing trip complaining of illness. She could easily have put the arsenic in his beer at any time.

Once she got the hang of it, she may have murdered her sister and mother to speed up her inheritance. She probably put the arsenic in her sister's soup and her mother's medicine. Grace was at each of the three deathbeds, a practice that gives perverted pleasure to some poisoners. At the death of her husband Grace inherited £1,200. When Vera died she inherited £2,000. On her mother's death she inherited £5,500, large sums in 1929.

No one was ever brought to trial for the Croydon Poison Mystery. Maybe the answer to it was lost forever on June 24, 1973, the day Grace Duff died. She was 87.

The Perfect Murder

To get away with murder is no easy task, but it does happen. The most successful murder of all, at least from the perpetrator's point of view, is a death that is never detected as murder. The untimely demise is attributed to an accident or natural causes and is never investigated. There is another category, where the act of murder is obvious, but every investigative avenue leads to a dead end and the murderer goes free.

Nora Fuller was an unlikely victim. In 1902 she was a teenager looking for a job, preferably in the entertainment industry. She had performed on the stage in high school, and applied for any job openings involving the theatre. Work wasn't easy to come by. After some weeks she decided to take a stop-gap job. That's how she came to answer an advertisement in a San Francisco newspaper: "Young girl to take care of baby; good home and good wages; Box 120—Chronicle."

The next day Nora received a postcard: "Miss Fuller, In answer to yours in response to my advt., kindly call at the Popular Restaurant, 55 Geary Street, and inquire for Mr. John Bennett at 1 o'clock. If you can't come at 1, come at 6. J. B."

Nora had to rush to get to the restaurant by six. She grabbed an apple, said goodbye to her mother and brother, and hurried out of the house to keep her appointment. An hour later, her brother Louis answered the phone. It was Nora. She told her brother that she had met Mr. Bennett, and was starting work immediately at his residence at 1500 Geary Street Louis shouted the news to his mother and said goodbye.

At about 5:30 that same day, Mr. Krone, the owner of the Popular Restaurant, was told by one of his patrons that he was expecting a young girl to call on him. The man asked Krone to send her to his table. After waiting a half hour he left the restaurant and was seen pacing up and down outside the front door. Krone later stated that the man in question had often eaten in his establishment. He was about forty years old, five feet eight, and weighed about 160 pounds. He had a brown moustache, and was always well-dressed.

When Nora failed to return that night, her mother reported her missing to the police. After a complete investigation they assumed that Nora had kept her appointment with Mr. John Bennett, but from there it appeared as if Nora had fallen off the edge of the earth. John Bennett didn't exist. The address at 1500 Geary Street was a vacant lot. With no new clues coming in, the investigation wound down.

On February 8, almost a month after Nora ran out of her house eating an apple, her body was found. A real estate representative, whose job it was to inspect houses before renting them to new tenants, was to scrutinize a house at 2211 Sutter Street. The house had been rented for one month, which would be up the following day. The real estate agent went through the property, which appeared never to have been occupied by the previous tenant. He gingerly opened the door to a tiny back room. Inside, lying on a bed, was the nude, mutilated body of a young girl. The real estate agent ran from the vacant house directly to the first policeman he could find. The dead girl was Nora Fuller.

Investigating detectives learned of the efforts that had been made to trace the missing girl, and how that investigation had bogged down. They learned that two days before the advertisement appeared in the *Chronicle*, a Mr. C. D. Hawkins had leased the house on Sutter Street from the real estate firm of Umsen & Company. When questioned about references, Hawkins stated that he and his wife had been living in a hotel for years. To circumvent any inconvenience, he would pay the first month's rent in advance. Money talks. The deal was consummated then and there. The salesman from Umsen & Company described his client as being about forty years old, five foot eight inches, well dressed, and having a brown moustache. Obviously Hawkins and Bennett were the same man.

Hawkins' movements were traced further. He purchased furniture on the same day that he rented the house. He systematically went about outfitting one room, the room in which Nora Fuller was to die. He paid cash and demanded that his furniture be delivered that same night. Pillows, sheets, and blankets were purchased from another store. All were paid for by cash with the stipulation that they be delivered immediately. Both stores did deliver their wares to the empty, eerie house. The delivery men were met by Hawkins and led to the little back room. The bed was set up. The following night Nora Fuller was to occupy it.

The vacant house and the murder room were examined without concrete results. Attempts to trace the murderer proved frustrating. All efforts came to an abrupt stop with the purchase of the furniture and the bedclothing. Even the original postcard was missing. Nora had taken it with her on her appointment with death. The killer had taken it from her purse. The details of the card were provided by Nora's mother.

An autopsy revealed that Nora had been strangled. Her last intake of food was the apple she had taken from her house. She had been killed on the same day. The vacant house had no water or gas hookup. No fire had been lit in the fireplace. It became obvious that the killer had placed the ad, leased the house, and bought the furniture all for one night's use.

After a frustrating investigation, the police got a break. A clerk, Charles B. Hadley, had disappeared. His employer reported that Hadley had been fixing the books and that he was several thousand dollars short. Hadley's girlfriend, Ollie Blasier, told the police that her boyfriend had flown the coop immediately after Nora Fuller's disappearance. One day he just walked out on her. Another interesting bit of information was that Charlie habitually wore a false moustache. He fit the description of Bennett-Hawkins. When the killer, using the name Hawkins, leased the house on Sutter Street, he had to sign a document. Ollie Blasier came up with Hadley's signature on a photograph he had given her. The two signatures were compared and were both written by the same man.

Hadley had worked for fourteen years at the same job. In recent years he had lived with Miss Blasier. Even she was amazed to find out how little she knew about him. Hadley was a loner. The police were unable to trace anyone who could shed any light on his past.

The man who had set the stage for murder, and killed his victim, effectively disappeared and has never been found or punished. He had committed the perfect murder.

Lydia Lost Her Head

The city of Detroit, Michigan, has long been associated with murder. The incidence of homicide per capita in Detroit is one of the highest of any city in the world. It takes more than a run of the mill murder to jar the citizens of the automobile city, accustomed as they are to murder on a daily basis. The Lydia Thompson case caught and held their attention for months.

Lydia was born in Russia. At the end of World War I she met Victor Thompson in Constantinople, where he was stationed with the British Army and where she was employed as a nurse. The attractive pair married and headed for Detroit to start a new life. From the very beginning they prospered. Vic gravitated toward the automobile industry, and eventually came to own a profitable agency. In addition, the couple owned a laundry and a garage.

In keeping with their financial success, they acquired an impressive executive home in Orchard Lake, an exclusive area just outside the city. The Thompson home had all the amenities of affluence—a swimming pool, tennis courts, pool tables, and well-stocked bars. To an outsider or even a casual acquaintance, it appeared that the Thompson's long marriage had been made in heaven. From

Lydia's point of view the union may have been created in more nether regions.

By 1945 Lydia, at forty-seven, had begun to notice those telltale grey hairs and wrinkles on her otherwise attractive visage. It seemed to her that Vic stayed away from home more often with each passing month. Things had not gone well since the beginning of the Second World War. Cars were in short supply, and Vic's business activities slowed down. As a result, he had time on his hands, and it appeared to Lydia that her husband chose to spend this time away from her.

Lydia accused her husband of engaging in dalliances with other women. The situation was so bad that Vic's comings and goings became an obsession with his wife. Lydia would stay in her home for weeks on end crying and otherwise making herself miserable. Her only conversation with friends was about her husband. She would pour out her troubles to anyone who would listen.

Instead of bringing Vic closer, her possessive nature drove him further afield. One of the directions Vic headed toward was Helen Budnik. Helen had at one time been Thompson's secretary, but the working friendship had soon developed into a far closer and warmer relationship.

The more Lydia nagged, the more Vic ran to Helen's welcoming arms. Lydia became so distraught she had detectives follow her husband. She didn't believe their reports, and ended up tailing the detectives herself. A few classic confrontations took place between Lydia and Helen. Helen told Lydia she couldn't help it if Vic didn't love her anymore. To these expressions of comfort, Helen added that maybe Lydia should stop bugging Vic. Despite this warning, Lydia kept on making herself and everyone around her miserable.

On October 13, 1945, the turbulent domestic lives of Lydia, Vic, and Helen made front-page news. That was the day three mushroom pickers found the body of Lydia Thompson in a lonely marsh, not far from suburban Pontiac. Someone had cut off her head. She had icepick stab marks on her chest and back.

Investigating officers questioned Vic Thompson and Helen Budnik, both of whom came under suspicion from the moment the body was found. They readily told the police of their relationship with the dead woman, and claimed they had nothing to do with Lydia's death. Both took lie detector tests, which indicated they were telling the truth; and both had airtight alibis for the night of Lydia's murder. Vic and Helen were released from custody after questioning.

Lydia's diary was found. It revealed the hopeless situation that existed between her and her husband. The diary was of no help in identifying her murderer, but it did indicate that she had a premonition of her death. She made several references to this in her diary and had even purchased a gun for protection.

An extensive search of the area where the body was discovered was conducted by Boy Scouts in an effort to find the murder weapon, but it was never found. A purse that Lydia usually carried was also missing.

The murder investigation wound down, as no new clues to the mystery were uncovered. Four months after the murder, in February 1946, Vic married Helen Budnik. While Vic was cleaning his home in preparation for his new wife's occupancy, he moved an icebox. Out popped his dead wife's purse. Later he found Lydia's gun in a little-used cupboard. Both of these discoveries shed no light on the identity of the killer.

There were no new developments for another year, but many thought that Vic, acting alone, or with Helen's help, had murdered his first wife. Seventeen months after the murder, Mr. and Mrs. Thompson were arrested and charged with Lydia's murder. The police had come up with a pots and pans peddler who claimed he had been hired by Vic to do the actual killing. The obvious motive was to get rid of Lydia in order to marry Helen.

There was one little catch. It was proven in court that the pots and pans peddler was lying. He had concocted the whole story to scare his girlfriend. Charges against the accused pair were dropped. The Thompsons were released.

And that's where the case stands to this day.

Was Captain Hart Guilty?

It is doubtful that many people have heard of Tenants Harbour, Maine. Situated about ten miles from Thomaston, Tenants Harbour is a quaint little crossroads by the sea. Nothing of interest has ever happened there, with one exception.

In 1877 the village was the scene of one of New England's most famous and mysterious murders. Five years later, in nearby Massachusetts, a young lady named Lizzie Borden was to stand accused of taking an axe and chopping up her mother and father. The Borden case was to become one of the most written about and analyzed crimes ever perpetrated, while the Sarah Meservey case of Tenants Harbour has been relegated to dim memory.

Before the turn of the century inhabitants along the coast of Maine were primarily sailors. They would take off from the northeast coast of the U.S. in schooners and travel the world. Voyages lasting over a year were not uncommon.

In October 1877 Captain Luther Meservey boarded his schooner, the Bickmore, for a four-month long sea voyage. His thirty-seven-year-old wife Sarah was quite accustomed to her husband's lengthy absences. Sarah, a slim, tall, no-nonsense woman quickly fell into her usual routine when the captain was at sea. She knitted, sewed, and cleaned the house. Chores neglected for months were now completed. Seldom did she leave her home other than to make her regular pilgrimage to the post office each day to collect her mail.

Two months passed without any changes. But December 22 was to be the last day of Sarah Meservey's life. It was a Saturday. As dusk was falling over Tenants Harbour, Sarah walked down the street to the post office. Once there she learned that her neighbour, Mark Wall, had picked up her mail. Sometimes he brought her mail home with him and she would pick it up later at his house.

Sarah started off on the five-minute walk home. She paused and passed the time of day with a few friends on the way. She decided not to pick up her mail that evening. Instead she entered her house and closed the door.

Next morning, Mark Wall sent his young son to Sarah's house with her mail. The boy noticed that the curtains were drawn, which was rather unusual. He pounded on the door, but received no reply.

In the days that followed, Sarah Meservey didn't take part in the Christmas activities of the village. Snow fell. No one cleared a path to Sarah's door. Mail piled up for her down at the post office.

It wasn't until January 29, a good five weeks since Sarah was last seen, that anything was done. The lack of curiosity exhibited by the inhabitants of Tenants Harbour is one of the mysteries surrounding the Meservey case. It is almost beyond comprehension that in such a small community not one person would act after a few days, let alone five weeks. No mention or reason for this time lapse is reported in the many newspaper accounts of the case, which was covered extensively at the time of the crime. We can only assume that small towns and villages are more private places than we are led to believe.

On January 29, Captain Albion Meservey, a cousin of Sarah's husband, brought the matter of her absence to the attention of a village politician, one Whitney Long. The two men crawled through a window into the freezing Meservey residence. Entering the bedroom the men found the floor strewn with glass from a broken mirror. Furniture was overturned and a great deal of blood was on the floor and walls. In the middle of the room was the frozen body of Sarah Meservey, rolled snugly into a quilt.

Next day the coroner reported that a scarf had been wrapped around Sarah's neck, causing death by strangulation. Several bruises were evident about the head. The victim's hands were tied behind her back with cod line. The knots themselves were obviously seamen's knots. Sarah had been fully clothed in an overcoat and overshoes when she met her death. This indicated that she had been killed shortly after she had returned from the post office weeks before. Bloody handprints were all over the house. On the kitchen floor police found a note that was almost illegible. Dated December 24, the letter stated that the killer hadn't murdered Sarah for money, but for some other reason that he didn't state. Despite the note, the house had been ransacked. Police believed Sarah had surprised her killer in the act of robbing the house. The residents of Tenants Harbour were aghast at the thought that one of them was a killer.

On February 16, Captain Luther Meservey returned home to learn of his wife's murder.

Three days later Mrs. Levi Hart received a letter from Philadelphia dated February 10 and postmarked February 16. The letter urged her husband, who was actively helping the police in their investigation, to stop assisting the authorities. It also stated that the killer would never be apprehended. Police believed that the letter had been written by a citizen of Tenants Harbour who had managed to have it mailed from Philadelphia.

Sheriff A. T. Lowe, in charge of the investigation from the outset, had four local men write out a phrase that had been included in the first letter found on Sarah's kitchen floor. The phrase was "i kiled her." Based on a handwriting comparison the Sheriff arrested Captain Nathan F. Hart.

As time went on it became common knowledge that Sheriff Lowe had found a particular type of wooden match on the floor of the Meservey kitchen. In the entire village, only Captain Nathan Hart used this distinctive type of match.

Captain Hart stood trial for murder on October 1, 1878. He swore he knew nothing of the murder of Sarah Meservey. Prosecuting attorneys attempted to prove that Captain Hart couldn't account for his actions on the evening of December 22 when he had strangled Sarah with her scarf. Worried about this, the Captain sneaked back into the house on December 24 and planted the note dated the 24th so that police would be led to believe the murder took place on that date. The Captain had an ironclad alibi for the evening of December 24.

The prosecution pressed on. They were able to produce witnesses who swore that Captain Hart had discussed the murder before the body was found. He had also described conditions that existed inside the house to other residents of the village.

Why would Captain Hart want to kill his friend and neighbour? The prosecution came up with a witness who claimed the Captain had made improper advances to Sarah some six months before the murder and had been repulsed.

The prosecution hit a snag when they attempted to prove that Captain Hart had written both the letter found on the kitchen floor and the one sent from Philadelphia. The handwriting expert, a Professor Dutton, who had caused Captain Hart to be arrested in the first place, now appeared in court for the defence. It appears that a ship's log, purportedly written by Captain Hart, had been used as a sample of his handwriting to be compared to the two incriminating letters. Professor Dutton still claimed all three documents were written by the same man.

The fly in the ointment was that the ship's log had been written not by Captain Nathan Hart, but by Captain Albion Meservey. Professor Dutton had gone to the trouble of bringing in other experts to corroborate his startling findings.

Captain Hart answered his accusers from the witness stand. He stated that he had dreamed that Sarah had been murdered. He also dreamed of the conditions inside the Meservey house, a not altogether impossible feat considering the conjecture running rampant through the village just before the body was found. Captain Hart admitted he didn't have an alibi for December 22. He simply was at home that night and hadn't been seen by anyone. He did state, and had his evidence corroborated by a friend, that on December 24 he had been afoot with his friend taking a gift to his granddaughter, who lived in a neighbouring village. Not too far from Sarah Meservey's house they had seen a stranger approaching from the opposite direction. The night had been snowy and the misty figure unrecognizable. The stranger seemed to be holding a coat over his head. Captain Hart thought nothing more of the stranger until the body was discovered and he was arrested.

After only two hours deliberation the jury returned a verdict of guilty of murder in the first degree. As there was no death penalty in Maine at the time, Captain Hart was sentenced to life imprisonment at Thomaston, Maine.

There were many who believed that Hart was innocent. Strong suspicion pointed to Captain Albion Meservey as the writer of the two letters and the actual murderer. Professor Dutton worked tirelessly on behalf of the convicted man. He wrote books, gave lectures, and generally kept the case alive as the years passed. Captain Albion Meservey further complicated matters by stating that he too thought Captain Hart innocent. Of course he swore he was not the author of the letters, and certainly not the killer.

On October 9, 1883, after five years imprisonment, Captain Nathan

Hart died. His body was transported back to Tenants Harbour for burial. The entire village turned out for the funeral. Among the mourners was Hart's staunchest supporter, Professor Dutton, who swore to his dying day that an innocent man had been imprisoned for a crime he did not commit.

In the five years after Sarah's murder, the Meservey case and its rather unsatisfactory conclusion was the chief topic of conversation in New England. Then that God-fearing, church-going young lady named Borden "took an axe and gave her mother forty whacks." Everybody stopped talking about Sarah and began talking about Lizzie. You see, Lizzie was alive, and Sarah was very very dead.

Demerol Was Deadly

To all outward appearances Dr. Charles Friedgood had the world by the tail. A successful surgeon, he owned a large eighteen-room home in the affluent Kensington section of Long Island's North Shore, was the father of a grown, well-educated family, and above all was the husband of Sophie, his loving wife of twenty-eight years.

It just wasn't that way at all. Dr. Friedgood, who was in his mid-fifties, neglected his wife. He arrived home late for meals, sometimes by hours. No matter what the occasion, Sophie never started a meal without him. She waited, and when he finally arrived, she argued, she screamed, and she bickered. To make matters more frustrating, Friedgood ignored his wife's outbursts, and never offered any excuses for his tardiness.

In 1967 Friedgood became infatuated with his Danish nurse, Harriet Larson. Although Harriet wasn't a beauty, she was attractive. Initially the doctor kept his relationship with Harriet a secret, but soon he was carrying on an open affair. For years his daughters, Toba, Esther, Beth, and Debbie had believed that Harriet was nothing more than a faithful employee. Gradually the truth became known to them. Typically,

Sophie was the last member of the family to accept the fact that her husband was keeping another woman.

All semblance of secrecy crumbled when Harriet became pregnant. Early in 1972 she flew to Denmark, where she gave birth to a boy, who was named Heinrich after Dr. Friedgood's dead father. When she came back to the U.S., Friedgood set Harriet and Heinrich up in an apartment not far from his home. He paid her an allowance of $1,000 a month. Two years later Harriet found herself pregnant once more. Again she returned to her native country. This time she gave birth to a girl, Matte, with Friedgood at her side. He had told his wife that he was attending a medical convention in Arizona, when in reality he flew to Denmark.

When Harriet and the two children returned to the U.S., Friedgood obtained a larger apartment for his second family, again quite close to his home in Kensington. He helped furnish it with older pieces from his own home that Sophie had discarded. Friedgood was under pressure from Harriet to obtain a divorce from Sophie. He convinced his mistress that because of financial difficulties incurred while he was purchasing a hotel, he had signed over everything he owned to Sophie, almost a million dollars in stocks, bonds, and cash. As soon as the deal cleared the courts, he would be free to marry, but in the meantime Sophie legally owned everything.

At the same time, the doctor tried to explain away Harriet to his wife by telling her that he couldn't dismiss his nurse because she had been witness to several documents he had signed concerning the same financial deal.

As the Friedgood girls grew up they came to know and like their father's nurse. Sometimes they were puzzled when little Heinrich would hug their father and call him Papa. Later they realized that the child was named after their own grandfather, and that besides, he bore a striking resemblance to one of their brothers. One by one the Friedgood girls married. Each of their husbands eventually learned of the strange, rather open, relationship their father-in-law had with his nurse. Occasionally one of his daughters would approach her father and beg him to explain his relationship with Harriet. Friedgood wouldn't hear of such scandalous talk. He assured them that it was nothing more than that of doctor-nurse. He was so convincing that sometimes his children believed him.

Naturally, Sophie, who over the years had been humiliated by her husband literally hundreds of times, fought back in the only way she knew. She screamed at him, "Go to your whore!" "Sneak away to your bitch." Friedgood had the exasperating habit of calmly reading his newspaper during these tirades.

The tense relationship between Charles and Sophie Friedgood could not continue indefinitely. Things came to a head on June 17, 1975. That evening Charles and Sophie had a date to meet for dinner at Lundy's Restaurant in Brooklyn. Sophie was in good spirits, having heard that Harriet was in Denmark. She arrived promptly at 6 p.m. Typically, Friedgood was late. Sophie sipped wine as she waited for him for over an hour.

After dinner, at approximately 8 p.m., the couple drove in separate cars to their accountant's home, where they were expected. They arrived at 8:30, stayed one hour, and then drove home. At 11 p.m. Esther called her parents from New Jersey. It was an exciting time for her. She and her husband had both just received their law degrees. Esther had a good chat with her mother and father. Moments later Charles and Sophie retired to their bedroom. They were alone in the big house.

We will never know exactly what happened in the Friedgood bedroom after 11 p.m. that night. Later, at Dr. Friedgood's trial, a medical examiner reconstructed the events as they must have unfolded.

Sophie and Charles undressed. Sophie lay in bed while Charles went to a filing cabinet in his study. From the top drawer of the filing cabinet he removed a long needle and syringe. He then filled the syringe with demerol.

Sophie, lying on her back in bed, had no way of knowing she had only moments to live. Charles pounced on his wife, firmly grasping one out-stretched arm above her head. As Sophie struggled, Charles injected the demerol up under her armpit. The doctor then held his wife helpless for the ten or twelve minutes it took the demerol to take effect. Sophie screamed frantically. The big house was empty. There was no one to hear.

A few minutes passed. Sophie became drowsy. Her efforts grew weaker. Charles lifted his wife's other arm, and once more jabbed the needle under her armpit. Injections in her thigh and buttocks followed. She lay quiet, but was still breathing. Charles turned his wife's limp form over. He gave her one last injection between the ribs directly into the liver. Sophie stopped breathing.

Dr. Friedgood replaced the needle and syringe in the top drawer of his filing cabinet and returned to his bedroom. He went to sleep beside the lifeless body of the woman who had been his wife for so many years.

Next morning Dr. Friedgood went to work as usual. Lydia Fernandez showed up for work at the Friedgood residence as she did every day. She tidied up around the house, and found it a bit strange that Mrs. Friedgood had not left her a note telling her when she should be awak-ened. Later that day, at 1 p.m., Lydia found Sophie Friedgood dead in her bed.

Dr. Friedgood was notified of his wife's death. He hurried home. He told of Esther's call the night before, of going to sleep, of waking up, of Sophie kissing him goodbye. It was shocking. His wife must have had a stroke after he left her. Because Sophie had suffered a stroke years before, it was assumed that she had suffered another one.

In keeping with the Friedgood's religion, steps were quickly taken to have Sophie buried in her hometown of Hazleton, Pennsylvania, the following day. Dr. Friedgood signed his wife's death certificate.

News of Sophie's death spread throughout Kensington. Something clicked in Police Chief Raymond Sickles' memory. While he didn't know the Friedgoods personally, he recalled that one of the Friedgood daughters had once frantically called him because her mother and father were having a terrible row. When one of his men arrived at the Friedgood residence they found nothing more than the usual family dispute. Sickles learned that Dr. Friedgood had signed his wife's death certificate. Although there was no law preventing a medical doctor from signing a spouse's death certificate, it was unusual. Normally another doctor would have been called upon to sign the certificate.

Sickles decided to inform the Nassau County Police of his suspicions. Officials felt that Dr. Friedgood's actions were so unusual that they consulted Dr. Leslie Lukash, the County Medical Examiner, who agreed that the funeral should be delayed long enough for an autopsy to be performed. Detective Thomas Palladino was dispatched to Hazleton to see to it that the burial did not take place as scheduled.

While he was mourning at the funeral chapel, Dr. Friedgood was first made aware that the police were concerned about the manner of his wife's death. Under threat that a court order would be obtained granting the autopsy, Dr. Friedgood gave his permission to proceed. He had no choice.

A post mortem was performed at St. Joseph's Hospital, while Detective Palladino looked on. Unbelievably, Dr. Friedgood insisted that he be allowed to observe his own wife's autopsy.

The autopsy revealed that at the time of death Sophie's stomach had been full. How could that be? The meal she had eaten the night before at 8 p.m. would have been digested long before 9 a.m. when the doctor left for work. Sophie must have died within six hours of having eaten the meal. Dr. Friedgood must have been lying when he stated his wife returned his parting kiss the morning after she consumed that meal. She was positively dead at that time.

Dark red bruises were found under the armpits, on the thigh, buttocks, and on the chest. Testing indicated that demerol had been injected in each bruised area. A lethal amount had been injected directly into the liver.

Detectives returned to Long Island hoping to find the needle and syringe in the Friedgood home. While detectives searched the first floor rooms, Dr. Friedgood was able to whisper to Esther, "Upstairs! File cabinet—bottle, syringe—top drawer." Esther looked in her father's eyes. The surgeon held her stare. A father was to be obeyed and protected. Esther calmly strolled upstairs to her father's study. From the top drawer of the filing cabinet she extracted two bottles and a syringe and placed them in a paper bag. Trembling, she lifted up her dress and put the death kit inside her underpants.

Back downstairs Esther told her sister Toba her terrible secret. After the detectives left she showed her sister the contents of the paper bag. One of the bottles was marked demerol. The Friedgood children discussed their father's plight and his obvious guilt with their husbands that night. Meanwhile, Esther had hidden the syringe and bottles in an upstairs closet. She revealed their location only to her father. The death kit promptly disappeared from its hiding place.

A few days later Dr. Friedgood forged his wife's signature to documents dated prior to Sophie's death, giving him access to several of her safety deposit boxes. He forged authorization to sell several of her securities as well. In all, he gathered up $600,000 in cash, negotiable bonds, and jewellery. He then called his daughter Debbie and told her that his doctor had advised him to get away for a few days. No amount of questioning could get him to reveal his destination. Debbie's husband, realizing that his father-in-law's mistress was in Denmark, was convinced that Friedgood was about to skip. He called the police.

Teams of detectives manned the phones calling Kennedy Airport, canvassing overseas flights. There was no one named Friedgood, or anyone matching Friedgood's description flying to Denmark, but the airport computers did come up with a Friedgood flying to London.

Just as Dr. Friedgood's plane was about to take off, it was instructed to return to the terminal. Friedgood was taken off the plane. A search of his luggage revealed the $600,000 horde. Dr. Friedgood was arrested and charged with the murder of his wife. At his murder trial, his children testified against him. In January 1977 he was found guilty and received the maximum sentence possible—twenty-five years to life imprisonment.

In 1978 New York State passed a law known as the Dr. Friedgood Bill, making it illegal for doctors to sign death certificates for relatives.

Dr. Cross Loved Effie

D r. Philip Cross surveyed his domain from his fine old home in Dripson, Ireland. The doctor had recently retired from the British Army after serving for many years in India. Now in the winter of 1886 the old man could look forward to many peaceful, if not somewhat boring years, with his wife, Laura, his children, and his retirement estate known as Shandy Hill.

It was not a future that promised much excitement, but many men work a lifetime for just such twilight years of contentment. The doctor was a gruff, introverted man who apparently tolerated the matronly Mrs. Cross as long as she conveniently stayed out of his way. Then again, the British Army does develop character.

When twenty-one-year-old Effie Skinner joined the staff of Shandy Hill as governess to the Cross children the doctor paid little attention. It is hard to believe the doctor ignored the new governess, for Effie was a peach. Her complexion was unblemished, and when she smiled, two pink dimples appeared on each cheek.

It is unclear exactly when the kindly doctor did take notice of this breath of spring. A smile, a touch, a hidden kiss, who knows? At first the embarrassed Effie rejected the doctor's advances. But old Dr. Phil slowly won Effie to his side both literally and figuratively. Stolen kisses in the hall of Shandy Hill led to more basic acts behind closed doors. Dr. Cross and Effie became lovers.

As was inevitable, Mrs. Cross found out about her husband's dalliance with the hired help. Laura could have become indignant, but instead, she decided to let bygones be bygones. After all, Phil had never before acted in this unfaithful manner. Mrs. Cross did the practical thing. She gave Effie her notice. This may not appear to be a major calamity today, but an unemployed governess without references before the turn of the 20th century could literally end up begging on the street.

To the rescue came Dr. Cross. Effie was understandably grateful for any help. The doctor's proposition was simple enough. He would provide the necessary cash for a flat in Dublin and would visit his paramour at every opportunity. Effie became Dr. Cross' mistress.

This new and convenient arrangement went along famously for several months. There was just one thing. The spry old doctor was in love with Effie and wanted to be with her all the time.

Meanwhile, back home at Shandy Hill, Mrs. Cross began to suffer from the most annoying stomach cramps. Sometimes her distress was so severe as to bring on attacks of vomiting. Phil ministered to his wife for several weeks before bringing in Dr. Godfrey, a cousin and friend of the family, for another opinion. Phil explained to his colleague that Laura was suffering from a slight attack of typhoid fever. Dr. Godfrey examined Mrs. Cross and quickly concurred with the older and more experienced doctor. After all, who would detect typhoid fever if not a former military doctor who had spent years in India?

On May 24, 1887, when the local clergyman Reverend Mr. Hayes called to pay his respects to the ill Mrs. Cross, he was told by the kindly doctor that she had just dropped off to sleep. A most distressing week passed for Mrs. Cross. She suffered greatly from nausea and vomiting.

On June 2, the maid, Mary Buckley, was awakened by the frantic doctor. Mrs. Cross had mercifully passed away.

Dr. Cross signed the death certificate without delay. Mrs. Cross was laid to rest two days later. The brief ceremony, conducted at graveside at the ungodly hour of 6 a.m., was thought by some good citizens of Dripson to be decidedly odd. It mattered not what the Dripsonites thought, for Dr. Cross was off to his true love.

Like a man possessed, he gathered up Effie in Dublin and sped to London, where the older gentleman and the twenty-one-year-old governess became man and wife. Dr. Phil and Effie tiptoed through the English countryside on their honeymoon. Back in Ireland news reached Dripson that the doctor had married the former governess, and only two weeks after Mrs. Cross had given up the ghost. A relative wrote Dr. Cross informing him that his friends and neighbours had not taken kindly to his actions. The doctor felt that he had better return to Shandy Hill for appearances' sake.

Once ensconced in his old home, the doctor kept a low profile. But nasty rumours failed to abate. There were those who remembered that Dr. Cross had tended to his wife in her final illness. Then there was the hasty funeral. Bad news travels fast. It wasn't long before Inspector Tyacke of the Royal Irish Constabulary heard the rumours.

The Inspector spoke to the coroner, who felt there was enough monkey business taking place to order an inquest. In conjunction with the inquest Mrs. Cross' body was exhumed. An autopsy indicated that she had never had so much as a touch of typhoid fever. What she did have was a massive quantity of arsenic, accounting for the nausea and vomiting she suffered before death.

Dr. Phil was arrested and charged with the murder of his first wife. He didn't have a chance. The prosecution produced one of those chemists who have a habit of taking the witness stand and pointing at the accused. They usually say, "That's the man I sold the poison to." In

Dr. Cross' case the chemist added the word "positively." The motive—Effie—was there for all to see.

On January 10, 1888, Dr. Cross, whose hair, incidentally, had turned chalk white during his confinement, was hanged for the murder of his wife.

Mrs. Morell's Will

D r. John Bodkin Adams, fifty-eight, had practised medicine for over thirty-five years in the resort town of Eastbourne, England. He never married, and lived alone in a large Victorian home with only a housekeeper to care for his needs. The doctor had a lucrative practice and was considered to be a pillar of the community. Yet he was to become the central figure in one of the most sensational murder cases ever to unfold in England.

The doctor's life was to become entwined forever with that of a patient, Mrs. Edith Alice Morell. An elderly lady, Mrs. Morell was visiting her son in Cheshire in June 1948, when she suffered a stroke. Taken to the Cheshire General Hospital, she was in great distress, and was given a quarter grain of morphine each day for the nine days she stayed in hospital. On July 5 she was transferred by ambulance to Eastbourne, where she came under the care of Dr. Adams, who remained her doctor until her death on November 13, 1950, at the age of eighty-one. Mrs. Morell's body was cremated, and that, for all intents and purposes, was that.

Six years passed before any further notice was paid to Mrs. Morell and the manner of her death. In 1956 rumours spread in and around

Eastbourne that many of Dr. Adams' patients who had died had left him bequests in their wills. These rumours came to the attention of the authorities and it wasn't long before Scotland Yard dispatched senior investigators to look into Dr. Adams and his medical practice. As a result of their inquiries the doctor was arrested and charged with Mrs. Morell's murder.

The murder case that unfolded captured the imagination of the English-speaking world. While many doctors have stood trial for murder in England, rarely had a doctor been accused of murder while ministering to a patient. In fact, the last such case took place over a hundred years earlier, when the infamous Dr. Palmer of Rugelay was convicted of murder. The Adams trial lasted seventeen days, making it the longest murder trial to take place in England up to that time.

Mrs. Morell's stroke had left her partially paralyzed. Eventually she was able to get around with assistance, but required nurses around the clock. Although the alleged crime was six years old at the time of the trial, the nursing records detailing frequency of injections and quantities of drugs administered were available. All medication, whether injected by the nurses or not, was given under the doctor's instructions.

It was established that Dr. Adams was a beneficiary in Mrs. Morell's will. He stood to gain a pre-war Rolls Royce, as well as an amount of silver valued at £275. After Mrs. Morell's death Dr. Adams did, in fact, come into possession of these two items.

From the time Mrs. Morell came under Dr. Adams care she received a quarter grain of morphine and a quarter grain of heroin daily. No doubt she became somewhat addicted to the good feeling these drugs gave her, for generally speaking, Mrs. Morell was an irritable and demanding patient.

During September 1950, when Mrs. Morell had only seven weeks to live, her medication was drastically altered by Dr. Adams. He instructed that she be given increased quantities of both morphine and heroin. Mrs. Morell received ten grains of heroin on November 8, twelve grains on November 9, and eighteen on November 11. On November 12, the day before she died, Mrs. Morell received three and a half grains of heroin and two grains of morphine.

Was Mrs. Morell's dosage of these drugs increased in order to end her life or was the doctor doing everything possible to alleviate pain for a dying patient? The line is a thin one, which many physicians have to walk. Maybe it was even thinner in 1950 than it is today.

Other pertinent events that occurred during Mrs. Morell's illness came to light. Dr. Adams had known he was in his patient's will. At one point he had gone to Scotland for a vacation and Mrs. Morell, in a fit of anger, changed her will, leaving him nothing. Later Dr. Adams returned to her good graces and was placed back in her will. There is little doubt that Dr. Adams was concerned about his patient's will. He had discussed the matter with Mrs. Morell's lawyer on several occasions, and at one point suggested that the lawyer draw up a new will and get Mrs. Morell's son to agree to it at a later date. Mrs. Morell's lawyer turned down such a shady proposition.

Conversely, there was the matter of the competent nurses who took care of Mrs. Morell during her long illness. Not one of them spoke up or suggested that during her last weeks Mrs. Morell's dosage was too high. Even Dr. Adams' partner, Dr. Harris, who filled in for his colleague while he was in Scotland, continued the regime of morphine and heroin. His explanation was that it is customary, all things being equal, to continue medication as prescribed by the regular doctor.

What could be the doctor's motive for murder? He had a lucrative practice and was well respected. Why would he purposely set out to destroy a partially paralyzed elderly woman who had a limited life expectancy? There were those who believed that Dr. Adams set out to make Mrs. Morell totally dependent on him after he realized that she was addicted to drugs. By abruptly increasing her dosage he intended to influence her in any way he wished concerning her will. It must be remembered that Mrs. Morell was an extremely wealthy woman. When her will was finally probated, her estate amounted to £175,000. A tidy sum today, in 1950 this amounted to a fortune.

Detectives uncovered a form, signed by Dr. Adams, which had secured Mrs. Morell's cremation. One of the questions of the form was, "Have you, as far as you are aware, any pecuniary interest in the death of the deceased?" The doctor answered in the negative, although it is quite clear that he was aware he would receive the Rolls and the silver under the terms of Mrs. Morell's will. Mrs. Morell was cremated the day after her death.

It took six years before the doctor was asked his reason for lying on the cremation form. His only explanation was that he had not lied from any sinister intent, but only to circumvent red tape and get on with the cremation.

On the day of Dr. Adams' arrest he made a statement that was to haunt him throughout his trial. In response to being advised of his rights he told a Scotland Yard detective: "Murder? Can you prove it was murder?" Not exactly the utterance of an innocent man.

During the Adams trial it was revealed that Mrs. Morell was not in pain while under the doctor's care. Expert medical opinion stated that morphine and heroin should be used only if the patient is suffering agonizing pain. Mrs. Morell was irritable and had trouble sleeping. Other drugs should have been used, and furthermore, Dr. Adams, as a competent physician, would know this. In fact, two expert medical witnesses swore that the dosages prescribed by Dr. Adams were certain to cause death.

Dr. Adams' defence attorneys produced experts of their own, who stated that it is impossible to tell exactly how an eighty-one-year-old partially paralyzed woman died. Remember Mrs. Morell's body had been cremated, so it was impossible to perform an autopsy. The defence doctors claimed that it is quite common for an individual who has suffered one stroke to suffer a second, fatal one. In fact, this was suggested to the jury as an alternative to murder.

This theory was ridiculed by the prosecution and contributed the only levity to an otherwise grim affair. Crown attorneys likened this second stroke theory to the instance of a man walking on a railroad track and being struck by a train. Is it reasonable to assume he had a heart attack a moment before the train struck, and therefore death was not due to a train accident but to a heart attack?

The crux of the Adams' trial revolved around the definition of murder. Murder is an act in which the intent is to kill, and that does in fact kill. A doctor attending a dying patient is compelled to take those measures necessary to relieve pain and suffering, and if his efforts incidentally shorten life, that is not murder. If he deliberately and knowingly cuts off life, that is murder. In the Adams case it was totally irrelevant if life was shortened by a day or by a year. If the intent to kill was there, it was murder. If a doctor errs in his judgement, and institutes measures that effectively terminate life, that is not murder. Intent was of the essence in the Adams case.

Despite the suspicious circumstances surrounding Dr. Adams and his particular brand of medicine, he received the benefit of reasonable doubt. The jury took only forty-four minutes to find him not guilty.

The trial of Dr. Adams for Mrs. Morell's murder stands alone, and I have tried to relate the salient points of the tedious trial as fairly as possible. However, the reader should know that, at the time, Dr. Adams came under strong suspicion for the deaths of two other patients. In fact, at the preliminary hearing that preceded the Morell trial, it was alleged that Adams murdered two other rich patients, a Mr. and Mrs. Hullett. While Adams was in custody, the bodies of these two suspected victims were exhumed, but as the Crown took no action against Adams in this regard, we can only assume nothing incriminating was found.

After his acquittal of the murder of Mrs. Morell, Dr. Adams was arrested and charged with sixteen counts of forging medical prescriptions and contravention of the Cremation and Dangerous Drugs Acts. He pleaded guilty to fifteen of these charges and was fined £2,400.

As a result of these disclosures, the General Medical Council of England had Dr. Adams' name struck off the Register of Medical Practitioners. John Bodkin Adams never practised medicine in England again.

The New Orleans Axeman

It is rare that the murderous frenzy of one man can hold an entire city in terror. Jack the Ripper did it in London in the autumn of 1888 when he mutilated and murdered five prostitutes. The Boston Strangler, Albert DeSalvo, managed to keep the greater Boston area in a state of fear when he sexually attacked and murdered thirteen women. In recent years David Berkowitz, better known as Son of Sam, kept New York City in a state of near panic as he wounded seven innocent victims and murdered six others.

Another mass murderer, not as well known as the ones mentioned here, may have been the strangest of all. The Axeman of New Orleans first struck in 1911.

A hardworking Italian grocer named Cruti went to sleep above his store and never woke up. During the night someone gained entrance to his living quarters and, using Cruti's own axe, beat his sleeping victim about the head until he lay dead in a pool of his own blood.

Cruti's murder appeared to be an isolated incident until another grocer named Rosetti was murdered in exactly the same manner. Rosetti's wife became the third Axeman victim as she lay sleeping beside her husband.

That same year the Axeman claimed victims number four and five. Tony Schiambra and his wife were cruelly bludgeoned to death with their own axe as they slept. Police scrambled to find the madman who only killed Italian grocers.

As suddenly as the strange killings began, they abruptly stopped. It wasn't until May 23, 1918, seven years later, that the Axeman struck again. On that night Joseph Maggio and his wife went to bed early in the living quarters behind their grocery store. They were never to leave their bedroom alive. During the night someone chiselled a panel out of the back door of their apartment. The madman entered the apartment carrying an axe he had picked up in the Maggios' yard. He proceeded directly to the bathroom where he found Maggio's straight razor. Quietly entering the bedroom, he swung the axe first at Maggio's head and then rained a blow upon the sleeping Mrs. Maggio. He leaned over both his victims and slit their throats. Both bloodstained weapons were found in the backyard where the killer had discarded them.

Initially some suspicion fell on Maggio's two brothers, Andrew and Jake, who lived in the same building. Both were able to prove that they were elsewhere on the night of the attack and were quickly exonerated. Police scanned the records of the old 1911 unsolved murders, but believed that the current axe murders were not connected with the older crimes, despite the similarity of the victims.

A little over a month later, on June 28, a baker, John Zanca, delivered bread to the back door of Louis Bessemer's living quarters behind his grocery store. Just as Zanca was about to leave, Bessemer opened the back door. Blood was streaming down his face from a vicious looking scalp wound. Zanca shouted to Mrs. Bessemer. Receiving no reply he made his way into the bedroom where he found Mrs. Bessemer unconscious on her bloodsoaked bed. Zanca called the hospital and the police. A blood-stained axe was found in the bedroom.

Bessemer was treated at hospital and released. His wife was more seriously injured but still alive. Bessemer could shed little light on the identity of his attacker or the motive. He explained to the authorities that the woman believed to be his wife was in reality a Mrs. Lowe, with whom he had been living for some time.

All Bessemer could tell detectives was that he had received a vicious blow to the head with his own axe. When his head cleared he got out of bed and found Mrs. Lowe moaning on the balcony. He carried her to her bed and was just leaving for help when Zanca showed up at the door.

Mrs. Lowe was able to give authorities their first description of the axe murderer. She had been attacked as she stood on her balcony, and had caught a glimpse of her axe-wielding assailant before being struck. She described him as being white, with dark brown hair, quite tall, and heavy set.

Mrs. Lowe's condition grew steadily worse. Doctors felt that an operation was necessary if she were to have any chance of survival. Unfortunately the operation was not successful, and Mrs. Lowe died on August 5.

That very night the Axeman struck again. Edward Schneider returned to his home to find his pregnant wife lying in a pool of blood in her bedroom. Edward rushed his wife to the hospital, where doctors were able to save her life. She told of waking up to see a shadowy figure lurking over her bed. An axe flashed, and that was all she remembered. A week later this remarkable woman gave birth to a healthy baby girl.

On August 10 the Axeman claimed another victim when he caved in Joseph Romano's head as he slept. By now the residents of New Orleans waited in dread for the Axeman to strike. The Italian community in particular was close to panic. Who could figure out what manner of man was going about in the middle of the night, obviously seeking out Italian grocers to butcher in their sleep?

On March 10, 1919, grocer Charles Cortimiglia, his wife and two-year-old daughter were the recipients of the madman's wild machinations. A competitive grocer on the same street, Iorlando Jordano and his eighteen-year-old son Frank, heard the Cortimiglias' screams from across the street and ran to their aid. They found the two adults soaked in blood from scalp wounds. Mrs. Cortimiglia held her daughter in her arms. The child was dead.

Rushed to hospital, both parents survived. They had seen their attacker and gave general descriptions of the Axeman. Mrs. Cortimiglia amazed detectives when she declared that she knew the killers. They were none other than Iorlando Jordano and his son Frank. She claimed that Frank was the axe-wielding killer.

Mr. Cortimiglia stated that his wife was definitely wrong in her identification of the two Jordanos. Despite this, both men were arrested and charged with murder. The rift between the two Cortimiglias became so heated that they separated over their diametrically opposed identification of the attackers. Mr. Cortimiglia claimed that there had been only one attacker and that his wife must have become insane at the shock of seeing her own daughter murdered.

At the murder trial that followed, Rosie Cortimiglia received much sympathy because of the loss of her daughter. The jury was inclined to believe her rather than her husband. Both Jordanos were found guilty. Frank was sentenced to hang, while his father received life imprisonment. It is hard to fathom the reasons for the Jordanos being brought to trial. Surely all the Axeman's trademarks were evident in Cortimiglia's attack. The door panel had been chiselled; the bloody axe owned by the occupants had been left behind.

Meanwhile there was no let-up in the activities of the Axeman. On August 10 Steve Boca staggered out of his home after being attacked with an axe. He could shed no light on the identity of his assailant. The panel of his back door had been removed by a chisel. Two months later Mike Pepitone and his wife were attacked. Mrs. Pepitone survived, but Mike died from head wounds.

Abruptly the attacks stopped. Mike Pepitone was the Axeman's last victim.

In the interim the Jordanos lawyers had appealed their convictions. Father and son languished in jail. It was now a year and nine months since the night they had gone to the Cortimiglias' aid only to find themselves convicted of murder.

On December 7, 1920, Rosie Cortimiglia walked into the office of a New Orleans newspaper and blurted out her story. "I lied, I lied! God forgive me, I lied; I hated the Jordanos because they were vicious business competitors, but they did not kill Mary." After the legal necessities were dispensed with, the two Jordanos were released. The only evidence against them had been Rosie's positive identification.

Who was the mad Axeman? Unlike the Jack the Ripper case there is every reason to believe that the murders have been solved in a strange and unusual manner.

On December 20, 1920, a native of New Orleans, Joseph Mumfre, was strolling down a Los Angeles street in broad daylight. Suddenly a woman approached Mumfre, and without saying a word, pointed a revolver at him and didn't stop shooting until the gun was empty.

The woman claimed that Mumfre was the New Orleans Axeman. When New Orleans detectives were contacted, they checked Mumfre's prison record against the dates on which the attacks started and stopped. Sure enough, Mumfre had been at large in 1911 when Cruti, Rosetti, and Schiambra had been attacked. Then he was back in prison for seven years, and was released just before the date of the Maggio attack in 1918. All other lulls in the murderous spree coincided with Mumfre's numerous prison sentences.

Mumfre's killer was charged with murder. During her trial she claimed that she recognized Mumfre and knew he was the New Orleans Axeman. Although she pleaded guilty, her lawyers claimed that the homicide was justified. Mumfre's murderer was found guilty and received a sentence of ten years in prison. She was released after serving only three years.

Her name was Mrs. Mike Pepitone.

Man's Best Friend

Donald Hume was born at Swanage, England, in 1919, the illegitimate son of a schoolteacher, who had no use for him. As a result of this lack of motherly love, he spent most of his formative years in assorted orphanages. By the time he was fourteen Donald was a lone, brooding youngster, deeply aware of the stigma of not knowing the identity of his father. Many lads of his age might have accepted the cruel blow that fate had dealt them, but not Donald. He resolved to strike back at life, to claw his way into a station in society where he would be the dealer, not the receiver, of cruel blows.

All his early luck was not bad. While seeking his first job in London he met a Mr. Fox, a builder, who took a liking to him and hired him at twenty-five shillings a week. Taking a sincere interest in Hume's welfare, Mr. Fox went as far as getting him a place to stay with his foreman's wife. This woman was also fond of Donald, and he was immediately received as "one of the family."

At the age of fifteen Hume had friends, was learning a trade, and was living in good surroundings. But this was not enough for him. In an effort to make more money he took a second part-time job in a chemist's shop. To augment his earnings still further, he started to steal small items from the shop and sell them to his friends. Then he began to take cars for joyrides, and his circle of friends widened to include youngsters who felt that roaming the streets at night, mugging and robbing, was a normal pastime. As a result, his work suffered.

The ever-concerned Mr. Fox had a heart-to-heart talk with his protégé, but the grateful lad he had hired a few short years before had turned into a sullen, bitter young man who didn't take kindly to moral lectures. Inevitably, Mr. Fox's talk did no good, and he was forced to fire Donald in November 1937. To make the break complete, Hume moved out of his pleasant lodgings.

For the next two years he drifted from one menial job to another. When he was twenty, World War II broke out, and he joined the RAF. Almost immediately he contracted cerebrospinal meningitis and was discharged twenty months later, bitter and disheartened at being forced to give up his glamorous uniform. Rather than seek normal employment in the many arms factories that were crying out for workers, he decided to try his luck outside the law.

His first scheme turned out quite well. He made contact with a firm of manufacturing chemists and purchased quantities of surgical spirits. He laced this potent brew with some legitimate gin, put fancy labels on the bottles, and sold the stuff at an enormous profit to any nightclub which would pay his price, averaging over sixty pounds a week, which wasn't bad in 1941. The scheme lasted a year, but then his supply of surgical spirits was cut off and he found himself out of business.

When this happened Hume dressed up in an RAF officer's uniform, and started passing bad cheques at Air Force bases all over England. He was caught, arrested, and committed for trial at London's famous Old Bailey. The young man who stood before Sir Gerald Dodson that day was now twenty-three years old. For Sir Gerald's benefit, Hume played the repentant orphan. Good-looking, immaculately dressed, he made an excellent impression in the dock. His full crop of black hair squared off a not unpleasant face, though his expressive mouth turned down disturbingly at the corners. The full lips twitched into a smirk as Sir Gerald gave him a two-year suspended sentence.

After this harrowing experience, Hume took a job as an electrician's helper and soon progressed to doing electrical and plumbing work on his own, swindling his customers by using inferior products and overcharging for his services. These methods didn't help his reputation, but they did make him money. An interesting insight into Hume's unscrupulous intelligence may be found in the fact that while he was cheating his customers and using every trick in the trade to line his pockets at their expense, he picked up all the practical knowledge he could about electricity. He made so much out of his customers that by 1943 he opened his own electrical and radio store. The Hume Electrical Company was located at 620 Finchley Road, and business was so good that within one year he was expanding his premises and employing forty-five people, making money hand over fist.

When the war ended in 1945, Donald Hume, at the age of twenty-five, was a successful legitimate businessman. In the same year the British government relaxed its ban on the production of domestic appliances. Hume saw an opportunity and grabbed it. He designed a toaster that proved to be a winner. He called it the Little Atom, worked like a dog, and marketed fifty thousand of them.

He was now a rich man, but despite his wealth and obvious success, he couldn't resist the thrills of the criminal life. For kicks, he associated with known criminals and joined them in the odd robbery and hijacking. His deep-rooted compulsion to hold "straight" society up to ridicule was coming to the surface again. Every time he met with legitimate success, his craving for the thrill and excitement of illegal activities seemed to become more intense. Basically a loner, he only came in contact with his criminal friends when a caper was being planned; he had no intention of making a career out of petty crime. It was only the thrill that compelled him to duck behind the veil. He always came back.

Then he acquired a dog. If Donald Hume ever had sincere feelings about any living thing, they were for his dog Tony. As other men might enjoy a quiet evening at home with a female companion, Hume was content to sit before a fireplace with his Tony. He would actually confide his innermost thoughts to his canine friend. Tony, looking up at his master with understanding eyes, always seemed to sympathize. The dog was an intelligent animal, and whatever chemistry exists to bring dog and man to an understanding of each other existed in full measure between Tony and Hume.

In 1947 Hume met, fell in love with, and married a well-bred, beautiful young divorcee named Cynthia. Shortly after his marriage he took up flying as a hobby, and got his civilian flying license. His business started to suffer. He had lived high off the hog for his few good years, and didn't have much to show when the situation started to deteriorate. When in 1949 he met a wealthy car dealer named Stanley Setty, he was impressed. Here was a living example of what he himself wanted to be. Setty oozed success. He carried a huge roll of banknotes, and diamonds twinkled on his chubby fingers when he reached for his wad. His large frame was draped in an expensive suit, obviously the product of one of the better London tailors. At forty-six Setty carried his 200 pounds well enough, although his dark face was running to fat. He ran a large legitimate operation, but he also dealt in forged petrol coupons and ran guns to countries that would pay the price. Both men realized they were kindred spirits from their very first meeting.

Setty, who had been born in Baghdad and whose real name was Sulman Seti, took Hume into his confidence about his illegal operations. At the time they first met, Setty was selling war surplus trucks to Iraq. This fact stuck in Hume's craw. He was aware that he himself was no angel, but that Setty, a Jew, should be selling war materials to

Israel's enemies appalled him. It was as if he had aided Germany during the war. Still, reasoned Hume, money and expediency make strange bedfellows.

Setty, on the other hand, figured he had met a rather intelligent small-time crook whom he could probably use in his operations. Soon the pair started dealing in forged coupons and stolen cars. When Setty heard that Hume could fly a plane he immediately set him up smuggling contraband and illegal passengers to and from the continent. Setty was the contact man, lining up any deal that would make them money. Hume took most of the chances, but the money was good, and the life it enabled him and Cynthia to lead was worth the risk.

Sometimes their deals were no more complicated than picking up an illegal immigrant on the continent and flying him back to a secret landing field in England. No nosy customs inspectors, no passports to be checked—neat, smooth, and profitable. At other times, the deals were more complicated. Once, Hume arranged to have two Dakotas flown with full crews from the U.S. zone in Germany to Palestine. Accompanying one of the planes himself, he pulled off the mission without a hitch. He was also instrumental in supplying Palestine with other war materials. A cargo of guns would take off from England in Halifax freighter planes and land in Spain, where it would be transferred to fishing boats and eventually find its way to Palestine.

And so it went—anything for a price. While they didn't love each other, Setty and Hume were compatible partners. Then one fine day, while visiting Setty at his garage, Hume, accompanied by his dog Tony, was admiring a freshly-painted car. The dog brushed against the vehicle, leaving a noticeable scratch on the fresh paint. Setty became furious. He gave Hume a tongue-lashing, but worst of all he gave Tony a vicious kick. Hume took his dog and left the garage. From that time on the relationship between the two men was never the same. Hume, whose fondness for his dog bordered on the obsessive, never forgave

Setty. His hatred for his associate smouldered within, ready to explode into murder at the first provocation.

On the evening of October 4, 1949, Setty paid a visit to Hume's maisonette. The two men began to quarrel bitterly. Hume grabbed a German ss dagger off the wall and stabbed Setty repeatedly until he was dead. The struggle only took a few minutes, but it left Hume physically and emotionally drained. He looked down at what a few moments before had been a living human being. The dead eyes stared back, seeming to say, "What now, chum; what do you plan to do with me, a body in your living room?" Hume's answer was makeshift at best. He carried the body to the coal cupboard which was located on the same floor at the rear of the flat. He then straightened out the furniture and washed the blood from the floor, took Setty's car keys, drove the car to Setty's home, parked it, and got away without being seen. Once a safe distance away, he hailed a cab and returned to the maisonette.

Sleep didn't come easily. He tossed and turned, trying to figure out what he would do with the corpse in the coal cupboard. He knew he would never be able to lift the big, heavy-set body out of the apartment by himself.

Next morning he got up and wiped the apartment clean of any fingerprints that Setty might have left. Then he noticed that despite his washing, his carpet was bloodstained. He rolled it up and took it out to be cleaned and dyed a deep green. At the same time he bought some varnish and applied it to his floor. Busy boy that he was, he checked Setty's pockets and found £1000 in five-pound notes. Most of them were bloodsoaked and shredded by his dagger thrusts, and he managed to salvage only £90. Revenge was the obvious motive for Hume's crime, but if he could make a few quid on the side, so much the better.

While Hume was scurrying about getting rid of incriminating evidence, Cynthia was upstairs in the flat, oblivious of her husband's activities and the weird events that were taking place in her home.

Finally she prepared lunch, and Donald had to sit there making small-talk. His grey eyes darted round the maisonette. It seemed to him that evidence of murder was everywhere. A stain here, a splash of varnish there, and of course Mr. Setty, not so very far away in the closet. But Cynthia, blissfully unaware of what had happened, saw nothing amiss.

Hume waited until early in the afternoon, when she went out of the house, once more to confront the annoying Mr. Setty. By now that gentleman was stiff as a board with rigor mortis, and it was no small task to lug the body out of the coal closet and into the area the Humes called the breakfast room. Then Tony, his faithful companion, watched as he coolly cut off Setty's legs with a linoleum knife and a hacksaw. Neatly wrapping the legs in felt, he tied the large parcel with cord. Next he cut off Setty's head and put it in a cardboard box. He weighted the packages with bricks, then wrapped the torso in a blanket and shoved it back into the coal cupboard to be dealt with later.

Hume cleaned the place thoroughly and drove away from the flat with his two grisly parcels. He went straight to Elstree Airport. Leaving Tony in his parked car, he hired a little Auster aircraft that he had often rented before. Once over the English Channel he dropped his parcels over the side and watched as they disappeared under the water. They sank like rocks. Then he tossed the dagger, knife and hacksaw that he had used on Setty overboard, returned the plane to the airport and drove home.

A murderer's work is never done. The following day he was faced with the task of getting rid of the torso. Not being completely pleased with the coat of varnish he had applied to the floor, Hume brought in a painter to do a more professional job. With a boldness born of desperation, Hume asked the decorator to give him a hand, as he had a heavy parcel to carry down to his car. As the unsuspecting painter and the murderer heaved and puffed with their awkward cargo, Hume noticed that the underside of the blanket wrapping was becoming bloodsoaked. The painter held firmly to the ropes that bound the parcel. Hume's eyes watched his every move, but not once did his hands change position. Had he groped for a better hold and inadvertently touched the bloodsoaked blanket, we can only guess what Hume's reaction might have been.

In the end the two men carried the torso down to the waiting car without incident. With Tony by his side, Hume made his second trip to the airport. He managed to heave his bulky parcel into the front seat of the plane, and Tony jumped into the back seat.

It is possible that in all the annals of crime no stranger threesome ever took off in an aircraft. There they were—a torso, a dog, and a murderer, flying over the English Channel. This time all did not go smoothly. When Hume tossed the torso overboard the lead-weighted blanket blew away, and the torso didn't sink. There was nothing Hume could do about it but return to the airport.

Meanwhile Setty was missed, and it was assumed that he had met with foul play because of the large amount of money he was carrying when last seen.

On October 21, the torso of Stanley Setty was found by Sidney Tiffin, out after geese in his boat, on a mudflat near the Essex village of Tilingham. Six days later, the police investigation turned up Donald Hume. They had meticulously checked every airfield for men with flying licenses who had police records. Upon checking further, they uncovered the connection between the dead man and Hume.

It has never been suggested that Donald Hume was not an intelligent man. As evidence of this, he decided upon a remarkable plan of action. He told the police a story which fitted all the facts that could be proved, and later repeated it to the jury at his trial for the murder of Stanley Setty.

Three men named Mac, Greeny, and The Boy, he claimed, had offered him £100 in five-pound notes to fly over the Channel with two parcels and drop them overboard. The next day they offered him a further £50, again in flyers, to do the same thing with a third parcel. Hume agreed that all the evidence of renting a plane, dropping the parcels, and coming back to his flat, was true. His story explained his actions just as well as the Crown's assertion that he was a murderer. There were none of the murdered man's fingerprints to be found in his flat, no murder weapon, no knives or saws for cutting up the body. Hume claimed that the larger parcel had dripped blood on his carpet and stained his floor. He admitted that he knew he was being used to dispose of the much-publicized missing Setty. And faced with the painter, he admitted that the man helped him carry the larger parcel to his car. In fact, Hume confessed to everything except murder. He gave a detailed description of Mac, Greeny, and The Boy, but they were never found. In one fell swoop Hume had accounted for all his actions and all the evidence.

The jury couldn't agree as to his guilt or innocence. They were immediately dismissed by the judge, and a new jury was sworn in. The judge in his wisdom ordered them to return a verdict of not guilty of murder. Then he read the charge indicting Hume as an accessory after the fact of murder. Hume pleaded guilty to this lesser charge and received a sentence of twelve years in jail.

Eight years later, Donald Hume was released from Dartmoor Prison. He was now thirty-eight years old. His wife Cynthia had divorced him. Even his dog Tony had been put to sleep. Only Donald Hume's irrepressible lust for life and the pleasures money could bring was alive and well. The sensational aspects of his crime were still remembered by the public at large, and Hume received several offers for the full and true story of his part in the murder of Stanley Setty.

One fine day he walked into the office of the Sunday Pictorial in London, England, and told them that he was willing to sell his confession. The exact amount paid has never been made public, but we do know he struck a hard bargain. The sum he received was enough to convince him that he could start a comfortable new life under an assumed name in another country. A reporter lived with Hume for three weeks at a hotel, recording his every thought concerning the killing of Stanley

Setty. Hume demanded, and got, ten days' lead time to get out of the country before the newspaper broke the story. In his confession he outlined, and had corroborated, every detail of the murder he had committed. He revealed that his very vivid descriptions of Mac, Greeny, and The Boy were the true descriptions of three of the investigating officers. Here, too, Hume's basic intelligence showed through. Had he made up fictitious descriptions and had to repeat them at a later date, he could quite easily have tripped himself up. By picking three men who actually existed, his memory was constantly being refreshed when he actually came in contact with them.

With the money from the sale of his confession, he left the country. He changed his name, forged new identity papers and lived for some time in Switzerland as a Canadian named John Stephen Bird. When he had sold his confession in England, he had sported a moustache and eyeglasses. Now he looked completely different. Dapper Johnny Bird was clean-shaven and wore no glasses. He passed himself off as a test pilot, and in this glamorous guise he frequented Zurich night spots and went the wine, women and song route until the cash from the sale of his story started to dwindle. Along the way he met a real beauty, Trudi Sommer. She had auburn hair, an open smile that showed off her even white teeth, and an hourglass figure that drew appreciative glances from every man who came in contact with her. Never one to do things by half measures, Hume promptly fell for her and moved into her apartment.

He now needed money and needed it fast. And what could be quicker than robbing banks? But he would have to operate without Trudi's knowledge. His fertile mind wasn't stymied by this one either. He decided to tell her he was a spy working for the United States against the Russians, which would account for his absences from Zurich. Trudi was actually thrilled by her boyfriend's glamorous occupation.

Hume decided to go into his new profession right away. His plan called for him to go to another country, using yet another alias, rob a bank and head back to Switzerland. He returned to London and cased the Midland Bank on Boston Manor Road in Brentford. A short time later, armed with a pistol, he managed to rob the bank, but ran into trouble, shooting and wounding an employee. Still, he made good his escape, and the next day was back, safely bedded down with Trudi in Switzerland. The take from his first venture into the robbery business was £1500.

Then Trudi started to pressure Hume, alias Bird, toward the altar. Donald, alias Johnny, put her off as long as possible. Finally he was forced to become engaged to the girl, and really planned to get married. First, though, he figured he needed more cash. Another bank robbery was planned, and again he headed for London. This time, when he entered the bank an employee grappled with him as he scooped up some bills. His pistol went off and the man fell wounded to the floor. Hume made it safely back to Zurich, only £300 richer for his trouble. Such a paltry amount didn't last him long.

On Friday, January 30, 1959, he walked into the Gewerbe Bank in Zurich. Located on the Ramistrasse, the austere stone structure was designed to give the impression of stability, but for all its Swiss solidity it was not built to prevent a robbery. It was exactly 11:30 a.m. when Hume marched through the massive doors carrying a small cardboard box in one hand and a gun in the other. For no apparent reason, he shot and wounded an employee named Walter Schenkel. The wounded man managed to set off the burglar alarm. Hume, nervous and desperate, grabbed at some bills and ran from the bank with employees hot on his trail. A taxi driver, Arthur Maag, saw what was happening and joined the chase. Hume turned, pointed his pistol and shot Maag dead. A group of men overpowered the fugitive, and he was immediately taken away to the police station, where his real identity was quickly uncovered.

Hume stood trial in Zurich for the murder of Maag. Since Switzerland does not have capital punishment, he received the maximum sentence of life imprisonment at hard labour. In the fall of 1976, he was transferred to the famous Hospital for the Criminally Insane at Broadmoor, England.

By the age of thirty-nine, Donald Hume had led quite a life. He had wounded three people, murdered two, and robbed three banks. We mustn't forget he also had the rather unique experience of dissecting one of his victims. Who knows, we may yet hear more from that well-known Canadian playboy and test pilot, John Stephen Bird.

Down the Drain

John George Haigh was born in Stanford, Lincolnshire, on July 24, 1909. It was a difficult time for the family. John, Sr., was an electrical engineer and had been out of work for several months. Being deeply religious (the family belonged to an austere sect known as the Plymouth Brethren) they were too proud to ask for help from friend or neighbour.

Their affairs took a turn for the better when Haigh Sr. obtained employment at the Lofthouse Colliery. He was to stay in their employ for the next twenty-five years, but the new job necessitated a move to Outwood, a small village near the city of Wakefield. Here they moved into a comfortable house that came with the job.

The Haighs have come under close scrutiny in hindsight, but nothing detrimental can be conjured up about them. John and Emily were a deeply religious couple, and no doubt the severity of their beliefs sometimes spilled over into the upbringing of their only son. Young George was brought up to respect authority in the puritanical atmosphere of their home. His parents were kind and loving to a point, but at the same time they were harsh and stern when it came to the qualities they and the Brethren deemed sacred. Qualities such as punctuality and obedience were deeply instilled in the young lad, and no doubt he chafed at the bit under the strict rules.

When he became a teenager he mastered the organ and piano. His voice was better than average, and soon he was singing in the choir in Wakefield cathedral. The proud and pious Haighs delighted in listening to their John sing—a bizarre picture of domestic bliss in view of the grim events that were to befall the family in later years.

But for the moment, time passed pleasantly enough for the respectable Haighs and their respectable son. In his last year at school John won a prize for studies in divinity. He became very interested in automobiles and at the age of eighteen got his first job as junior salesman at Appleyards, a car dealership in Wakefield. This position lasted about a year.

Something of a loner, Haigh had no close friends or social life. He was a strange fellow, but no worse than many blokes struggling to make a living. He was of average height, had a full crop of black hair, was always neatly dressed, and generally made a good impression on those he met.

For the next two years John moved from job to job and showed a distinct lack of interest in bettering himself. Then, when he was twenty-one, he and a partner started a business in Leeds, a combination advertising agency and real estate firm. For a short while it prospered, but then the tiny company fell on hard times. In order to keep the business going, John tried to obtain funds by false pretenses. He glibly misrepresented some buildings he was trying to sell, and obtained advances based on his misleading claims. The police picked him up, but because it was a first offense the charges were dismissed.

He then joined a combination car rental and insurance company, again based in Leeds, and again did very well at the outset. In fact, he was remembered as the ace of the staff. Then the bombshell fell. John was making up and signing fraudulent contracts, and had been doing so since joining the company. He had actually started up a dealership to perpetrate his frauds. He would sell a non-existent vehicle from his garage, and send the hire purchase contract to the company he represented. They in turn would send Haigh's garage a cheque, and of course Haigh would receive his commission from the company for bringing in the business. He had to keep meticulous records in order to make sure that all his fraudulent contracts were being paid each month, as it obviously wouldn't do to have someone trying to contact one of the false names and addresses which appeared on the contracts. One wonders if Haigh's penchant for forgery wasn't practice for bigger and better things that were to follow.

When his frauds were uncovered, his father made arrangements to pay the company the money that was missing and keep his son out of jail.

Haigh moved to Leeds, where he met, wooed and married Beatrice Hamer. He hadn't known the twenty-one-year-old Beatrice very long, and the marriage was not a gala affair as John's parents didn't approve of the union and the bride's parents were not thrilled with John. The young couple exchanged vows without benefit of parents at a registry office on July 6, 1934.

Fifteen months later John was again charged with fraud. Unbelievably, he had managed to secure employment with a branch of the same company from which he had previously been fired. He even used the fraudulent contract scheme again. This time he received fifteen months in prison. While he was serving this sentence his wife gave birth to their baby. John was never to live with his wife again, nor was he ever to lay eyes on his child; he abandoned them without a thought for their welfare. He got three months off for good behaviour, and was out after serving one year. His parents, who by now were feeling the disgrace of their son's petty crimes, still stood behind their only off-spring. He swore that he was turning over a new leaf, and like parents everywhere, they believed him.

Haigh's father introduced him to a man who owned a dry-cleaning plant in Leeds. John told the truth about his past, and because of his sincerity, got the job. As always, things went well at first and John soon became assistant manager. Then, following his previous pattern, he was found to be promising people jobs for small cash considerations. He was fired on the spot, and moved on to bigger and better things in London.

He got a job as manager of an amusement park in Tooting. For twelve months he worked diligently for the owner, William McSwan, and his son, Donald. Then Haigh got that old urge to take another short cut. He left the McSwans and somehow or other hit upon a novel get-rich-quick scheme.

He would find the name of a legitimate lawyer in one town, and set up a law office in another, using the legitimate lawyer's name. He would then write to a selected list of clients that he was winding up an estate. This fictional estate would have some stocks that would be offered at slightly less than the current market price. For a small deposit Haigh would hold the stock for the proposed buyer. After he had accumulated enough cheques, and just before his clients started to demand delivery of the stocks, Haigh would close shop and set up in another town under another name.

On November 24, 1937, the authorities caught up with him. This time he got four years in Dartmoor. He received time off for good behaviour and was released in 1940. In the summer of '41 he sold some furniture that didn't belong to him, for which indiscretion he received twenty-one months in Lincoln Prison. Upon being released in 1943 John moved to Crawley, where, with the help of forged references and educational documents, he got a job with a light engineering firm owned by a Mr. Stevens.

Stevens was so taken with Haigh that he invited him to stay with his family, and John was quick to accept his offer. The Stevenses had two daughters. The younger of the two was usually underfoot, but Barbara was another story. She was an attractive young girl, and she and John became good friends. Barbara, like Haigh, loved good music, and the two of them spent many pleasant evenings discussing various compositions and composers. Sometimes Haigh played the piano while the entire family sat around and listened attentively.

John left the Stevens home and employ after six months, had some personal cards printed that read "J. G. Haigh, B.Sc., Technical Liaison Officer, Union Group Engineering," and started a light engineering firm on his own in London. At first he did rather well, and in 1944 he moved to the Onslow Court Hotel in South Kensington. He had devised another get-rich-quick scheme, and this time it included murder.

One day John bumped into young Donald McSwan on the street, and the two men struck up a conversation about the good old days when they had worked together in the amusement park in Tooting. Donald was a pleasant enough lad, somewhat taller and more extroverted than Haigh. In the course of making small talk with Haigh he mentioned that he had sold his share of the amusement park and had invested his money in some property. No doubt Haigh's interest in his old friend blossomed with this information, and they got along so well that Donald invited John over to his home to have a meal with his elderly parents. Haigh accepted this invitation, and the McSwans were genuinely happy to see him again.

Donald and Haigh became chums. They would meet every so often for a meal or just to pass the time of day. There is no doubt that the friendship was being cultivated by Haigh for his own devious purposes, and on September 9, 1944, these purposes became clear enough. Haigh invited Donald over to his workshop at 79 Gloucester Road, sneaked up behind his chum and hit him over the head with a piece of pipe. He later claimed that it was only then that he thought of the perplexing problem of getting rid of the body. The idea of submerging it in sulphuric acid came to him the next morning. He had been using the acid to scale metal, and it was "mere coincidence" that two carboys of acid were at hand.

The next morning Haigh placed the body in a drum. He then had the rather difficult task of taking sulphuric acid out of a carboy and transferring it, with the aid of a pail, into the drum containing the body. It was a tough job, and several times the burning fumes were too much for him and he had to go out to get fresh air. But slowly and surely the drum filled with sulphuric acid, completely immersing the body. Haigh was sure that he was removing both the body and all traces of the murder. What he didn't know is that certain parts of the human body, as well as foreign materials, take varying lengths of time to disintegrate. Gallstones may take a very long time to disappear completely, and human fat will remain for years. Haigh was later to refer to this fat as sludge, and it was this that proved beyond a doubt that a human being had been disintegrated in his workshop.

Haigh left his gruesome deposit and travelled to Scotland. Here he forged letters to the elder McSwans in their son's handwriting, saying that he had skipped to Scotland in order to avoid being called into the service. Donald had mentioned his reluctance to enter the armed services before, so the old couple had no reason to be suspicious.

Then Haigh came back to his workshop in Crawley and poured the now dissolved Donald down the drain. With commendable patience, he waited twenty months before he invited the elderly McSwans to 79 Gloucester Road on a warm July day and killed them both with vicious blows to the head.

Conscientious monster that he was, he had now outfitted himself with the tools of murder. He wore a mackintosh when he struck the fatal blows, in order to keep the blood off his clothes. He had also outfitted the workshop with a stirrup pump to transfer the sulphuric acid from the carboy into the drum. With two bodies on his hands, he now had two drums to fill, and had taken the precaution of wearing a gas mask to protect himself against the fumes.

Having disposed of their mortal remains, he equipped himself with

forged power of attorney documents and ingeniously went about liqui-
dating and transferring all the McSwans' assets to himself. They had
two properties, a bank account, and some stocks.

When questioned about the missing couple, he would quickly produce personal letters in the McSwans' handwriting. These letters gave
plausible excuses for their absence and assured anyone who inquired
that they were fine. In order to make legal contracts, Haigh would produce the necessary forged documents demonstrating that his dear
friends had empowered him to make transactions in their names. No
one became suspicious. The McSwans were an unobtrusive lot who had
never harmed anyone. It was just their bad luck that they crossed the
path of our friend, John George. Haigh realized about £4,000 from the
deaths of the three McSwans, and went home for Christmas, satisfied
and now prosperous, to visit his mother and father.

Throughout all his activities Haigh was writing and seeing his old
girlfriend, Barbara Stevens. He treated her with the utmost respect,
and at no time was he anything but a perfect gentleman to her. A deep
and lasting friendship developed between them. He confided many of
his innermost thoughts to her, and a strong attachment grew between
the couple. Dashing John was the greatest thing that had ever happened to Barbara. The well-groomed, mature charmer was very
different from the awkward local lads her own age. They took in sym-
phonies and plays, and had intellectual conversations on a variety of
topics. This rather weird relationship got to the stage of discussing
marriage, but of course we know that Haigh was already legally married. Not once did Barbara ever suspect that her boyfriend was
anything other than he seemed.

At this stage of his career John had money in his pocket, a pretty
girlfriend, and had successfully murdered three innocent people.

At about this time he decided to give up his shop at 79 Gloucester
Road, the scene of his three murders, and take up a new location on

Leopold Road in Crawley. He told the company he rented the premises from that he planned to conduct several experiments there.

In September 1947, Haigh answered an advertisement offering a house for sale at 22 Ladbroke Square, London. The home belonged to Dr. Archibald Henderson and his wife, Rose. Haigh didn't buy the house, but soon became a close friend of the handsome and wealthy Hendersons. For six months he cultivated their friendship and stored away all the personal bits and pieces of information he could. When he knew enough about the Hendersons, it would be time to kill them.

Haigh picked his spot. He waited until they were on vacation. Then one day he dropped in on them at the Metropole Hotel in Brighton, and suggested that the doctor might care to visit his "factory" in Crawley. It wasn't much of a drive, so the doctor accepted. As soon as they entered the storeroom, Haigh shot Dr. Henderson in the head from behind. His now familiar, macabre procedure was set into motion. The stirrup pump transferred the sulphuric acid from the carboy into the drum, and Haigh scurried about the small building in his gas mask, much like a busy chef overseeing a gourmet feast.

He then rushed back to Brighton and told Mrs. Henderson that her husband had suddenly been taken ill. On this pretext she accompanied him back to Crawley. Once in the storeroom he shot her in the back of the head and proceeded to dispose of her body in the same manner as that of her husband. Haigh had taken the liberty of stripping both bodies of a substantial amount of jewellery before placing them in the sulphuric acid, and he later sold the jewellery for £300.

A few days after these murders, on February 16, Haigh showed up at the Metropole Hotel in Brighton. He had a letter, apparently signed by Dr. Henderson, instructing the hotel to give him the Henderson's baggage. Haigh had studied the doctor's handwriting and forged the letter.

Mrs. Henderson's brother soon contacted Haigh regarding the whereabouts of his sister and brother-in-law. Haigh told him the couple had had a very serious disagreement in Brighton and had decided to go away by themselves to work out their marital difficulties. To facilitate their rush to privacy, Haigh told Mrs. Henderson's brother, he had loaned the couple £2,500. He added that if they didn't return in sixty days the Hendersons were to give him their car and home. He showed the brother a document to this effect, apparently signed by the doctor.

The brother didn't like this story one bit, and insinuated that if he didn't hear from his sister soon, he would go to the police. Haigh dashed off a forged letter from Rose to her brother. Cunning devil that he was, he had learned and stored away very personal family matters. He even copied her style of writing. This letter substantiated Haigh's story, and set Rose Henderson's family at ease, for the time being at least.

Haigh followed up with postcards and telegrams, and set up a fictitious situation that was extremely believable. Finally he forged a fifteen-page letter from Rose to her brother, postmarked Glasgow, Scotland. In the letter Rose explained that due to personal financial problems, she and the doctor were going to South Africa. The letter carefully stated that the brother should settle the £2,500 debt to their friend, John Haigh, and take his advice in clearing up all money matters.

Scotland Yard maintain that this letter, in the exact style and handwriting of Rose Henderson, is one of the most brilliant forgeries they have ever encountered.

Rose Henderson's family now considered Haigh a dear friend who had done many favours for the doctor. It is estimated from Haigh's bank statements that he realized over £7,000 from the Henderson murders, but within a year he had blown the money on high living, and was looking around for more people to kill.

The Onslow Court Hotel catered mainly to elderly ladies who had been left considerable incomes. Most of the ladies were there on a more or less permanent basis. They passed the time sitting on wicker chairs, sipping tea and recalling days gone by. John Haigh, a permanent resident himself, was popular with his more senior associates of the opposite sex. In fact, one might say that many of them doted on him.

Mrs. Durand-Deacon was typical of the residents at the Onslow Court. Grey-haired and matronly, she could have been typecast for the part. She and John Haigh sat at adjoining tables at breakfast and often passed the time of day. Sometimes Mrs. Deacon expressed an interest in Haigh's engineering business. In fact, Mrs. Deacon had the bright idea that she wanted to manufacture artificial fingernails. Haigh, who had the patience of Job and would wait until his victims almost begged to become entwined in his net, expressed keen interest in this. He thought it might be a good idea if she were to accompany him one day to his factory in Crawley.

On February 18, Haigh was having lunch at the Onslow Court when Mrs. Durand-Deacon suggested that it would be as good a day as any to visit the factory in Crawley. Haigh thought the day was just perfect. Mrs. Durand-Deacon told her good friend Mrs. Lane that she had an appointment with Haigh later that afternoon.

Haigh left the hotel heading for Leopold Road, carrying a hatbox, which, unknown to the occupants of the hotel, contained a revolver. He entered his workshop with Mrs. Durand-Deacon. Two sides of the main room had workbenches running the length of the walls, and three carboys of sulphuric acid took up much of the available space. By 5:30 that same afternoon Haigh had gone through the preliminary portion of his macabre routine. He had donned his mackintosh, shot Mrs. Deacon, and placed her body securely in the empty drum. Then, exhibiting a quirk that most normal people have difficulty comprehending, John Haigh got hungry. He slipped over to Ye Olde Ancient Prior's Restaurant in the Square in Crawley and had poached eggs on toast and tea. This brief respite is well documented, as he chatted with the owner of the restaurant.

Then, back to work. He donned rubber gloves and gas mask, started up the stirrup pump, poured in the sulphuric acid, and poor Mrs. Deacon was well on her way to disintegration in the drum.

Haigh was back in London by ten o'clock that night. When Mrs. Durand-Deacon didn't show up for dinner, her friend Mrs. Lane was mildly alarmed. When her friend didn't show up for breakfast, she approached Haigh for an explanation. He had a story ready. He told Mrs. Lane that he had an appointment to meet Mrs. Durand-Deacon in front of a store, but she didn't show up. He waited for her for over an hour, then decided that she must have been delayed or changed her mind, and went on without her.

He left the worried Mrs. Lane and went to Crawley to check on the disintegration of Mrs. Deacon and pay a visit to his girlfriend Barbara Stevens. Both Barbara and her mother were to state later that on this particular visit John looked ill and had a hoarse voice. The hoarseness of the voice we can attribute to too many acid fumes, and the peaked condition could be laid at the doorstep of the inquisitive and annoying Mrs. Lane back at the Onslow Court Hotel.

Haigh should have known better. Surely one of the first rules in the mass murderers' handbook should be never, never mess with little grey-haired ladies. If either the victim or a friend of the victim's falls into this category, the entire operation is invariably ruined. Ladies of this ilk simply tend to spoil everything.

But let's get back to it. For the first time, one of his victims was missed by someone who didn't accept his glib explanations. The next morning was a Sunday, and Haigh knew he would have to face the troublesome Mrs. Lane at breakfast. He decided to be aggressive, and was the first to inquire as to the whereabouts of Mrs. Durand-Deacon. He suggested they go and report the missing woman to the police. Haigh offered a lift in his car, and Mrs. Lane accepted.

The police took a routine report from Mrs. Lane, and a woman sergeant was dispatched to the hotel to question all the guests, including

Haigh, who had been one of the last residents to see the missing woman. The policewoman came away from the hotel with a nagging suspicion about this glib Haigh fellow. It bothered her so much she emphasized her suspicions in her report to her superior, Division Detective Inspector Shelley Symes. His first move was to check Haigh's record, and, of course, he uncovered his lengthy criminal past. Inspector Symes decided to pay him a visit. On Monday Symes interviewed Haigh and was given substantially the same story as his sergeant had received. He obtained a picture of the missing woman and circulated it to the press.

The next day, Tuesday, Haigh checked the drum in Crawley, and discovered that the body was completely dissolved. He poured the liquid sludge out into the yard. On Wednesday Haigh was again questioned by the police. Again he gave the same story.

By Saturday the police had located Haigh's landlord and decided to break the lock on the "factory" door. Inside they found a revolver and ammunition. They also found documents belonging to Mr. and Mrs. McSwan and their son, Donald. Further documents were found belonging to a Doctor Henderson and his wife, Rose. They also found a dry-cleaning receipt for a Persian lamb coat. Mrs. Durand-Deacon was last seen wearing such a coat. When it was retrieved from the cleaners, the detectives found that there was a patch on the sleeve. Inspector Symes searched Mrs. Deacon's room at the Onslow Court Hotel, and inside a sewing basket he found the same material that was used to patch the coat. Because of the publicity the case was now receiving in the press, a jeweller came forward with jewellery sold to him by Haigh. Mrs. Durand-Deacon's sister identified it as belonging to the missing woman.

The police picked up Haigh outside his hotel and took him to Chelsea Police Station. Inspector Symes produced the fur coat and jewellery, and asked Haigh for an explanation. Haigh was starting to give a cock-and-bull story to his adversary when Symes was called out of the office. Left

185

alone with Detective Inspector Webb, for some reason Haigh started to talk. The conversation bears repeating here. Remember, at this point no one actually knew a murder had taken place.

Haigh said, "Well, if I told you the truth, you would not believe me; it sounds too fantastic. Mrs. Durand-Deacon no longer exists. She has disappeared completely and no trace of her can ever be found again."

"What has happened to her?" asked Webb.

"I have destroyed her with acid. You'll find the sludge which remains at Leopold Road. I did the same with the Hendersons and the McSwans. Every trace has gone. How can you prove murder if there is no body?"

Webb got Symes back in the office, and in front of Haigh told him what had transpired. Haigh interjected, "That's perfectly true, and it's a very long story and will take hours to tell."

Haigh spewed forth every detail of how he killed not only Mrs. Durand-Deacon but the McSwans and the Hendersons. These former murders were unknown to the police. He elaborated on his diabolic behaviour by adding the fact that he had made a tiny incision in each victim's throat. From this incision, he claimed, he extracted and drank a glass of blood.

The authorities converged on Haigh's factory once more. Now they knew what they were looking for, and they found all the paraphernalia of murder. On the ground outside the workshop there was a greasy area where the drums of sludge had been emptied. After a minute examination of the yard (it was all actually lifted up and taken to Scotland Yard) some gallstones and a plastic denture were found. The denture was identified as belonging to Mrs. Durand-Deacon by her dentist. She had also suffered from gallstones. Tiny particles of eroded bone were also found.

There was no doubt about it. Haigh was what he claimed to be—a monster. Realizing that his one chance to live was to appear insane, he maintained that he had killed for a glass of blood and not for material gain. Due to the rather large sums of money he diverted to himself, this reason proved hard to swallow. When questioned by psychiatrists he told about dreaming of Christ with open wounds bleeding into his mouth, and claimed that in this way he acquired the uncontrollable urge to drink blood. No one believed the blood theory. It was obvious that Haigh was trying to feign madness.

While awaiting trial he received a letter every day from his mother. Barbara Stevens wrote to him and visited him often. She was the one exception in his life—the only one he had ever treated decently. In his way, Haigh seemed to be genuinely fond of her. She in turn shared his affection, and remained loyal to him until the last.

On July 18, 1949, Haigh stood trial for the murder of Mrs. Durand-Deacon. Huge crowds gathered outside the courthouse to catch a glimpse of the mass murderer. He pleaded not guilty. The defense tried to prove him insane, and the prosecution tried to prove him sane. The jurors obviously believed the prosecution. They took exactly fifteen minutes to find him guilty.

Facing death by hanging, Haigh took great pains to bequeath his clothing to Madame Tussaud's Chamber of Horrors. There were certain stipulations. Vain to the end, he insisted that his wax image be kept in perfect condition, hair combed and pants pressed.

He was executed on August 10, 1949.

The Jigsaw Murder

It all started in New York City in 1897 on a sunny Saturday afternoon in June. Two young lads, James McKenna, thirteen, and John McGuire, fourteen, were swimming at a disused dock at the foot of East 11th Street when they saw a brightly-wrapped parcel floating in the water. They swam out and succeeded in pushing the parcel into shore. The bright wrapping proved to be red oilcloth with small golden stars; really quite a joyous-looking prize. The boys eagerly opened the parcel. It contained the joyous trunk of a man, or rather the shoulders, arms and chest of what had once been a man. Mysteriously, a patch of skin had been neatly cut away from the area below the left breast.

The boys called off their swimming for that day, but for the rest of their lives they were able to relate how they found the first piece in what was to become New York's famous Jigsaw Murder.

The next day another pair of boys, picking berries with their father near East 176th Street on the Bronx side of the Harlem River, came across a parcel wrapped in red oilcloth with a pattern of gold stars. When the Bronx cops opened this little treasure, they found the lower part of a torso. While the neck had been cut neatly and professionally, the legs were severed from the trunk in a most haphazard manner, because as anyone in the dismembering business knows, you can cut a head off rather easily but legs are a tiresome task. This lower portion was matched up with the first find, and they fitted perfectly. Not only that, but the cut edges of the oilcloth also matched up.

There was more to come. In the middle of the same week some sailors on the USS *Vermont*, over at the Brooklyn Navy Yard, found some brightly-wrapped legs. They matched up with the previous two pieces. If you are keeping close track of all the parts, we now have everything except the head. Everyone was baffled. Even in little old New York, it's not every day they find pieces of people scattered hither and yon over several boroughs. All the daily newspapers in New York featured the story on Page One. Each time a new fragment turned up it fostered new theories and kept the story fresh and exciting.

The New York papers were extremely competitive at this time, and some of their ace reporters were as good as top detectives at cracking murder cases. The papers featured pictures of pieces of the corpse, as well as theories by learned medical men. The main dailies ran contests offering cash rewards to the public for furnishing the clues that would crack the case.

What they had to go on was as follows. The man's weight was estimated to be 180 pounds, with big powerful arms. The chest was husky and well-developed, and he was in perfect health. His flesh was white and untanned, but his hands didn't go with the rest of his powerful physique. The hands came under close scrutiny as a means of figuring out his occupation. The fingers were small and uncalloused, indicating that he was not accustomed to hard manual labour. The fingernails were carefully trimmed and cut short; not at all like the long polished nails found on the society dudes of that era. The tip of each finger was slightly shrivelled. It was estimated that the first section of the body to be found had been in the water for less than a day. The best police officers, top reporters, and the public all had a crack at guessing the man's occupation, and none of them came up right. Only one boy, fresh out of his first year at medical school, came up with the correct answer. His name was Ned Brown and he had a summer job as a cub reporter with the New York *World*. By correctly deducing the occupation of the victim, he went on to solve the murder.

If you want to play detective and try to guess the occupation of the corpse, review the facts, no peeking below, and give it a try.

Ned correctly figured out that the well-built corpse had been a masseur or "rubber" in one of the hundreds of Turkish baths that dotted New York at the turn of the century. The heavy, muscular, well-built chest and arms came from massaging twenty to thirty men every day. His work kept him indoors all day, which accounted for the lack of a tan. Carefully trimmed fingernails were a necessity in order to avoid scratching his clients. If you go swimming for any length of time or even take a long shower, take a look at your fingertips and you will notice a crinkling effect. This feature of the fingers, coupled with the general condition of the hands, left Ned with the correct occupation.

He started canvassing the Turkish baths to try to find one that had a rubber missing. On his fifth try, an attendant told Ned that one Willie Guldensuppe had taken the previous Friday off and hadn't shown up for work since. Ned got the missing Willie's description and it exactly matched the jigsaw corpse. It seems Willie had a tattoo under his left breast. Remember the piece of skin that was missing? Ned figured it was taken away to remove the tattoo. He went to Willie's address, and found it to be occupied by a fine cut of a woman, standing five feet, six inches tall, and weighing in at 200 pounds, give or take a bulge. Her name was Mrs. Augusta Nack, and she had formerly lived with Willie. Unfortunately, poor William was now missing. Mrs. Nack had a not-so-new lover, one Fred Thorn.

Subsequent investigation proved that the 200-pound Augusta led an active sex life. She had originally been married to Mr. Nack, a baker, whom she had left. He never entered this case except to express relief that his head was on his shoulders, and to imply that this might not still be the case had he remained under the same roof as the ever-loving Augusta. Augusta then took up with Fred Thorn, whom Willie threatened and scared away. Thorn moved out, and Willie moved in. Well, not exactly. You see, Fred became a thorn in Willie's side by dropping in to see Augusta during the day when Willie was busy rubbing down stiffs at the bath.

The reason the overweight Mrs. Nack was able to command so much attention from her suitors was because of her lucrative profession of midwife, supplemented, it is suspected, with the odd abortion. In any event, she was a fine means of support for any man who could stomach her.

Mrs. Nack and Fred Thorn were arrested, but knowing the identity of the victim and the suspicious lives of the accused was not proof of murder.

Enter my friend, the duck.

In a sparsely populated area in the suburb of Woodstock, there was a man who owned a beautiful white duck. One day he noticed the duck came home with all its feathers coloured a bright red. He followed the duck the next morning, and beside a house he found a little pond with blood-red water. The duck had stumbled onto the scene of the murder.

Mrs. Nack and Thorn started to talk. She had lured Willie out to the isolated house on the pretence that they would set up a prostitution operation. Thorn was waiting in the house. He shot Willie in the back of the head and placed him in a bathtub, where he cut his throat with a razor. They cut up the rest of Willie right there and then. The reason the head was never found is that it was encased in plaster of Paris, and as a result sank beautifully. The murdering couple, for some reason, thought the other bundles would sink without the plaster.

Thorn had kept the water running in the bathtub all the time in order to get rid of the blood. How was he to know that the pipes were not connected to any sewerage system, but ran directly into the little pond beside the house?

During the trial Mrs. Nack's most embarrassing moment came when a shopkeeper positively identified her as the purchaser of several yards of bright red oilcloth. Mrs. Nack turned state's evidence against her lover, and was allowed to plead guilty to manslaughter in the first degree. She received the relatively light sentence of fifteen years. Fred Thorn was electrocuted in Sing Sing in August of 1898, possibly the first and only murderer to have the dubious distinction of being placed in the electric chair by a duck.

Ned Brown, the first-year medical student who really cracked the case, got a five-dollar bonus from his paper. He never went back to medical school, and his summer job with the New York *World* lasted thirty-four years.

Murder in the Air

Three times a week, a Quebec Airways flight left Montreal for Seven Islands, with stops at Quebec City and Baie Comeau. It was so punctual and reliable that people along the route used to set their watches by the roar of the engines.

On September 9, 1949, Patrick Simard was fishing for eels near his home at Sault-au-Cochon, Quebec. He glanced up, idly following the flight of the Douglas DC-3 as it approached Cap Tourmente. Then he heard a loud explosion, and as he watched in horror the plane veered crazily to the left and went into a power dive, heading straight for the peak of Cap Tourmente. Simard ran through thick bush towards the crash; it took him an hour to get to the scene. Scattered among the wreckage of the aircraft were the remains of the passengers and their luggage. Surprisingly, there was no fire, but the ominous smell of leaking gasoline hung over the entire area. The propellers had been turning when the plane smashed vertically into the ground. There was no swath of torn trees, just the aircraft with its wings ripped off and its horribly mangled nose sticking into the earth.

The plane had held four crew members and nineteen passengers. Simard checked to see if there were any survivors. Finding none, he started down the mountain for help. He met some men who were working on railway tracks nearby, and they took the news to St. Joachim, where it was relayed to Quebec City. Within hours Canadian Pacific Airlines, the patent company of Quebec Airways, had their investigating officials at the scene of the crash.

The left front luggage compartment showed signs of an explosion, and it was this explosion that had destroyed the control system of the aircraft, causing the disaster. They examined everything aboard the aircraft that could have caused an explosion. Items such as fire extinguishers and storage batteries were checked, but none of these was found to be the cause of the crash. The four crew members and nineteen passengers had been killed instantly upon impact, but the lack of fire made identifying the bodies relatively easy, and the next of kin were quickly notified. Because of the explosion in the baggage compartment, the authorities concluded that they were dealing with a criminal case and not an accident. On September 12, the entire matter was turned over to the RCMP. The Mounties were to be assisted by the Quebec Provincial Police and the Quebec City Police Force.

The left front compartment had been loaded in Montreal with cargo destined for Quebec City. It was completely emptied in Quebec City and reloaded with cargo destined for Baie Comeau. This was routine practice, and was employed to reduce unnecessary delay during the flight's many stops. The authorities realized that the explosive material must have been put into the left front baggage compartment at Ancienne Lorette Airport in Quebec City.

The passenger list of the ill-fated craft was closely scrutinized, as was the list of insurance policies taken out on the passengers' lives. A cursory check turned up nothing unusual, and the police decided to place all relatives of victims who boarded the plane in Quebec City under observation and to conduct an investigation into their private lives.

Undertaking the investigation from another direction, the police started with the plane on the ground in Quebec City and the left front baggage compartment empty. They questioned Willie Lamonde, the freight clerk who had been on duty on September 9, but he could recall nothing of significance except that several pieces of freight had been placed on the aircraft in addition to the passengers' regular luggage. From company records the police were able to obtain the names of the senders and prospective receivers of all the air freight shipments, and they set about checking every name on the list. This approach bore fruit with the discovery of a 28-pound parcel sent by Delphis Bouchard of St. Simeon, Quebec, to Alfred Plouffe, 180 Laval Street, Baie Comeau. Neither sender nor addressee existed, so it seemed reasonable to assume that someone had walked up to Willie Lamonde with a bomb and shipped it air freight to Baie Comeau.

The police begged Willie to try to remember who had given him the parcel. Willie's memory was now jarred by names and addresses he could relate to, and he came up with a mental picture of the person who had given him the bomb. He said it was a fat woman who had come to the airport by cab. He remembered this because the cabbie had carried the parcel to the scale for the fat lady. The cost of shipping the 28-pound parcel to Baie Comeau was $2.72, which she paid to Willie, who gave her a receipt. The police started the tedious task of questioning every cabbie in Quebec City, and almost immediately they found the right man.

Paul Pelletier, who worked for the Yellow Cab Company, had picked up the fat lady on September 9 at the Palais Railroad Station. He described her as middle-aged and overweight, with dark hair and eyes. She didn't say one word to him on the trip to the airport, but because she was returning to the city with him, he had carried the parcel to the freight clerk. When they returned to the city she got out of his cab at the rear of the Château Frontenac Hotel, and Pelletier recalled seeing her walking toward Lower Town or the older section of the city.

Then, upon checking the relatives of victims, the police for the first time heard the name of Albert Guay, whose wife Rita had died in the crash. Albert had been fined $25 for causing a scene some months previously in a restaurant, where he had brandished a revolver at a waitress named Marie-Ange Robitaille. It was a small and relatively insignificant incident, but one that couldn't be overlooked by the authorities. The girl still worked at the restaurant and the police decided to question her about her relationship with Guay. The detectives confronted an attractive, shapely young girl who would have caused heads to turn anywhere.

Marie-Ange openly admitted knowing Albert Guay, and when asked if Guay had anything to do with a fat middle-aged woman, she immediately gave the police the name of Marguerite Pitre who lived at 49 Monseigneur Gauvreau Street. The police stationed the cab driver outside Marguerite Pitre's house, so that when she came out he would be able to identify her. On September 20 a taxi drove up and Pelletier had a good look at Marguerite as she got in. He positively identified her as the lady he had driven to the airport on September 9. Marguerite had taken an overdose of sleeping pills, and the taxi had been summoned to rush her to Infant Jesus Hospital. The police decided to arrest her as soon as she was released.

Who was this strange woman? What circumstances tied her to the young waitress, Marie-Ange Robitaille? How was Albert Guay connected to the two women?

The tangled web started to unfold. Albert Guay was born in 1917 to a working-class family. As a child, he liked games in which he played the part of a ship's captain or commander of great armies, and always had illusions of power and wealth. By the time he was twenty-two he was working in a war plant and selling watches as a sideline. During the war he married the former Rita Morel, and when peace came he gravitated to the jewellery business as a full-time occupation, opening up a shop in Seven Islands, Quebec. In 1948 he closed this store and opened a shop on St. Sauveur Street, which he soon owned.

Guay was having a prolonged affair with Marie-Ange. It is almost certain that Rita Guay had knowledge of the affair, but being wise to the ways of men with wandering eyes, she figured Albert would have his fling, tire of the waitress, and return to her. Marie-Ange had lived in a room in Marguerite Pitre's house, and it was here that Albert Guay would come to make love to his mistress, with Marguerite's complicity. The heavy-set Marguerite, who always wore black, and as a result came to be known as The Raven, had met Guay during the war when they both worked in the same munitions plant. Another member of the Raven's family, her crippled brother Genereux Ruest, worked for Guay as a watch repairman in his jewellery shop. The Raven had come under Guay's influence when she started borrowing small amounts of money from him during the war. This led to more and more loans until finally she was compelled to comply to his every wish. When questioned, the Raven at first denied taking the bomb out to the airport, but when faced with the cab driver she confessed that she had delivered the explosives. Once started, the Raven continued to sing. She admitted getting in debt to Albert until finally she owed him $600. He always demanded favours of her, and when Marie-Ange was only sixteen she had set the good-looking young girl up in her own apartment at his insistence. The Raven claimed that Guay promised he would forget the debt if she would get him some dynamite, knowing that her neighbour had acquaintances in the construction business who had access to explosives. The Raven told her neighbour that if she could get her hands on some dynamite it would be her chance to get out of Albert's clutches once and for all. Guay had told the Raven that he needed the dynamite for a friend who was removing tree stumps. In the end the Raven succeeded in obtaining 10 pounds of dynamite and nineteen blasting caps.

On September 23, Albert Guay was arrested and taken into custody. He admitted everything except murder. Albert said he knew the Raven very well because she brought him leads for watch sales, and her crippled brother worked for him. He even admitted having the affair with Marie-Ange, but claimed it was over before the plane crash. Through it all he swore he loved his wife dearly, and that the Raven was a barefaced liar.

The police descended on Genereux Ruest's workshop to search it for any evidence that a bomb had been manufactured there. They found an insignificant piece of corrugated cardboard coated with black deposits. It was the only thing in the shop that looked unusual in any way, and it was rushed to a Montreal laboratory for testing. In the lab, blasting caps were exploded using a piece of corrugated cardboard as a shield. The explosions left black deposits on the cardboard matching the ones on the cardboard taken from Ruest's workshop. The same tell-tale black deposits appeared on the inside of the left front luggage compartment of the downed aircraft.

Armed with this incriminating evidence, the authorities faced Ruest. Finally he confessed that he had constructed a time mechanism, and that he and Albert had experimented with setting it off. He claimed Albert had brought him all the materials for the bomb, and that he had no idea that Guay planned to use it for anything other than clearing stumps. He said he was afraid to volunteer the information earlier because he thought the police would believe he knew of Guay's intentions.

Meanwhile Marie-Ange Robitaille added her chapter to the increasingly well-documented life and loves of Albert Guay. She said she had met Guay at a dance in 1947, when she was sixteen years old. She thought he was a glamorous man-about-town in the jewellery business, and even though she knew he was married, it wasn't long before they were having sexual relations. Rita Guay had even complained to the girl's parents, but Marie-Ange moved out of her parents' home and moved into a spare room that the Raven provided. Several times she tried to break up with Guay, but each time he went after her and brought her back. There is little doubt that Marie-Ange was physically attracted to Guay, but in the end she could see no future with a married man. She had only seen Guay once since the crash. On that occasion he had begged her to come back to him, pleading that since his wife was now dead, no obstacles stood in their way. She told him their affair was over, and she now told the police that she knew nothing about any bomb.

Despite the incriminating statements of the Raven and her brother, Albert steadfastly maintained his innocence. On February 23, 1950, Albert Guay stood trial for murder. The jury took only seventeen minutes to find him guilty, and he was sentenced to death by hanging. Once in Bordeaux Jail awaiting death, he made a full confession, implicating the Raven and her brother as willing accomplices. Both had been motivated by money he had promised them from a small insurance policy he had taken out on his wife's life, and both had been well aware that he planned to blow up the aircraft.

Albert Guay was hanged on January 12, 1951, and Genereux Ruest followed him to the gallows in 1952. The Raven was hanged in 1953.

Where's Helen?

Arthur Kendall, his wife Helen, and their five children, Jimmie, twelve, Margaret, ten, Ann, eight, Jean, five, and Mary, one, lived on a farm in Elma Township in southern Ontario.

In the spring of 1952, Arthur and a neighbour put in a crop of flax. Arthur looked around for some way to supplement his farm income during the summer months while the flax grew to maturity. He went on a fishing trip to the Bruce Peninsula on the 24th of May, and met Ashford Pedwell, who owned a sawmill. The elderly Pedwell took a liking to the stocky, serious Kendall, and when Arthur volunteered that he was a carpenter as well as a farmer, Pedwell offered him a job running the sawmill. Kendall accepted the job with the proviso that he had to return to his farm in September to harvest his flax. This was agreeable to Pedwell, who told Kendall that he needed more hands for the mill, and asked Arthur to bring help with him when he came back.

The mill was located a few miles to the south of Tobermory on a side road, known as the Johnston Harbour Road, that led to Lake Huron. On May 26 Arthur started his new job; he had brought Jim Baillie, the son of a neighbour, with him, and the next week he hired two more boys, Gordon Neabel and George Hislop. The four men worked the mill and lived in a shack directly across the road. The shack came with the job, and was to be used as living quarters. It wasn't long before Baillie tired of the work and returned home.

Then Arthur asked his wife and children to join them. Not many women would feel that crowding into a shack measuring twelve by fourteen feet with five children and three adult men was much of a vacation, but Helen Kendall didn't see it that way. They could all stand a change from the farm. The children were out of school, and there was a lake close by for swimming. All in all, the whole family liked the idea. Sleeping arrangements were a bit of a problem, but everyone seemed to fit comfortably enough into the shack. There were upper and lower bunks on each side of the single room. The two men slept in the upper bunk on the west side, while Arthur, Helen and eighteen-month-old Mary slept in the lower bunk on the east side. Jim and Jean had the top bunk on the east side, while Margaret and Ann shared the bottom bunk on the west side. They had a small stove and a table that could seat five.

Both the hired men were very impressed with Helen Kendall. Despite trying conditions, she managed to serve good meals and always kept the little shack clean and tidy. She was meticulous about her own appearance, and her children were always clean and neatly dressed.

Mrs. Kendall had no way of knowing that before she arrived on the scene, Arthur had met a waitress named Beatrice Hogue at the Olympia Restaurant in Wiarton. Beatrice was an attractive redhead who had a total of seven children, two of whom were from a previous marriage. When Arthur met her, six of the children were living with her at her home in Wiarton. Thomas Hogue, her husband, was a sailor on the Great Lakes and was away from home a great deal. Kendall saw a lot of Beatrice during the early summer, and it soon became obvious to friends and acquaintances that they were having an affair.

On July 26, Neabel and Hislop finished at the sawmill for the season. Helen served them dinner, after which Arthur gave them a lift down to Elma Township. He went by way of Wiarton and picked up Beatrice and her six children. Then he dropped the two men off and proceeded to his own farm, where he and the Hogue family stayed the night. Next morning he paid a visit to a neighbour, Martin Barker, and inquired if he would like to hire Beatrice to look after his house and children. Barker replied that she had too many children and let it go at that. Kendall then returned the Hogue family to Wiarton and went on to the little shack on Johnston Harbour Road.

The next we hear of Arthur and his family is when he and his children returned to their farm. They arrived back prematurely, as the flax wasn't ready to be harvested and it was still several weeks until school opened. Their appearance surprised the Kendall's immediate neighbour, James Broughton, and he went over to speak to his friend Art. Instead of greeting him warmly, Kendall was sullen and sharp. The children, who were normally great friends of Broughton, tried to avoid him. Helen was nowhere to be seen, but Beatrice Hogue and her children were very much in evidence. Broughton inquired after Helen. Art explained that his wife had left him, but Broughton found this hard to believe, being aware of Helen's deep affection for her children. Arthur said that he and his wife had had a fight in the shack. Angry words had been exchanged and Helen had thrown a cup of tea at him. He had then stormed out of the shack with the idea of driving his car off the wharf at Tobermory, but when he got there there had been too many cars and he couldn't get to the edge of the wharf. When he returned to Johnston Harbour it was early in the morning and young Jimmie had told him his mother had left right after he had driven away. Kendall claimed he never saw his wife again.

It was now Friday morning; he made breakfast for the children and went to work at the mill. On Saturday night he dropped his children off at Mrs. Hogue's and went on to his farm. On Sunday night, he said, he slept with young Jimmie in his car outside Wiarton. He hung around

Wiarton all day Monday, and on Monday night slept in the shack at Johnston Harbour with his son. On Tuesday he loaded his car with some belongings and left Johnston Harbour.

Jim Broughton couldn't get Arthur's story or the children's strange behaviour out of his mind. It was as if Arthur was talking about some other person, not Helen, the devoted wife and mother. Nothing seemed to fit. After a few days he decided to visit Arthur again. This time, accompanied by Lloyd Machon, another neighbour, he again inquired about Helen. Arthur was evasive but gave the impression that she might be with her mother in Brantford. Later that day Broughton called Brantford and asked Helen's brother, Ross Cameron, if she was there. Her brother told him that she was not in Brantford, and the story of her disappearance so upset him that he decided to visit Arthur. That same night Ross Cameron went to the Kendall farm in Elma Township. Arthur came out of the house and met him in the yard. He avoided Ross' direct questions about Helen and didn't seem to want to talk about her. The children, who were usually underfoot making a fuss when their uncle visited, were nowhere to be seen. Finally Ross Cameron left the Kendall farm and went to the Sebringville Ontario Provincial Police Office, where he had previously arranged to meet Jim Broughton. The two men reported Helen Kendall as a missing person.

Arthur was questioned by the police but didn't give any new information. Helen's description was taken and her picture was distributed to police outlets across Canada and the United States. She had blue eyes, blonde hair, stood five feet seven inches tall, weighed 132 pounds, and was considered to be an attractive mature woman. The Kendall children were also questioned, but seemed reluctant to volunteer any information of a concrete nature. Mary was too young to interrogate, but Ann and Jean were questioned extensively, and each time they were gently pressed for an answer about their mother's disappearance, they burst into tears. Margaret, the eldest daughter, corroborated her father's story in every way, as did twelve-year-old Jimmie. The police felt the children were not telling the complete truth and came to the conclusion that the Kendall children feared their father. The little shack and the family car were both examined, with no results. Everyone questioned knew of Kendall's relationship with Beatrice Hogue, but could offer no explanation as to what had happened to Helen.

On September 3, approximately a month after Helen's disappearance, John Krugel was cutting bush on his property not far from the Kendall farm when he came upon a cardboard box containing women's undergarments. He notified the police, who later identified the contents of the box as belonging to Helen Kendall. Arthur Kendall appeared to be as mystified as anyone else at the weird discovery. During the month of September, the police were actively looking for Helen Kendall's body. The bush surrounding the shack at Johnston Harbour was thoroughly searched, and likely areas were also combed; but all to no avail.

Months passed, and the authorities began to receive complaints about the care of the eleven children living on the Kendall farm. On January 7, 1953, they received a report from Dr. C. E. Connors of Listowel that Margaret had been attacked by her father with a whip. Evidently she had been warned not to stop off at the farm of Clarence Ronenburg on her way home from school, and when she did drop in on the farm, her father went over and gave her a horse-whipping. Kendall was arrested for this mistreatment of his daughter, but was later released when Margaret said that she had only received a slight punishment for disobeying her father.

The Children's Aid Society was successful in gaining custody of the Kendall children, and they were taken away from the Kendall farm for a full year. Arthur appealed this decision, and the children were eventually returned to him.

Kendall and his family moved several times to get away from the derogatory rumours that dogged them wherever they went. In 1954 Thomas E. Hogue was granted a divorce from his wife Beatrice, naming Arthur Kendall as co-respondent. The years sped by, and in 1959 Kendall's lawyer was successful in having Helen declared legally dead. Three months later Arthur married Beatrice Hogue.

It was now nine years since the happy Kendall family left their farm for what was to be a pleasant vacation in the bush. Margaret, the oldest girl, was married to a private in the Canadian Army stationed in Winnipeg. Ann was living away from home, and Jimmie was now a strapping twenty-one-year-old working for Canadian Canners in Exeter. The two children still living with their father, Jean, now fourteen, and Mary, now ten, were of deep concern to Ann, who felt that they were being discriminated against, particularly now that they were the only Kendall children still at home.

Then the police received a telephone call from a friend of Ann's, advising them that Ann would now talk to them. They rushed to interview her. She now stated emphatically that she and her older brother and sister had seen her father kill her mother. In front of the officers she called her sister in Winnipeg and told her what she had done. The answer came back sharp and clear, "Ann, I've wanted to do it for years, but I never had the guts!"

Ann then told her story in detail. She said:

"After George Hislop and Gordon Neabel left, our sleeping arrangements were my mother and father in a lower bunk at the back of the cabin on the right as you walked in; my sister, Margaret, and I in the upper bunk above them. On the left of the cabin at the back, Mary and Jeannie slept in the lower bunk, with Jimmie in the bunk above. A curtain hung between the bunks.

"I don't remember details of going to bed the night before we left Johnston Harbour, but my mother always insisted that we go to bed as soon as it was dark. About dawn—daylight was coming through the one and only window in the cabin—I was awakened by a commotion under our bunk and I heard mother cry, 'No, Art, please don't.'

"I didn't hear my father say anything. I looked down over the bunk and I saw my father go from the lower bunk and lay a butcher knife on the table which was only one or two steps from the bunk. I saw blood on the knife. My dad was wearing only his work shirt; my mother her nightgown. When I awoke, Margaret was already awake and she put her hand over my mouth.

"I saw my father grab my mother around her shoulders; she was limp. He dragged her out the door. There was only a screen door on the cabin; I remember it slammed shut. I remember my mother's feet were dragging on the floor. I saw my father go past the window towards the bridge—east. I could see him dragging my mother on the road—walking in the direction of the mill.

"Dad was away about twenty minutes or half an hour. As soon as he came back he dressed, then he cleaned up the blood on the floor at the bunk. He took off the bedsheets and the pillow slips and he gathered my mother's clothes. He wiped the floor with my mother's clothes, then wrapped them up with the bedclothes and the butcher knife. He bundled them all up, put them in a shopping bag and went away. I saw him walk past the window. He was away a few minutes longer than the first time.

"As soon as he came back the second time he scrubbed the floor with a brush and rainwater from the tub filled from the cabin drainpipe. I had never seen him clean a floor before, either at the cabin or at home. While washing the floor he told us to get up and get dressed. It had always been a very strict rule in the house that we kids should never make a noise or get up until we were called. He then took Margaret away in the car to get drinking water from the spring. I remember he put the milk can we used for drinking water in the car."

Officers flew to Winnipeg, and Margaret's statement was in substance the same as Ann's. It concludes:

"Dad drove me to the fork in the road. As you go from the cabin towards the highway you come to the mill gate, a culvert over the road where there is quicksand, a hill and a turn, then you reach the fork where my dad stopped.

"He told me to tell anyone who asked about mother that she left Thursday night when he was in Wiarton—the night he told us he took Mr. Pedwell for a shot in the arm. Dad told me to say that my mother and he had a quarrel, she threw a cup of hot tea at him, and after he left she walked out, taking her clothes in a shopping bag. I was to say that she told us she would never return.

"Dad told me not to make porridge; the old stove was in poor condition. I was to go to Charlton's store for corn flakes. Dad didn't actually threaten to kill me but when he told me to do or say anything, I knew better than to disobey him.

"Dad drove me back to the cabin. Before he went to work he told us kids to pick wild strawberries for dinner. I walked to the store for corn flakes and I had to knock to wake up the Charltons. We kids had breakfast. We didn't talk about mother but I recall a general feeling that she had gone to hospital. It was only when we reached Mrs. Hogue's place that night that I realized mother wasn't sick in Wiarton.

"Dad came home for dinner at noon. Ann and I had picked strawberries and we had killed a rattlesnake. We laid it out on the ground for dad to see. I had made a stack of sandwiches and we had berries. There was no conversation about mother. Dad went to work and quit earlier than usual. He came to the cabin and told us to put on our good clothes, we would have supper where we were going.

"He drove us fast to Wiarton. On the way he loaded some wood in the car and unloaded it in Mrs. Hogue's woodshed. I remember my father saying, 'Beatrice, this is my family.' Then he shaved. We had supper—spaghetti and margarine—I had never tasted either before.

Dad and Mrs. Hogue appeared to have known each other before, and she also knew my brother, Jimmie."

Arthur Kendall was arrested on January 27, 1961, nine years after his wife disappeared. A preliminary hearing was held on March 3, and Kendall was committed for trial. His trial began in Walkerton on Tuesday, October 24, 1961.

Jimmie Kendall took the stand and told of the night his mother was murdered.

"The last night we were at Johnston Harbour Dad left the cabin in the car, saying he was taking Mr. Pedwell to the doctor. At dawn I woke up when I heard my mother cry, 'Don't, Art!' She said it three or four times. I was sleeping in the top bunk. I remember looking over the bunk. My mother looked kind of stunned. She was wearing a light coloured nightgown. I saw my dad take my mother out of the cabin. He had his arms under her armpits and she was kind of limp. I believe my mother was still saying, 'Don't, Art,' as my dad took her down the road in the direction of the highway. I think she was still living when she passed the window. I haven't seen my mother since.

"I was frightened and I wondered if my dad was coming back to do the rest of us kids in. Dad came back alone within an hour. He was wearing hip rubber boots. He didn't speak. I noticed a butcher knife on the kitchen table with blood on it. Dad wiped the blood up off the floor with a rag. It took him about ten minutes. I was scared."

Arthur Kendall sat unmoved as his three children testified against him. The jury took only two hours to find him guilty of capital murder. He was sentenced to hang on January 23, 1962. Seven days before he was to be executed, his sentence was commuted to life imprisonment.

Whatever happened to Helen Kendall's body? No one knows for sure, and it has never been found. The most popular theory is that Kendall disposed of his wife's body by placing it in Lake Scugog, which is located directly behind the Pedwell sawmill. The middle of the lake is blanketed with acres of green marsh grass, which lies about a foot under water. The rooting of the grass is so tangled it can almost support the weight of a grown man. If Kendall parted this mass and lowered his wife's body under the tangled root system into five further feet of water, the body would never rise to the surface. Mr. Pedwell claimed that he lost many logs in this manner when he ran his sawmill.

Arthur Kendall never once admitted to killing his wife. He claimed his children lied at the trial in order to lay their hands on their mother's small estate. Why did his children wait nine years to change their stories? They were questioned by mature members of the OPP. Surely they would have told the truth to these professionals, if indeed it was the truth. Why, Kendall asked, would he kill his wife in front of his children when there were so many other places to commit murder, surrounded as they were by wild bush country? These are, indeed, thought-provoking questions.

Don't Look in the Closet

When I decided to visit London, England, I swore I would never stay in one of those modern structures that contain every convenience designed by man. I checked into the Rubens Hotel on Buckingham Palace Road, and was relieved to see that the armchairs in the lobby were slightly frayed where thousands of elbows had rested in years gone by, and that the once-beautiful carpet had faded paths leading to doors, worn down by untold pairs of feet, scurrying to dine, scurrying to enter and scurrying to leave.

The year of my visit to England was 1972. I arose bright and early and briskly walked to the lift. Browning's line "Oh, to be in England now that April's there" came to mind. The lift descended ever so slowly to the lobby, and I dashed over to the hall porter.

I inquired of the young man, "Can you tell me how to get to 10 Rillington Place?"

"I never heard of that address myself, sir. Let me get a map," he replied.

I couldn't believe my ears—never heard of 10 Rillington Place! The lad must be pulling my leg. He returned with a street map of London.

"No, sir," he said, "there doesn't seem to be a Rillington Place at all."

"But," I stammered, "everyone knows 10 Rillington Place. It's Reg Christie's place—you know, the murderer."

"The name Christie does seem familiar. Let me get the manager, sir," the young man offered.

A tall balding man with a moustache looked down at me and said, "Yes?" in a manner which seemed to demand an explanation.

"Have you ever heard of 10 Rillington Place?" I asked.

"Certainly, sir," he said.

This was more like it.

He took me aside, and in the confidential manner made famous by movie spies giving the secret password to enemy agents on street corners, he said to me, "They changed the name, you know. It was so notorious after the murders it was changed to Ruston Close. Nothing much there now, but I'll tell you how to get there."

One hour later, I was looking at the demolished houses that had once been Rillington Place. At last I was standing on the same ground as that most classical of all murderers, Reginald Christie.

Reggie was born in Halifax, England, in 1898, to normal parents. There is nothing in his early life that can even vaguely be construed as a hint of what was to follow. He was a boy scout and eventually became an Assistant Group Leader. In his teens he was a choirboy, and to many I am sure this activity will seem an admirable one. As I have said, the disproportionate number of choirboys who later in life go around killing people has always made me wonder.

Christie left school at the age of fifteen, and got his first job as a projectionist in a Halifax movie theatre. It was around this time that he induced a young lady to accompany him to a local lovers' lane for what was to be his first try at sex. Later the young lady, who was apparently a blabbermouth, told one of Christie's chums that Reggie couldn't get it up. From across the streets of Halifax came shouts of "Reggie no dick" and "Can't make it Christie." It seems that after this incident Reggie always felt inadequate around women, and while this experience may not have actually caused his inhibitions, it serves to illuminate the fact that he was never quite normal when it came to members of the opposite sex.

Christie enlisted in the army in September, 1916, at the age of eighteen. He now stood five feet eight inches tall, with blue eyes and reddish-blond hair atop a round, full, ruddy face. The young soldier was a model rookie to everyone with whom he came in contact. We suspect that he gave an external impression of efficiency to his superiors and cheerfulness to his acquaintances, but inside smouldered a deep resentment for women. When he looked at the painted young girls flaunting themselves at the uniformed soldiers, we wonder if deep down he still heard the taunts of his chums of a few years back.

In April 1918 Christie was sent to the front, and towards the end of June a German mustard gas shell knocked him unconscious. When he regained consciousness he discovered that he had lost his voice. Though he later claimed that he never said a word for over three years, in reality his muteness lasted only a few months and finally gave way to a low whisper. The army doctors diagnosed his affliction as functional aphonia, which means that the explosion scared the wits out of him and left him speechless.

Christie was discharged by the end of 1919, and returned to civilian life to pick up the pieces in Halifax. On May 10, 1920, he married a neighbour, Ethel Simpson Waddington. The young couple, both twenty-two years old, had known each other for some time. Ethel was a plump, matronly type of individual, who did not stand out in any particularly memorable way.

Reggie, who now had a nondescript job as a clerk, moved into a new house with his bride. He did not have full use of his voice at this time, and it's fascinating to imagine the whispering Reggie explaining to the frigid Ethel that he really wasn't that good at this sex business. We wonder who was more relieved, Reggie or Ethel.

To better his lot Christie changed jobs and became a postman. Almost immediately he started stealing postal orders, and almost immediately he got caught and received three months in jail. When he got out things went along routinely enough, but in Reggie's eyes Halifax held no chance for advancement so he headed for London, leaving the wife with relatives in Sheffield.

Once in London Reggie held a series of dull clerical positions. He took to breaking the law regularly, and just as regularly he received jail sentences for these indiscretions. In 1924 he received a three-month sentence, followed by six months, for two charges of larceny. In 1927 he was caught stealing and received nine months in jail. Two years later Reggie shacked up with a prostitute. Like many men before him who couldn't hack it with normal women, he seemed to be in his element with prostitutes. No inhibitions here; his sex partners quite simply didn't give a damn one way or the other. One day he had a temper tantrum and hit a prostie over the head with a cricket bat, an indiscretion which earned him six months at hard labour for malicious wounding. In 1933 he got three months for stealing a car; it didn't help him that the owner of the vehicle happened to be a Roman Catholic priest.

After ten years of trying to get ahead of the game and finding nothing for his efforts except jail, Reggie decided to import the wife, who was still staying with those relatives in Sheffield. He wrote to Ethel from prison, and the pair reached a reconciliation during a visit at the jail. Coinciding with the reunion with his wife, Christie was released from prison and became a patient of Dr. Matthew Odess—not that he had any major illness, but he lived in fear of recurring muteness and suffered from such ailments as nervousness and stomach trouble.

In 1938 the sickly Reg and the nondescript Ethel moved their belongings into 10 Rillington Place. Situated in Notting Hill, Rillington Place was a dead end street, coming to an abrupt stop at a factory wall. Number 10 was the last building on the left-hand side. Because of the light traffic, Rillington was an active, alive street. Children could play games and dogs could scamper in relative safety from vehicles. Number 10 consisted of three flats, of which the Christies occupied the ground level. The whole structure was in a state of visible decay. Over the years everything had been painted many times, and was now sadly chipped and cracked; soot from the factory had rained down over the street, coating everything with a greasy deposit.

The flat above the Christies' was occupied by a partially blind old man named Kitchener, and the top flat was vacant. The three flats were connected by narrow stairs that started in the narrow passageway that led to the ground floor past the open door of Christie's flat. Reggie's front room had a bay window covered by curtains. In the evenings, he would part these curtains to watch the goings-on out in the street.

The passageway and stairs were common territory to the tenants of all three flats, but you were almost in the Christies' flat when you were coming and going. Their front room and back room were both only accessible through the passageway or hall. Behind these two main rooms, the Christies had a kitchen with an empty alcove that was used to store coal, and sometimes other things. Behind the kitchen was a wash-house that was mainly used as a storeroom, measuring four feet by four feet. Attached to this section of the house was a lavatory for the use of all the tenants. The rest of the lot, measuring about twenty feet square, was to become famous as the garden. To gain a proper perspective of the Christie flat, one must try to realize that everything was undersized. Two people couldn't pass comfortably in the hall or on the stairs; the rooms were cramped and small. There was little in the way of comfort at 10 Rillington Place.

Shortly after moving into his new premises, Reggie joined the War Reserve Police. He was assigned to the Harrow Road Police Station, wore a crisp official uniform, and all in all cut a dashing figure. This was more like it. Reggie was a good, efficient cop, and quickly gained a reputation for being very strict with those who didn't obey the air raid regulations.

It was during this rather happy and contented time in Reggie's life that he met, quite by chance, a young lady named Ruth Fuerst. She was an Austrian student nurse who had found herself in England when the war broke out and decided to stay in England rather than return to Austria. When she met Reggie she was working in a munitions factory and living in a furnished room at 41 Oxford Gardens, in the same neighbourhood as the Christies. This lonely twenty-one-year-old, who spoke English with a slight accent, was a tall, pretty girl with brown hair and brown eyes. It wasn't long before she and Christie were seeing a great deal of each other.

In the middle of August 1943, Ruth visited Reggie at 10 Rillington Place. Though we only have Reggie's word for what took place that fateful afternoon, in this instance his account is probably accurate. Ethel was away visiting her relatives in Sheffield. While he was having intercourse with Ruth in the bedroom, Reggie strangled her with a piece of rope.

Pause and reflect on Reggie's state of mind when, as he lies spent, just having had intercourse (we must assume he enjoyed it) and having just strangled a naked woman (we can only assume that some perverted thrill was attached to his act) there came a knock at the door. The blood pounding in his temples, Reggie made himself presentable and answered. It was a telegraph-boy with a telegram. The message was from Mrs. Christie. She was returning home from Sheffield that evening with her brother.

Bothersome bodies indeed!

Christie was frank about how he solved the problem: "I took her from the bedroom into the front room and put her under the floorboards. I had to do that because of my wife coming back."

A few hours later Ethel and her brother, Henry Waddington, arrived.

215

Ethel and Reggie slept in the bedroom and Henry slept in the front room, just a few feet from the remains of Ruth Fuerst. Next morning Henry went back to Sheffield, and in the afternoon Ethel went out visiting. At last! Reggie retrieved the body from under the floorboards and removed it and Ruth's clothing to the wash-house. Then Reggie decided to do a little gardening; he dug a grave. That night, on the pretence of going to the lavatory, he moved Fuerst's body from the wash-house and put it in the hole he had dug. Next morning he tidied up, raking over the grave site and burning Ruth's clothes in a dustbin with some other rubbish.

In September Ruth was reported missing to the police. No one pressed the matter. She had no relatives, no close friends. The bombs had claimed many victims who were not found for months, even years. Then again, she could be a young girl on the loose. She had probably taken a lover and gone away without telling anyone. No one gave her another thought, except Christie.

Let's let him tell it.

"Months later I was digging in the garden and I probably misjudged where it was or something like that. I found a skull and put it in the dustbin and covered it up. I dug a hole in the corner of the garden, and put the dustbin in the hole about eighteen inches down. The top of the dustbin was open, and I still used it to burn rubbish."

In December 1943, Christie got word that his application for employment at the Ultra Radio Works, Park Royal, Acton, had been accepted. He left the War Reserve Police, and early in the new year took up his new job. Ethel had gainful employment with a lightbulb factory, and again the Christies settled into that humdrum way of life so typical of many who have stubbed their toes on the ladder of success.

Reggie ate his lunch in the company canteen, and it was here that he met Muriel Amelia Eady, a respectable, thirty-one-year-old spinster. Muriel had brown hair and eyes and was rather stout and short. Christie

216

overheard that she had a steady boyfriend, so he asked Muriel to bring him over to 10 Rillington Place to have tea with himself and Ethel. A sort of friendship developed, and Muriel brought her boyfriend over to the Christies on more than one occasion. In the course of idle conversation Muriel complained of catarrh, and Reggie told her he had an inhaling device that would ease her difficult breathing if she cared to try it.

One fine day in October 1944, Ethel was away visiting her brother in Sheffield when Muriel knocked on the door of 10 Rillington Place, wondering if the kind Mr. Christie would let her inhale some of his cure.

"Come right in," said Reggie. He had planned the whole thing for just such an occasion. His inhaling device consisted of a glass jar with a metal screw top that had two holes in it. The jar contained Friar's Balsam, and a rubber tube was inserted into one hole so that Muriel could breathe through the other end of the tube and inhale Friar's Balsam. Another tube was attached to the gas stove, and the other end of this tube was inserted into the second hole on top of the glass jar. Reggie sat Muriel in a chair so she wouldn't see what he was doing, and she relaxed and breathed deeply. Gas rushed into the jar and through the tube to Muriel's lungs, soon rendering her unconscious. Reggie carried her into the bedroom, placed her on the bed, took off her panties, and had intercourse with her as he strangled her. When it came to disposing of the body, this time he could afford to work more leisurely since Ethel wasn't rushing home. Muriel's body was taken out to the wash-house, and that night it was buried in the garden.

Miss Eady was reported missing by relatives, but no trace of her could be found. No suspicion was ever cast in Christie's direction.

The war ended and Christie changed jobs again. He obtained a position as a clerk in the Savings Bank at the post office. The years passed, and Reggie kept running to Dr. Odess with his minor ailments. Nothing of a serious nature was ever uncovered by the doctor. Perhaps

Reggie used these visits to gain a brief respite from his boring existence at home.

A break in the monotony came when another tenant took up residence at 10 Rillington Place. At Easter 1948, Timothy Evans and his wife Beryl moved into the upper flat. Beryl was nineteen, three months pregnant, and quite pretty, while Tim was twenty-four and not too bright. He was employed as a van driver and could only read with great difficulty, though he was by no means a simpleton, and had definite ideas on world events as he saw them unfold around him. If his interpretations were erroneous, who are we to criticize? He spent many a night at the pub, and prided himself on his capacity for beer. He was also a congenital liar, as everyone who ever came in contact with him is quick to point out.

Six months later Beryl gave birth to a little girl whom the Evanses christened Geraldine. The cramped quarters, the lack of toilet facilities, the dirty diapers and the inadequate wages Tim brought home were all conducive to bickering. The bickering led to arguments and the arguments led to screaming fights. What had started out for the young Evanses as a happy, carefree life together had deteriorated to the point where Tim was spending more and more time at the pub and Beryl was slaving away to keep some semblance of a home at 10 Rillington Place.

In the late summer of 1949 Beryl found herself pregnant again, and resolved to try to bring on a miscarriage. She tried various pills and home remedies without success, then decided to have an abortion. She told several people about this, including the Christies. By now the Evanses and the Christies were seeing each other quite often. Tim and Beryl liked the Christies, and the Christies seemed to take to the young couple living above them. But seeing an attractive girl like Beryl on a daily basis must have played havoc with Reggie's perverted urges. Every time she entered the house, went up the stairs, or went to the lavatory, she had to pass a doorway leading to Reggie's rooms. Only he knew of the two ladies who had been resting comfortably for years in the garden. Later, Reggie was to say he never thought much about the two bodies. Once, while digging in the garden, a human femur popped to the surface. He nonchalantly used it to prop up the sagging fence bordering his property. The weather-beaten bone was to remain exposed in this way for years.

In October and November, a series of seemingly common, everyday events started to unfold that were later to come under meticulous study. Mr. Kitchener's sight became so bad that he went to the hospital for an operation. He remained in the hospital for five weeks, and was therefore absent from the scene during the crucial weeks that were to follow.

Toward the end of October the landlord at 10 Rillington Place hired a firm of builders to carry out some repairs to the building. These men were in and around the house on and off for the next fifteen days. During this time Beryl Evans told a friend that considerate Mr. Christie was going to perform an abortion on her, despite her husband's objections. The atmosphere between husband and wife was strained over the operation and over a sum of money that Tim had given her to make a payment on their furniture, but which Beryl had spent on something else.

On November 7 it started to rain early in the morning, so the builders, who were not actively engaged in working on the roof, knocked off for the day. When Evans came home from work his wife told him that Christie would be performing the operation on her the following morning. The Evanses argued about the abortion all that evening. Next morning, Tim went to work. The weather had cleared and the workmen were back doing their repairs at eight o'clock. Mrs. Christie went out. Beryl waited upstairs, preparing herself for her operation. Finally, Reggie appeared carrying a rubber tube, which he attached to an outlet on the side of the fireplace. He told Beryl that a few gulps of the gas would make the operation less painful.

We do not know exactly what happened next, but it is very possible that Christie made an unmedical improper move, because at this moment she realized what was happening and started to struggle. Christie struck her several blows to the head and strangled her with his rope. He then turned off the gas and had intercourse with her remains.

There was a knock on the door. God, how scared Christie must have been! Remember the telegraph boy arriving at the exact moment he killed Ruth Fuerst? This time Reg didn't know what to do. A friend of Beryl's, Joan Vincent, was surprised to find the door to the flat closed. Beryl had never kept it closed before. She felt her friend was inside and didn't want to see her. Somewhat annoyed, she expressed her feelings through the closed door and left. Reg Christie breathed a sigh of relief.

All the while workmen were scurrying about on the ground floor, in the wash-house and lavatory. Reggie moved Beryl's body to the bedroom and covered her with a quilt. When Tim came home from work Christie met him at the door and explained that the operation had been a failure, and that Beryl was dead. He showed Tim his wife's body laid out on the bed, explaining that she had poisoned herself by trying to induce a miscarriage and would have died in a few days had he not tried to abort her. Evans, a bit slow-witted, accepted this explanation and went about changing his baby's diapers and giving her something to eat. Christie explained that he was in a jam for trying to do Beryl a favour, and needed Tim's help. He said that they would dispose of the body and this way no one would get in trouble. Evans, stunned, scared, and slow to comprehend, put himself in Christie's hands. The two men carried the body down to Mr. Kitchener's vacant flat. Evans inquired of Christie just what he planned to do with the body.

Christie replied, "I'll dispose of it down one of the drains."

Both men went to bed in their own flats. The next day the sun's rays couldn't break through the overcast, dreary sky as Tim Evans awoke in his flat and Reg Christie got dressed on the ground floor. It was

Wednesday, November 8, and there was the important matter of an infant child to contend with. Evans and Christie met in the hall, and Christie told him not to worry, he would look after the baby for the day, maybe even make some inquiries about adoption. Tim went to work a troubled, confused man. At eight o'clock the workmen arrived again and went about their tasks. By four in the afternoon they had finished, and stored their gear in the wash-house for the night. When Evans returned, Christie informed him that he had found a couple who would make a good home for Geraldine. Reggie told him to dress and feed the baby before leaving for work the next day, and when the couple came around for the child in the morning he would let them in and give Geraldine to them. Christie told Evans that if he ever received any inquiries about Beryl and Geraldine he was to say they were away on vacation. On Thursday, November 10, Reggie strangled the child with a necktie and placed it beside its mother in Mr. Kitchener's flat. Evans got fired from his job that same day and arrived home by 5:30. Christie told him everything had gone well, the couple had come and picked up the baby. Christie, good friend that he was, had thought of everything— he had even arranged to sell Evans' furniture, so there would be nothing keeping Evans from leaving London. On Friday, November 11, the workmen finished their repairs and cleaned out all their gear from the wash-house, leaving it bare. That evening Christie, knowing the workmen would not be returning, placed the bodies of Beryl and Geraldine in the wash-house.

By Sunday Evans had sold the furniture (which he didn't own) and said good-bye to the Christies. He told them he was going to Bristol, but actually he caught a train at Paddington for Cardiff and Merthyr Vale to visit his uncle and aunt, Mr. and Mrs. Lynch. Tim said that he and his boss were touring the area for some vague business reason and had had car trouble in Cardiff. He was wondering if he couldn't stay with them until the car was repaired. In passing, he mentioned that his wife and baby were vacationing in Brighton. Evans stayed with the Lynches for the next six days. He acted perfectly normally, went shopping with Mrs. Lynch and to the pub with Mr. Lynch. Once he talked to his aunt about getting his daughter a Christmas present.

On November 23, Evans showed up on Christie's doorstep inquiring about his daughter. Christie replied that she was well and happy with her new parents, but that it was too early to see her. Disappointed, Evans returned to Merthyr Vale. He had to make up more lies to pacify the Lynches, and told them a not-too-convincing tale to the effect that Beryl had left him and that he had left his daughter with friends. On November 27, Mrs. Lynch wrote to Tim's mother saying that he was staying with them and that they felt something was wrong because they couldn't get a straight answer from him. Tim's mother wrote back that she hadn't seen Beryl or the baby for a month. Mrs. Lynch read this letter to Tim and accused him of lying to them. Evans, beside himself at being caught in his web of lies and childlike in his indecision and lack of planning, decided to go to the police.

He walked into the police station in Merthyr Vale and told the officer on duty, "I want to give myself up. I have disposed of my wife, put her down the drain."

The officer on duty took this statement from Evans:

"About the beginning of October my wife, Beryl Susan Evans, told me that she was expecting a baby. She told me that she was about three months gone. I said, 'If you are having a baby, well, you've had one, another won't make any difference.' She then told me she was going to try and get rid of it. I turned round and told her not to be silly, that she'd make herself ill. Then she bought herself a syringe and started syringing herself. Then she said that didn't work, and I said, 'I am glad it won't work.' Then she said she was going to buy some tablets. I don't know what tablets she bought because she was always hiding them from me. She started to look very ill, and I told her to go and see a doctor, and she said she'd go when I was in work, but when I'd come home and ask her if she'd been, she'd always say that she hadn't.

"On the Sunday morning, that would be the 6th of November, she told me that if she couldn't get rid of the baby, she'd kill herself and our other baby Geraldine. I told her she was talking silly. She never said no more about it then, but when I got up Monday morning to go to work she said she was going to see some woman to see if she could help her, and that if she wasn't in when I came home, she'd be up at her grandmother's. Who the woman was she didn't tell me.

"Then I went to work. I loaded up my van and went on my journey. About nine o'clock that morning I pulled up at a transport café between Ipswich and Colchester. I can't say exactly where it is, that's the nearest I can give. I went up to the counter and ordered a cup of tea and breakfast, and I sat down by the table with my cup of tea waiting for my breakfast to come up, and there was a man sitting by the table opposite to me. He asked me if I had a cigarette I could give him. I gave him one and he started talking about married life. He said to me, 'You are looking pretty worried, is there anything on your mind?' Then I told him all about it. So he said, 'Don't let that worry you. I can give you something that can fix it.' So he said, 'Wait there a minute, I'll be back,' and he went outside. When he came back he handed me a little bottle that was wrapped in brown paper. He said, 'Tell your wife to take it first thing in the morning before she has any tea, then to lay down on the bed for a couple of hours and that should do the job.' He never asked no money for it. I went up to the counter and paid my bill and carried on with my journey.

"After I finished my work I went home, that would be between seven and eight. When I got in the house I took off my overcoat and hung it on the peg behind the kitchen door. My wife asked me for a cigarette and I told her that there was one in my pocket, then she found this bottle in my pocket, and I told her all about it.

"I got up in the morning as usual at six o'clock to go to work. I made myself a cup of tea and made a feed for the baby. I told her then not to take that stuff when I went in and said 'Good morning' to her, and I went to work, that would be about half past six. I finished work and got home about half past six in the evening. I then noticed that there was no lights in the place. I lit the gas and it started to go out, and I went into the bedroom to get a penny and I noticed my baby in the cot. I put the penny in the gas and went back in the bedroom and lit the gas in the bedroom. Then I saw my wife laying in the bed. I spoke to her but she never answered me, so I went over and shook her, then I could see she wasn't breathing. Then I went and made some food for my baby. I fed my baby and I sat up all night.

"Between about one and two in the morning I got my wife downstairs through the front door. I opened the drain outside my front door, that is 10 Rillington Place, and pushed her body head first into the drain. I closed the drain, then I went back in the house. I sat down by the fire smoking a cigarette. I never went to work the following day. I went and got my baby looked after. Then I went and told my governor where I worked that I was leaving. He asked me the reason, and I told him I had a better job elsewhere. I had my cards and money that afternoon, then I went to see a man about selling my furniture. The man came down and had a look at my furniture and he offered me £40 for it. So I accepted the £40. He told me he wouldn't be able to collect the furniture until Monday morning. In the meanwhile I went and told my mother that my wife and baby had gone for a holiday. I stopped in the flat till Monday. The van came Monday afternoon and cleared the stuff out. He paid me the money. Then I caught the five to one train from Paddington and I come down to Merthyr Vale and I've been down here ever since. That's the lot.

(Signed) T. J. Evans"

The Merthyr Vale police put in a call to the Notting Hill police, who in turn sent a car over to 10 Rillington Place. Sure enough, there was a manhole in front of Number 10. It took three men to open the lid, but the drain was empty; there was no body. When the Merthyr Vale police told Evans, poor Tim was flabbergasted—the body must be there. Christie said he was going to put it down the drain. Caught in a lie again, he tried to brazen it out. The detectives asked him who helped him lift the manhole cover. Tim said he lifted the lid himself, which was an impossibility. Six hours later he gave another statement. This time he told substantially what he believed to be true, that his wife had died during an illegal operation. The police were again dispatched to 10 Rillington Place to make a thorough search, and this time they found the body of Beryl Evans behind some boards under the sink in the wash-house. Geraldine's body was found behind the door with the necktie still around her neck.

Evans was brought from Wales to London, and told of the gruesome find at 10 Rillington Place. He made a further statement telling how he had killed his wife and daughter. He gave plausible, exact details of how he tied the necktie around Geraldine's neck. He said he was happy to get the guilty knowledge off his chest. He kept up these pronouncements of guilt until he met with his lawyers, at which point he abruptly changed his story to put the blame on the shoulders of Reg Christie. Did the lawyers tell him to cut out his lying and tell the truth, one wonders? Evans' lies were designed to protect his friend Christie and make it appear as if he, Evans, was confessing to clear up a distasteful, unfortunate death that was unavoidable. Evans didn't start out confessing to murder. Read the words carefully. He only wanted to impart the knowledge that his wife's body was down the drain, not that he killed her. It isn't easy not to have murdered your wife and still to have put her down a drain, but poor Evans managed to confess to both without doing either.

On January 11, 1950, Timothy Evans stood trial for the murder of his daughter in London's Old Bailey. Reg Christie, the respected former policeman and neighbour to the accused murderer, was the chief prosecution witness. Evans, begging to be believed, testified that he had found out about his daughter's death only after he had been told by the police. When he was informed of her death he didn't care what happened to him, and confessed, incriminating himself as a double murderer. He started off trying to protect Christie, but now he had to tell the truth to save his own life. He said time and again, "Christie did it," but no one believed him. He further said that the details of the murders had been given to him little by little by the police. They had mentioned that Beryl had been strangled by a rope and Geraldine by a necktie, so that when time came for him to give his statement, he repeated the details. The police denied these accusations.

Evans made a hesitant, unbelievable witness in the dock. Reg Christie's straightforward aloofness was impressive. Wounded serving his country in the First World War, Reg was treated with deference by the presiding judge, even being given a chair to make him more comfortable in the witness box. No one took Evans' irresponsible accusations against him seriously. The jury took only forty minutes to find Evans guilty. All appeals failed, and on March 9, 1950, Timothy Evans was hanged.

And so the Christies returned to 10 Rillington Place. Month after dreary month Christie complained of minor ailments that necessitated continual visits to Dr. Odess. Black Jamaicans had rented the flat above him, and this increased his bad disposition. Mrs. Christie, too, couldn't stand the blacks coming and going all day long in her hall.

Reggie worked for two years as a clerk for British Road Services, and being back at work and away from home seems to have relieved his nervousness and minor ailments. Then in the spring of 1952 he became ill with fibrositis and was confined to hospital for three weeks. When his doctors decided his trouble was psychological rather than physical, he was released.

At this time, another real problem came to a head. He had abandoned sexual relations with his wife since Evans' execution. Not only that, but Ethel, nondescript, frigid Ethel, started to get on his nerves about being impotent. Did Reggie again hear those boys from the streets of Halifax shouting "Reggie no dick"? Did he lie beside Ethel night after night with his hands reaching to his ears as the boys' voices taunted him— "Can't make it Reggie"? He left his job, and was thrown together with his wife day and night.

On the morning of December 14, 1952, Reg took a stocking that was lying on a chair near his bed, leaned over and strangled Ethel. Her body was to lie in the bed for two or three days while Reggie decided what to do with it. Then he remembered—of course, the loose floorboards in the front room. He rolled back the linoleum, and under the floor she went. Christie covered the body with earth, put back the linoleum, and it was as if Ethel had gone away to Sheffield for another of her visits. To neighbours and friends who inquired after her, and there were a few, it being Christmas time, Christie explained that she had gone to Sheffield and he was following her there later as he had accepted a good job opportunity that had suddenly come up. Her friends thought it strange that Ethel didn't say goodbye, but passed it off as a rush trip and let it go at that.

Christmas and New Year's came and passed. Reggie, who by this time was sprinkling deodorant around the front room, made arrangements to sell all his furniture. He received only £12 for the lot. The used furniture buyer wouldn't even take some of the pieces, they were in such bad shape. Reggie stayed on in the flat a little while after the furniture had been removed.

It was now January, and Christie was alone. His wife lay under the floorboards in the front room, Fuerst and Eady were only skeletal

227

remains resting in the garden, the Evanses, mother and child, were gone, and Timothy had met his end at the hangman's noose. Even the furniture was gone. In Reggie's solitude, his mind turned to the necrophilic thrills that had almost faded from his memory.

On a night in the middle of January, at about eight o'clock, Christie went into the Westminster Arms, where he met a prostitute, Kathleen Maloney. He had met the twenty-six-year-old Kathleen before, and within a short time the pair was seen leaving the Westminster Arms together. Kathleen was quite drunk, and Reggie was taking her home. She didn't require the finesse of deception; Reggie merely sat her down on his chair, attached the rubber tube to the gas, and placed the exposed end of the tube close to her mouth so she was bound to breathe in some of the fumes. Soon Kathleen became drowsy and Reggie strangled her with his piece of rope. He removed her undergarments and had intercourse with her right in the chair. Then he brewed himself a pot of tea and went to bed. When he got up in the morning Kathleen was still in the chair.

Christie pondered a moment—what to do with this bothersome body? He pulled away a small cupboard, revealing an alcove he knew was off the kitchen. He bundled the body in a blanket, pulled a pillowslip over the head, then hauled the corpse into the alcove, where he arranged it with the legs in the air against the wall. He then covered it with some ashes and earth, and put the cupboard back in place.

The perverse thrill of long ago was now fresh in Reggie's mind, and he wanted more. A few days later he picked up an Irish girl named Rita Nelson, a twenty-five-year-old prostitute who had convictions for soliciting and drunkenness in Ireland. She ended up in Reggie's death chair inhaling gas, and she, too, was ravished after death and her body placed with Kathleen's in the alcove, resting on its neck and head, with the legs extended in the air, propped up against the wall.

About a month went by. Then, quite by chance, Christie met

Hectorina Maclennan and her boyfriend, a truck driver named Baker, in a café. When Christie found out they were looking for a flat he offered to show them his, which he told them he was about to vacate. It was sheer aggravation for Christie when Hectorina brought Baker with her to inspect the flat. Since they had nowhere else to stay, Christie gave them sleeping privileges and they stayed for three days and nights. On the fourth day Christie had had enough of Baker, and asked the couple to leave. Later the same day Reggie sought out the couple and invited Hectorina to visit him alone. He said he had something to tell her. Hectorina showed up at 10 Rillington Place, and Reggie poured her a drink. In a terrible state of nervousness he was fumbling with his rubber tube, connecting it to the gas, when she became suspicious and got up to leave. Christie caught up with her and strangled her in the hall. He lugged her back to the kitchen, and thinking she was still alive, gave her an application of his infernal inhaling mechanism. He then had intercourse with her and put her body with the other two in the alcove.

Baker grew uneasy when Hectorina had still not returned from 10 Rillington Place at 5:30, and he dropped over to inquire. Christie said that he hadn't seen her, and offered a sociable cup of tea. Later that evening, when Baker went looking for his girlfriend, Christie accompanied him.

Reggie papered over the entrance to the alcove, and set about subletting his empty flat. On the premises but not included in the inventory were the two skeletons still resting peacefully in the garden, Mrs. Christie under the floorboards in the front room, and the three bodies upside down in the alcove. Not on the premises but certainly the responsibility of Mr. Christie was the entire Evans family. Nine bodies in all.

While sauntering down Ladbroke Grove on March 13, Christie met a Mrs. Reilly who was looking at advertisements showing flats for rent. Christie, who never had any difficulty striking up a conversation, told

Mrs. Reilly that he had a vacant flat. She was delighted, and with her husband went to inspect the flat. On March 16 her husband gave Christie £7.13 for three months' rent in advance. Four days later the Reillys moved in, and after borrowing a suitcase from Mr. Reilly, Christie left 10 Rillington Place forever. That very evening the landlord showed up, and was amazed to find the Reillys living there. He informed them that Christie was several months behind with his rent, and that while they could stay the night, they would have to leave in the morning. The Reillys left the next day, unaware that they had spent the night at close quarters with six assorted corpses.

The landlord gave permission to use the vacant Christie kitchen to Beresford Brown, who was occupying one of the Evans' rooms upstairs. He used the kitchen for the next few days and started to tidy up the place. On March 24, he decided to put up a shelf to hold a radio. He was tapping to find a solid wall, but he kept getting a hollow sound from the alcove that Christie had thoughtfully wallpapered over. He tore off a piece of paper, pointed his flashlight into the alcove, and found himself a place in every book ever written about infamous murders. There, in the alcove, with their legs in the air, were the bodies of Kathleen Maloney, Rita Nelson and Hectorina Maclennan.

Scotland Yard descended on 10 Rillington Place, and the three bodies were meticulously removed from the alcove, being photographed at every stage of their removal. Someone noticed that the boards in the front room were very loose, and in due course a fourth body was removed from under the floor.

Old London Town has provided us with some weird murders, and the men who investigate them tend to become blasé with the passage of time. But even for them, four bodies in one house on one night was not a routine evening. The word went out; the police would like to question John Reginald Halliday Christie. The days passed and Christie's description was everywhere. The news reached new heights of sensationalism when Fuerst's and Eady's skeletons were discovered in the garden. Where was the elusive Christie? Not really elusive at all—he was wandering the streets of London. On March 31, Police Constable Thomas Ledger saw a man near Putney Bridge. Constable Ledger asked him a few questions and ascertained that the man was Christie. Reggie was taken into custody.

From the beginning Reggie confessed to all the murders, except that of little Geraldine Evans. He lied about the details to make himself look better, but he didn't deny killing the women.

Christie was charged with murdering his wife, and appeared, ironically enough, in Number One Court of the Old Bailey, the very court where he had been the chief prosecution witness against Evans nearly four years earlier. Christie's lawyers never for a moment denied his guilt; they pleaded that he was quite mad.

On July 15, 1953, Christie was hanged for his crimes. In January, 1966, Timothy Evans was granted a posthumous free pardon by the Queen of England.

Bluebeard's Ladies

Henri Landru was born in Paris on April 12, 1869, to honest, hardworking parents. His mother was a dressmaker who ran her business from her home on Rue de Puebla, and his father was a bookseller. These occupations did not place the Landru family in the highest income bracket, but it did allow them to lead comfortable, if frugal, lives. Henri attended a school run by Jesuits, and was a good, hardworking, intelligent student.

At the age of fifteen he was initiated into the delights of sex by the neighbourhood prostitute, but despite these attractions, he had eyes only for the daughter of a neighbour who lived not far from him on Rue de Puebla. Her name was Marie Catherine Rémy, and in his unique fashion Henri loved her. As a result of his affections she became pregnant, at which point Henri, coincidentally enough, left Paris and joined the French Army.

After three years of military service, Henri desperately wanted out. He wrote to Marie's father, who used his influence to get Landru a discharge. Henri came home, married Marie, met his two-year-old daughter, and got a job as an accountant. Within the next two years the couple were blessed twice more. Now twenty-six years old, Henri found himself in a dead-end job, with three children and a wife to support.

In the years between 1900 and 1910 Henri tried his hand at swindling women, using any ruse to gain possession of their money and furniture. It didn't seem to matter what he did, he always got caught, and received a series of short jail sentences for fraud. In between sentences Henri never forgot Marie—in fact, he remembered her to the extent of another bouncing baby daughter. The Landru family now totalled four children.

Henri's profession was that of con artist and thief, with no gainful employment other than the courting, wooing and fleecing of members of the opposite sex. He had a magnetic personality, but at this point in his life he had not yet perfected the fine art of escaping detection after the fact. From 1910 to 1914 he corrected this flaw in his operating procedure to a degree that put his frauds in the top professional category. He kept meticulous notes and records on every lady, her likes, dislikes, and habits. He categorized the potential degree of difficulty in fleecing them, and how big a financial reward was waiting to be plucked. Six days a week, Henri left his wife and four children to go to his work.

Only Henri knew that he was busy building up another life and another role, which he entered fully and completely. Sometimes when he left his family he would have to stay away for a few days. He always told Marie the length of his business trips, and if he was held up for any reason, he was always considerate enough to phone her. She never questioned his absences, nor did she inquire about the cyclical nature of his income. She had a general idea that her husband was in the used furniture business and had several warehouses which he visited. When he made a profitable deal the family shared in the good fortune, but when he had trouble putting together a lucrative transaction, the exchequer suffered. Marie was a perfect wife for Henri Landru; she cared for her brood, but more important, she didn't have an inquisitive bone in her body. The family moved frequently; this too she took in her stride without question. She knew her husband would be home at least one day a week, for on that day Henri opened his huge desk and did his bookwork.

At the age of forty-five Henri had grown a long, flowing red beard that was without a doubt his most outstanding feature. He had a rather long body for a small man, which gave him the appearance of being taller than he really was. His pale complexion contrasted sharply with his bright red beard, and he was bald as a billiard ball, with large, powerful hands for a man of his size and build.

In order to guarantee a constant supply of ladies, Henri used the simple but effective method of placing matrimonial ads in the newspapers. He studied the best ads, and by trial and error he developed the wordings that brought the best results.

On Bastille Day, July 14, 1914, the Landrus had just moved into another new home in Clichy. Henri had to go to work soon after they arrived in their new home, and this particular job was to be concluded in a most unique way. Using the name Raymond Diard, he had received a reply to one of his ads from Jeanne Cuchet. Jeanne fell into the exact category that rated an A in Henri's book. She had been married to a commercial traveller, who had unfortunately died of natural causes. She lived with her elderly parents and teenaged son, André. Best of all, she had a substantial nest-egg of 5,000 francs.

A tall, thin, plain woman, she was flattered and thrilled to be singled out, and soon became completely infatuated with Henri. An expert at his chosen profession, he knew the words, the topics and above all the manners that appealed to Jeanne. As Monsieur Diard he dined with her parents, careful to agree with her father's views on the conduct of the war, and careful to have an extra helping of her mother's *biscuits à la cuiller*. This milieu was Henri's business office, and in it he laboured as patiently and efficiently as any accountant. The couple announced their engagement, received congratulations from the family, and another plum of a set-up was ready to be plucked. The 5,000 francs would go a long way—wouldn't Marie be pleased at the successful conclusion of this piece of business!

In subsequent meetings with his fiancée, he let it be known that he was a qualified engineer who ran a small business currently making lighter flints. Lovestruck Jeanne's life had changed in three short months. It was too bad that her son André didn't take to Raymond; but never mind, he would doubtless grow to love him as much as she did. What a trusting man Henri was, thought Jeanne. He insisted that he put his money and hers together in the bank. The happy couple moved into a little apartment, and as soon as the money was safely placed in the bank, Henri cleaned out the account and took off.

Months later, quite by accident, Henri bumped into Jeanne, who was tossing flowers at the feet of passing soldiers during a military parade. One of the flowers landed at his feet, and when he looked up it was into her eyes. It was a tribute to his ingenuity and her stupidity that he was able to make up a story that placated her. He admitted to her that he had lied—he was really married and had two daughters—his divorce would become final any day now—the day he left her he had received word that his wife had balked at the divorce and was coming to Paris with his two daughters—he had held her money for her—it was safe in a Swiss bank.

Bluebeard was able to pull it off, and the pair took up where they had left off months before. In November, three months after his reunion with Jeanne, Henri rented a house in the country. It was a villa called The Lodge at 46 Rue de Mantes in Vernouillet, a small town just outside Paris. Henri took Jeanne to this villa. He usually only worked for profit, and there was nothing further to be had from Jeanne but her life. While lying in bed with Jeanne, Bluebeard leaned over, placed his large hands firmly on her neck, and strangled her to death. He then left for Paris with her bankbook. He had noticed that she had managed to save a paltry four hundred francs since her last plucking, and it was not difficult for a man of his experience to extract it from the bank. The next day he was back at Vernouillet, with a bothersome body on his hands.

The unheated lodge was cold and damp, and when Henri arrived he was altogether uncomfortable. But repeated trips to the woodhouse soon warmed him up. He piled the logs high in the stove, and the fire caught on his first attempt. Next, precise, exact Henri, operating according to his pre-arranged plan, cleaned out the bathroom tub, which was in the cellar. Revolted as he was at handling Jeanne's body, he managed to place it into the tub. Ditchdiggers don't necessarily like digging ditches, but it's their job. And this was Henri's. With crude household implements Henri managed to dissect the body in the tub. As he proceeded he decided he would never be this ill-prepared again, but after all, this was only his apprenticeship. If butchers learned how to dress game, he would learn to become as efficient as a butcher.

Over the next several days, Henri lugged his gruesome cargo piece after piece up the stairs and placed it ever so carefully in the stove. Black smoke billowed out of The Lodge's chimney, and the smoke was accompanied by a repulsive odour. The wind carried it to every nook and cranny of Vernouillet. Later, many villagers stated that they had noticed the smoke, and more particularly the offensive smell. Some even said it smelled like roast beef. One villager complained to an official, who knocked on Henri's front door to question him about the terrible smell emanating from his chimney. Henri told the official that the chimney was defective and promised to have it fixed immediately. This seemed to satisfy the official, and he went away.

Soon afterwards, while walking on the streets of Paris with the signs of war all about him, Henri was accosted by Jeanne's son André, in one of those chance meetings which plague murderers.

"Monsieur Diard, where is my mother?"

Henri had to shift into high gear in a hurry. Again it is a tribute to his guile that he convinced the lad that his mother and he were living together in Vernouillet, happy and contented. He placated André by telling him that his mother was planning to send for him, and now that they had met in this way he wanted André to accompany him to Vernouillet. Henri always liked to put a bit of frosting on the cake. "She is pregnant," he told her anxious son.

They arrived at Vernouillet; Jeanne, it seemed, was not in. Henri offered André something to eat. While the young man sat at the table Henri's strong hands firmly clasped his neck and squeezed the life from his body. This time the operation went more smoothly. Henri had bought a hacksaw, meat cleaver and mallet, so it was not long before the black smoke and offensive odour billowed forth from the chimney once again.

In December of 1916 Monsieur Diard closed The Lodge at Vernouillet and left it forever.

It is one thing to swindle women one at a time, but it is quite another to be playing many roles simultaneously. Henri always kept extensive notes to remember which lady knew him under which name. He couldn't afford a mistake, because sometimes he had to deal with bank officials, using his many aliases without the slightest hesitation. He even got into the habit of talking to himself, using the alias of the moment in order to implant the proper name in his mind. On many occasions he would rush from one apartment to another, consulting his notebook to refresh his memory as to which name and personality he had to assume.

In the summer of 1917 Henri rented a house in Gambais, not far from Paris. He picked it carefully. The house adjoined a cemetery; there were no inhabitants for miles around. Using the name of Paul Fremyet, he purchased a good stove and connected it to the existing smokestack. Then he set about enticing more women, making sure that they turned over their worldly belongings to him before they turned over their lives.

In all, Henri Landru strangled and burned eleven people—young André Cuchet and ten gullible women.

One of his victims, Anna Collomb, had invited her sister, Madame Pillot, to Gambais to visit the man she was soon to marry. After returning to Paris, Madame Pillot never heard from her sister again, though she wrote to her at Gambais. In desperation she wrote to the mayor of Gambais, who answered that he believed he had located the house mentioned in her letter, but that no one had ever heard of her sister's fiancé, Monsieur Fremyet. The mayor stated that the tenant of record of the house in question was a Monsieur Dupont. He volunteered that he had received another inquiry about the house from the sister of one Madame Celestine Buisson. The writer of the letter was Mademoiselle Lacoste, and the mayor suggested that Madame Pillot might find it useful to contact Mademoiselle Lacoste.

The two ladies did indeed meet and compare notes. No one could mistake that red beard. Diard, Fremyet, Dupont, Cuchet, the names went on and on. Landru was readily traced and arrested. The police found him trying to destroy a notebook in which he had the names and addresses of all his victims.

One woman, Fernande Segret, visited the house in Gambais and lived to tell about it from the witness stand. For some unknown reason the mass murderer put the pretty Fernande in the same class as his wife, Marie Catherine. They lived as man and wife, and she claimed he was normal sexually and in every other way. There was nothing perverted or sadistic about Landru, nor did he ever cheat or swindle her, as she had no worldly goods. But relatives and swindled ladies kept coming forward, and from these women and the detailed files Henri kept in his desk at Clichy it was estimated that he had had intimate relations with close to three hundred women in the five years before his trial.

On February 24, 1922, Henri Landru, now known throughout the world as Bluebeard, admonished his keepers for offering him a mug of rum and a cigarette. "You know I neither drink nor smoke," he said. The tired old man of fifty-two was still receiving over a hundred letters a day from women offering everything from a lock of their hair to proposals of marriage. His loyal and faithful wife visited him in jail, and it was only when he refused to see her that his ties with her were finally severed.

His keepers tied his hands behind his back as was the custom, and Henri walked steadily to the guillotine, taking his brief instructions from the executioner. Then his head tumbled into a basket of bran that had been placed in position for that purpose.

Castle of Death

Herman Webster Mudgett was born in 1860 to a respected family in the tiny New England community, where his father had been postmaster for over twenty-five years. Though young Herman early showed a vicious streak—neighbours of the Mudgetts were to recall seeing him setting a cat on fire—he had many redeeming features, not the least of which was his keen intelligence. His teachers remembered him as a bright, alert scholar. After his graduation with honours from Gilmanton Academy, he eloped with a farmer's daughter from the nearby village of Loudon, and paid his tuition at the University of Vermont at Burlington from a small inheritance his wife had just received. He transferred to the University of Michigan at Ann Arbor, where his wife gave birth to a son.

Mudgett started his criminal activities while still at university. He and another student concocted a scheme whereby Mudgett took out an insurance policy on his friend's life in the amount of $12,500. The friend promptly disappeared, leaving the way clear for Mudgett to steal a corpse from the dissecting room of the university, positively identify it as his missing friend, and collect the insurance. Shortly after the successful completion of this scheme, he qualified as a Doctor of Medicine and abandoned his wife and infant son. Mrs. Mudgett returned to Gilmanton, never to lay eyes on her husband again.

The doctor, now a tall, good-looking twenty-four-year-old with all the qualifications to be a legitimate success, struck out on his own. With his fashionable walrus moustache and his luminous brown eyes, he was altogether a distinguished-looking gentleman. And when he was decked out in his bowler hat, tweed suit and shiny shoes, Herman held more than a little attraction for the opposite sex.

For six years he wandered through Minnesota and New York, making a dishonest dollar wherever he could. The fact that he could have made a fine living at his own profession apparently didn't enter his mind. Records show that in St. Paul he was appointed receiver of a bankrupt store. He filled the store with merchandise purchased on credit, sold off the stock at cost price or less, and took off with the proceeds.

In 1885 he reappeared in Wilmette, a suburb of Chicago, as an inventor, using the name Henry H. Holmes for the first time. He met a dark-haired beauty named Myrtle Z. Belknap, who was not only a stunning looker but also had a father who was one of the wealthiest residents of Wilmette. Holmes married her without going through the annoying formalities of a divorce from his first wife. He succeeded in getting enough money out of Myrtle's daddy to build a house, and then started forging Mr. Belknap's name on cheques. Though the family was furious, they decided to sidestep a scandal and not to prosecute the scoundrel, for he still held a fascination for his wife, who stood beside him no matter what sort of scrapes he managed to get into.

Next, Holmes answered an advertisement in the local newspaper requiring a chemist for a store owned by a Mrs. Holden on the corner of 63rd Street and Wallace in Englewood, another suburb of Chicago. Mrs. Holden, who had been recently widowed, was thrilled to have such a highly qualified and handsome man apply for the position, and gave him the job without any qualms whatsoever. Almost at once she became disillusioned with her new employee and confided to close friends that she suspected him of theft from her store. Early in 1890 Mrs. Holden suddenly disappeared without mentioning anything to friends, except to Holmes, who claimed she had told him she was taking a long holiday in California. Then he soothed nervous acquaintances by telling them that she had sold the store to him and was staying on the West Coast. It seems that no one was interested enough in Mrs. Holden to delve deeper into her disappearance, and she was never seen again.

In the meantime, with his knowledge of medicine, Holmes was making the business prosper. He had a few sidelines, such as his own patent medicines which he sold at enormous profits, and things were going so well that by 1892 he figured there was nothing further to be gained from the Belknap family, so he left his wife and moved into rooms above his store. Then he commenced the construction of a monstrous building directly across the street. It was three storeys high, measured fifty by one hundred and sixty-two feet and contained more than ninety rooms. On the main floor Holmes opened a jewellery store, restaurant and drugstore. The false turrets gave the whole structure a somewhat mediaeval appearance, and the ugly pile soon came to be known as Holmes' Castle. Ostensibly Holmes built the structure to accommodate the huge crowds which were expected for the Chicago World's Fair in 1893, and the third floor of the castle was divided into apartments for this purpose; but the second floor had winding staircases, connecting hallways, trapdoors, and asbestos-lined rooms, some of them equipped with gas jets. Holmes had his own comfortable quarters on the second floor; inside his closet were valves that controlled the flow of gas to the various rooms. From his bedroom Holmes could gas a victim, turn a switch that controlled a trapdoor and plunge the body down a chute to the basement. The basement was equipped with a dissecting table, medical instruments, a crematorium, a huge vat of corrosive acid and two further vats of quicklime.

Into this veritable murder castle came Mr. Icilius Conner, his wife Julia, his sister Gertie, and his eight-year-old daughter Pearl. Conner was a jeweller by trade and was looking for ways to get into business. Holmes obliged by making a part of his drugstore available to him for the sale of jewellery, and by hiring Julia as his personal bookkeeper. The Conners were an extremely handsome family, particularly Julia, and it wasn't long before the cunning doctor had alienated her from her husband, and she had in effect become his mistress. Holmes let it leak to Conner that his wife had been sharing his bed, and Conner left Chicago in disgust. Mrs. Conner and her daughter Pearl were to live with Holmes for the next two years. During these two years Holmes took a trip to Texas, where he stayed for over six months, engaging in his usual activities of thieving and swindling, before returning to Chicago.

In 1893 the doctor received a visit from an acquaintance he had met during his stay down South. Her name was Minnie Williams, and her greatest claim to fame was the fact that she and her sister Nannie jointly owned property valued at $50,000 in Fort Worth, Texas. She was a welcome guest to the castle, and it wasn't long before she was Holmes' mistress. Coinciding with her coronation as queen of the castle, Julia Conner and her daughter disappeared. Holmes and his new flame lived together for a full year, and it was during this year that more visitors started to enter the death castle than were seen to leave it. It is difficult to believe that Minnie could have lived there at this time without having some guilty knowledge of what was going on. Holmes was easier to figure; if ever there was a born criminal it was Henry H. Holmes. He was motivated by lust and greed, not necessarily in that order, and seems never to have even considered leading an honest life.

The list of his known victims is a long one. A young girl, Emily Van Tassell, worked as a clerk in Holmes' drugstore for a month and then disappeared. Years earlier, while serving a three-month jail sentence in St. Louis, Holmes had met fellow inmates Benjamin F. Pietzel, a small time con artist, and a rather well-known train robber, Marion Hedgepeth. Pietzel was soon to be released to join his wife and five children, but Hedgepeth was awaiting transfer to a penitentiary and a lengthy sentence. Pietzel now showed up in Chicago and looked up his friend Holmes. He kept telling Holmes about a beautiful young girl he had met in Dwight, Illinois. Her name was Emeline Cigrand, and she had made a lasting impression on Pietzel, who told Holmes she was the most beautiful girl he had ever seen. Finally, at Pietzel's urging, Holmes corresponded with the girl and offered her a job at a salary far above the average. She couldn't resist the temptation, came to Chicago, entered the castle, and was never seen again. Her boyfriend, Robert E. Phelps, inquired about her at the castle, was invited in, and never left. Holmes was later to confess to Emeline's death, describing in detail how he kept her in a soundproof room for the sole purpose of having sexual relations with her. He claimed he didn't want to kill her, but Minnie got jealous and he had to do it. The boyfriend, Holmes said, was just too nosy to live.

Nannie Williams, Minnie's sister, came to visit. Holmes made love to her, got her to sign over half the property in Fort Worth, and killed her, in that order. He told friends of Minnie's that her sister had returned to Texas.

Now we enter an even stranger period in the saga of Henry H. Holmes. In the fall of 1893, he left his friend Ben Pietzel in charge of his various businesses and took a trip with Minnie to Denver. Using the alias of Howard, he married a Georgianna Yoke of Richmond, Indiana, without Minnie's knowledge. He spent many weeks in Denver, living alternately with the two women, neither of whom knew of the other's existence. Even after Georgianna returned to Indiana, Holmes visited her on many occasions during the next two years and seems to have become quite attached to her. She lived to testify at his trial, and was the only person to speak highly of him.

Before Christmas, 1893, Minnie made the same mistake as her sister Nannie; she signed away her half of the Fort Worth property and promptly disappeared. Later Holmes was to show the police where to find her skeleton and her sister's, in the cellar of the castle.

How was Holmes able to build a structure that was obviously custom-designed for murder? Firstly, he personally supervised the entire construction, from the cellar to the top floor. Then he only kept the same crew of workmen for a few days before he discharged them. A new crew would start, often entirely unaware of what had transpired before they appeared on the job. In this way, no one saw the master plan or knew that the cumulative effect of their labours was a bona fide murder castle.

When he had been in jail with Pietzel and Hedgepeth years earlier, Holmes told them that he had figured out a foolproof way of defrauding an insurance company. He said he needed a really smart lawyer to pull it off. Hedgepeth gave Holmes the name of his lawyer, Jeptha D. Howe of St. Louis, and received in return a promise of $500 after the scheme was successfully completed. Holmes kept this plan under wraps for a few years, and then took it out of mothballs in the early summer of 1894. The scheme was the same one that Holmes had used so successfully in university. Pietzel was to have his wife take out insurance on his life, and then he was to drop out of sight, while Holmes was to come up with a corpse which would be identified as that of Pietzel. Mrs. Pietzel would collect the insurance and the partners would divide the spoils. Everyone agreed that the plan had some merit. Pietzel took out a policy amounting to $10,000. Then he went to Philadelphia and set up shop as a patent attorney, using the name B. F. Perry. Within a month his body was found on the floor of his office, badly burned, particularly about the face. The police investigating the accident found a broken bottle of benzine on the office floor. The preliminary assumption was that an explosion had taken place, causing the accident. Then an autopsy was performed and the death was found to have been caused by chloroform. Jeptha D. Howe appeared on the scene and informed the authorities that the dead man was Ben Pietzel, and as Mrs. Pietzel's attorney, he was representing her in asking for any insurance money that was due his client. Pietzel's good friend Holmes arrived and also identified the body. The insurance money was paid off to Mrs. Pietzel; it was later divided up, with Howe getting $2,500, Mrs. Pietzel $500, and Holmes receiving the balance.

Holmes, the arch-criminal, had really murdered his friend Pietzel. The corpse was no stranger to him, but he managed to deceive Howe and Mrs. Pietzel, who throughout the con thought that Pietzel was in hiding. Howe returned to St. Louis assuming that the scheme was a complete success and that Mrs. Pietzel would be joining Mr. Pietzel in a few months and that everyone would be happy. He visited his client Hedgepeth in prison and mentioned how well the scheme had worked. Hedgepeth was furious, as he had been promised $500 by Holmes and never received a cent. Hedgepeth called for the warden and told the whole story. The warden called the insurance company, who in turn called in the Pinkerton Detective Agency to investigate the case. When Hedgepeth told the story he naturally repeated it as he had heard it from Howe; that it was a stranger's body that was found on the office floor, not Pietzel's. It didn't take long for the Pinkertons to realize that there was more than simple fraud involved, and they called in the police.

By this time Holmes had fled, and he proved to be an elusive quarry. He had talked Mrs. Pietzel into meeting him in Detroit. She took two of her children with her, while Holmes took the other three, Alice, Nellie and Howard. He told her they would all meet with Mr. Pietzel in Detroit in two weeks' time. Holmes arrived before the allotted time and placed the three Pietzel children in a boarding house while he scampered to Richmond, Indiana, returning with the lady who really thought she was his wife, Georgianna Yoke. Holmes set up three different groups while in Detroit. One consisted of the three Pietzel children, another consisted of Mrs. Pietzel and the other two children, while a third contingent was made up solely of Georgianna. Holmes would join any of the three groups, who at no time knew of the others' presence in the city. Finally he took all three households on the road, and it is a measure of his cunning that he managed to stay ahead of the police for two months. They finally caught up with Holmes in Boston on November 17, 1894. The other two detachments were accounted for when gullible Georgianna, who was innocent of any wrongdoing, was located by the police in Indiana where Holmes had stashed her, and Mrs. Pietzel and her two children were discovered living in Burlington, Vermont, waiting for the reunion with her husband that was never to come.

Only Nellie, Howard, and Alice Pietzel, the three children who were travelling with Holmes, could not be found by the police, and Holmes steadfastly refused to give them any information concerning the three children.

The interior of Holmes' murder castle was now exposed, and the police realized they were dealing with one of the most hideous monsters who ever lived. The search was on for the three children; the trail led from Detroit to Toronto to Cincinnati to Indianapolis, throughout the midwest and back into Canada. Finally, at 16 Vincent Street in Toronto, the authorities found a house that had been rented to a man with two little girls. The police found out that the man had borrowed a spade to dig a hole, supposedly to store potatoes. They were able to find the neighbour whose spade had been used, and he loaned the same spade to the police. The police dug up the same hole, and in it they found the pathetic bodies of Nellie and Alice Pietzel. In an upstairs bedroom of the house they found a trunk with a rubber tube leading from it to a gas outlet. Diabolical Holmes had enticed the girls to enter the trunk and had asphyxiated them. This discovery now accounted for all the family, except Howard. While questioning neighbours in the area of 16 Vincent Street, the police found one who had talked to the two girls.

This neighbour remembered that the girls had mentioned their little brother living in Indianapolis. The investigation moved to Indianapolis, where nine hundred houses were searched, and finally, in the suburb of Irvington, police found the house in which Holmes had lived for a week. It had been vacant since Holmes left, and the charred remains of Howard Pietzel's body were found in a stove in the kitchen.

Holmes made a full confession while in jail, but as it is sprinkled with proven lies it does not give an accurate account of his atrocities. While it seems that he operated basically for gain, when his castle was dismantled it was discovered that he had a rack which he used to try to stretch people, believing that he could make them permanently taller.

Holmes' trial for the murder of Ben Pietzel began on October 28, 1895. It was one of the most widely publicized trials of the last century. Every detail was reported in the press, for nothing quite like it had ever been perpetrated in the U.S. before. The jury were out for two and a half hours, but later a member of the jury was to state that the verdict was decided in one minute with a show of hands. They stayed out because it was a capital case, but no one wavered from their unanimous one-minute verdict.

While his appeals were being heard, Holmes embraced the Roman Catholic Church. All of his appeals failed, and on May 7, 1896, accompanied by two priests, Holmes mounted the scaffold at Moyanensing Prison. He made a short speech to the assembled onlookers but saved his last words for the gentleman who adjusted the noose around his neck.

"Make it quick," he said.

H. H. Holmes, one of the most notorious murderers who ever lived, would have been thirty-six had he lived nine more days.

The Perfect Hiding-Place

When Bela Kiss and his wife arrived in the tiny village of Czinkota, Hungary, they immediately bought the only imposing house in the area, a huge greystone structure on the outskirts of the village. Bela was about forty years old and his wife was fifteen years his junior when they took up residence. Mr. Kiss immediately impressed the locals with his acts of kindness towards the less fortunate in the village. He made it his business to find out who was ill and who needed assistance; nothing seemed too insignificant for the unselfish Bela to lend a hand. He owned a dashing red roadster, and many a night it would be seen roaring up the main drag, sometimes to deliver a food basket to a needy citizen, sometimes to bring some much-needed medicine to a sick friend. Everyone agreed that Bela was the greatest thing that ever happened to Czinkota. He seemed not to worry about money at all, though he had no visible means of support. But the villagers must have felt that it was not for them to look a gift horse in the mouth.

Despite his magnanimous gestures, Bela was a shy, introverted man, short of stature but with considerable presence. He sported a black handlebar moustache, which accentuated his oval face, and made him appear somewhat chubby. His wife, Marie, was a real knockout in the looks department, with a voluptuous figure to match. She and Bela hired two girls from the village to act as servants, but they only stayed during the day, returning to their own homes each night. As for Bela, he sometimes left in his red car for a few days, but generally could be found at home, in his great greystone house, living the life of a country gentleman.

It is too bad that such scenes of marital bliss and tranquillity should have to come to an end. In Bela's case the whole thing came to an abrupt stop when he learned that Marie was seeing an artist, Paul Bihari, on the side. Actually, she was doing more than seeing him; she was sharing his bed. Imagine Bela's disappointment when he found out that the one woman he ever cared about was being unfaithful to him, particularly since it coincided with his purchase of their new home and their good life in Czinkota.

At about the time that this revolting development came to Bela's attention, the village constable paid a social visit to the Kiss residence. Constable Adolph Trauber, who didn't have that much to do in the village anyway, occasionally did a little public relations work to pass the time of day. He wanted to know if there was any way he could be of service to the village's most illustrious resident. Bela said that he would appreciate it if Trauber would keep an eye on the property on those nights when he was away and Marie was left alone in the house, and the constable said that he would be delighted to do so. Trauber, a big, friendly man, immediately liked and admired Bela, and a warm friendship grew between the two men.

In the meantime, every time that red roadster disappeared over the hill, who would show up but Marie's lover, Paul. In a village the size of Czinkota it was impossible to keep tongues from wagging, and the townspeople passed the days wondering about the outcome of the triangle. All agreed that the shabby artist couldn't be half the man kind Mr. Kiss was, but there were a couple of things—the artist was tall, slender, and above all, the same age as Marie.

One day just before Christmas, when the two servants reported for work in the morning, they were surprised to find Bela in his study with his head buried in his arms. They gingerly asked him what was wrong. Bela passed them a letter written to him by his wife to the effect that she had left him for the artist Paul Bihari. Bela, beside himself with grief, informed the two servants that he wouldn't be needing them any more now that he was alone in the big house, and that anyway he wanted to be alone in his sadness.

As the weather grew colder and the grey house remained dark and quiet, the only break in the monotony of village life came when one evening a wagon pulled up at Bela's door and deposited two large metal drums. Then the cold winter descended like a blanket, leaving the villagers with only one piece of gossip to discuss during the long dark evenings—poor Bela's beautiful wife running off with an artist.

Weeks passed into months, and one day it dawned on Constable Trauber that he had not seen his friend Bela since his wife ran away. He decided to pay him a visit. When he knocked at the door, though he pounded long and hard nobody answered. He broke the lock and entered the dark interior. In the study he found Bela, looking half-starved, his clothes in rags and the house a shambles. It was obvious to Trauber that his friend had not taken care of himself or the house since his wife left him.

"I have nothing to live for, Adolph," said the downhearted Bela.

"Nonsense," said the constable. "First we will get someone to look after you and the house. You are both a mess."

The very next day an old woman knocked on Bela's front door, announcing that she was the widow Kalman and that Constable Trauber had sent her to take care of him and the house, and that was that. Under the widow's supervision Bela once more began to look like his old self. He started to gain weight, and with the improvement in his health, his old cheerful but reserved disposition returned. By spring he appeared to be back to normal.

One fine day, when the snow had melted and flowers were beginning to show their buds, Bela had a little tête-à-tête with the widow. He thanked her profusely for being such a great help to him, but felt that he was sufficiently recovered so that he no longer needed her at night. She could return to her home each evening and come back each morning. The widow didn't know whether to take this new arrangement as an insult or a compliment, but eventually she found out that when Mrs. Kiss lived in the house the two servants had returned to their homes each night, so all things considered she decided not to take offence. At least nice Mr. Kiss was well enough to take care of himself. Anyway, Mr. Kiss had some strange ideas, thought Mrs. Kalman. Take the upstairs closet which he always kept locked—she had once asked about cleaning in there, but was told that it wasn't necessary. It was none of her business, mind you, but a body couldn't help but be curious.

Shortly after Bela's little meeting with the widow he left the village in his smart red car and returned with a lady. The widow Kalman was given to understand that the visit would be a more or less permanent one. The Madame, as Bela called her, was an overweight blonde in her late fifties. She was just getting settled in when a wagon pulled up to the Kiss residence and deposited another metal drum. Bela had the delivery man carry it to the upstairs closet which already held the other two drums.

Kiss, who never ceased to amaze the widow Kalman, then offered to send her on a week's vacation with full pay. The widow took her boss up on the offer, and was on her way the same day the proposition was put to her. When she came back from her unexpected vacation, she noticed that the madame was nowhere to be seen. Bela nonchalantly told her that the madame had left. This puzzled Mrs. Kalman, because when she had set off on her travels a few days earlier it had appeared that the madame would be a permanent resident.

Maybe Bela realized the widow was having some misgivings about her boss, because he came to her and invited her into his study. The widow, who was becoming accustomed to their little chats, nevertheless shifted uneasily in an overstuffed chair. Bela coughed once or twice, and then confessed to Mrs. Kalman that he liked women and he intended to indulge himself with them. He was sorry if he shocked her, but out of respect for her he thought it best to let her know that he planned to invite several ladies to the house in the future. She could, of course, leave his employ if she wished, but Bela would rather—indeed, positively insisted—that she stay. To sweeten the pie, Kiss let it drop that there would be quite a few paid vacations during the coming months. The widow Kalman made up her mind. Women or no, she would be happy to remain in his employ.

Next day Bela took off in the red roadster and returned with a six-foot, 300-pound Amazon. He winked knowingly at the widow Kalman. "Madame will be with us for some time," he said. Mrs. Kalman nodded understandingly and started to unpack madame's bags. She then went on one of her periodic vacations, so she didn't see the wagon when it delivered the fourth steel drum. Upon her return she inquired after the new madame, and was told she had left. The widow Kalman nodded her head and went about her dusting.

One day Constable Trauber, who by now was justifiably proud of butting into Bela's life and bringing him out of the doldrums, paid his friend a semi-official visit. Two Budapest widows had mysteriously disappeared of late, and as Bela had recently entertained two ladies, would he mind answering a few questions? Evidently a man named Hofmann had enticed the ladies to his flat, and they were never heard of again. The Budapest police had found the flat, but Hofmann had long since gone. The police felt that the women had been murdered, because both had withdrawn their life savings immediately before their disappearance. Trauber and his friend had a good laugh. Such gullible women almost deserved whatever fate befell them. The two men had a glass of wine, a good cigar out of Bela's humidor, and spent a pleasant few hours, as good friends will. Bela told Trauber that he had something he had been wanting to show him. He took the constable upstairs and unlocked the closet door. Inside were four metal drums which Bela started to bang on with a stick. They all gave off a dull thud as if they were full of liquid. Bela took the cover off one of the drums and told his friend to look in.

"Petrol," Trauber said.

"Yes," replied Bela. He had a friend who could only pay off his debts in petrol, which was just fine with him. With the sabre-rattling that was going on throughout Europe, Bela explained, it was only a matter of time before the world would be at war and petrol would be better than hard cash. Trauber agreed, as Bela replaced the lid. Bela tapped the other three. "See," he said, "they contain petrol, too. Here, take the keys to this room. If anything ever happens to me, you take the petrol. I wouldn't want my wife and her artist friend to have any claim to it."

The two friends returned to the study to have a few more glasses of wine, Trauber protesting that nothing was about to happen to Bela.

In 1914 the war broke out. Time and time again Bela was seen with middle-aged ladies by his side as he roared from Budapest to Czinkota in his red roadster. Mrs. Kalman was taking more and more paid vacations, and the man with the drums kept reappearing at Bela's door. Bela, always an impressive figure around the village, distinguished himself by acting as a voluntary recruiting officer. The young, able-bodied men had to be on their guard if they shirked their duty, because Bela didn't take his job lightly.

Then one day it actually happened to him. He was taken without notice from his house to Budapest to join the army. He never even got a chance to return to his home to tidy up his affairs, and nothing further was heard from him. Often on a cold winter evening the very old, for they and the very young were the only people left in Czinkota in 1914 and 1915, wondered how their distinguished little neighbour was making out at the front.

In May 1916, Adolph Trauber received word that Bela Kiss had been killed in action at the front. Constable Trauber had lost a friend, the village its most illustrious citizen, and Hungary a true patriot, in one fell swoop. Having spent many an afternoon in his cups with Bela, Adolph felt that he had suffered a personal loss. He went down to the village square and inscribed Bela's name on the roll of honour. Grief-stricken villagers joined the constable, and with bowed heads they mourned the passing of Bela Kiss.

Not long after the touching scene in the village square, representatives of the government entered Czinkota looking for that most precious of all commodities—petrol. They looked up Constable Trauber and made their mission known to him. It was only then that the constable remembered the hoard of petrol which Bela had shown him so many months before. He took the soldiers to the austere grey house, and up the stairs to the closet where the petrol was stored. The soldiers tilted the first drum and one peered inside. He said, "My God," and started to stammer, pointing into the drum. The second soldier took a look, and he too became incoherent. Finally the constable looked into the drum and saw the well-preserved body of a woman, submerged in alcohol.

In all there were seven drums in the closet. All but two contained the bodies of middle-aged ladies; in the sixth was the body of Paul Bihari, and the seventh contained petrol—the same petrol that Adolph had peered into when Bela showed him his secret.

A top detective was dispatched from Budapest to take over the strange case of Bela Kiss. Detective Nagy pasted together the baffling pieces of the case. He searched Bela's house, and found his desk full of letters from women all over Europe. The mass killer had used the simplest of schemes, that of placing matrimonial advertisements in newspapers and luring rich widows to his home in Czinkota, where he had strangled each of his victims with a rope and pickled them in alcohol. Detective Nagy traced the supplier of the drums and found out that he had delivered many more than the seven that were found. As a result a thorough search of the entire area was conducted, and several more drums were uncovered. Each of them contained the well-preserved body of a strangled lady.

When news of Detective Nagy's gruesome find spread, several farmers came forward and told of turning up skeletons when they were ploughing fields adjoining Bela's property. In all it seemed that Bela Kiss had murdered twenty-three women, including his wife, and one man, the artist Paul Bihari.

Then, in 1919, people who knew his face reported seeing him in Budapest. The reports were so positive that Detective Nagy went to the hospital in Belgrade where Kiss had died of his wounds during the war. He was shocked to find out that Bela was a tall, blond, blue-eyed Nordic type. It was obvious that Bela had managed to switch papers with a critically wounded soldier. When the soldier died, Kiss had assumed the dead man's identity, and had been discharged at the war's end.

Cunning little Bela Kiss had made good his escape. Years passed without word of the mass killer, until in 1952, a deserter from the French Foreign Legion told of a companion named Hofmann who used to amuse his fellows in the desert with stories of how he had loved and strangled women in Hungary. When Detective Nagy heard these stories he recognized details that had never been made public, and he knew that the teller was in reality Bela Kiss. But by the time Nagy got in touch with officials of the French Foreign Legion, Bela had deserted.

Though some criminologists who have studied the Bela Kiss case believe he emigrated to the United States, he has never been apprehended.

How Does Your
Garden Grow?

B elle Paulsen's father was a magician who travelled the length and breadth of Norway with his magic act. Belle was born in 1859 and grew up to be a slim, well-behaved child who became adept at tightrope walking, delighting her father's audiences with daring stunts on the taut wire. When her father retired from the transient life of a magician and bought a farm, Belle 'found the change from being a performer to the solitude of rural life unbearably boring. Now an impetuous teenager, she decided to emigrate to the United States.

After she arrived in the U.S., Belle, a shapely twenty-four-year-old, met Mads Sorensen, a Swede, who courted her and won her hand in marriage. The couple settled in Chicago, Illinois, and the marriage commenced to bear fruit in the form of two offspring, Lucy and Myrtle. Two years after the marriage, Mads had a heart attack and died. There was a small group of friends and relatives in the close-knit Scandinavian community who never for a moment thought that it was a heart attack that had put an end to Mads. They whispered that he had been poisoned, and they fingered the widow as the administrator of the deadly potion. But even though Belle collected $8,500 in insurance money and sold Sorensen's home for $5,000, nothing came of the distasteful rumours.

The now well-heeled Belle and her two children moved to Austin, Illinois, where they purchased a new home. One cold night the house mysteriously caught fire, and while the insurance company suspected that the fire wasn't accidental, there was no proof of any monkey business and they paid off.

Belle moved back to Chicago in the grip of an obsession. She had somehow acquired a ravenous appetite, and ate to such an extent that she started to gain weight rapidly. She became fatter and fatter, until the scales tipped 200 pounds. This five-foot-seven-inch dumpling was no longer recognizable as the slender Norwegian girl who had married Mads Sorensen. Her face had been plain to begin with, but now it became bloated and ugly. In Chicago she purchased a candy store, which soon burned to the ground. Again with some misgivings, the insurance company paid off. We can imagine Belle, relaxing with a box of chocolates, figuring that the greatest prerequisite for success in the world of commerce was to have a quick hand with a match.

With the proceeds of her fires she purchased a forty-eight acre farm about a mile from La Porte, Indiana, and quite by chance had an unexpected addition to her family. Antone Olson had recently lost his wife, and felt ill-equipped to take care of his daughter Jennie. Belle, who had known the Olsons for years in Chicago, was only too happy to take Jenny in, and as she put it, "treat her like one of my own."

Belle soon ballooned to a substantial 230 pounds. She worked her farm like a man, and gained a sort of local fame by butchering her own farm animals, particularly hogs, and selling the meat in the nearby town of La Porte. In April of 1902 she met Peter Gunness, who, like Belle, was Norwegian. We don't know where Peter came from, but he settled in on the farm and appears to have been well-liked by his neighbours and people who came in contact with him in La Porte. The neighbours had only a short time to make any judgement about Peter, for only seven months after he married Belle, disaster struck. It came in the form of a sausage grinder, and it struck poor Peter square on the head, killing him instantly. The grinder sat on a high shelf and, as luck or whatever would have it, Peter picked a spot directly under the grinder to rest his weary bones. Coincidentally enough, the grinder chose this opportune moment to totter and fall, striking Peter a fatal blow to the head.

During his short but noteworthy appearance upon the stage with Belle, the unlucky Norwegian managed to accomplish three things. He changed Belle's name from Belle Brynhilde Paulsetter Sorensen to Belle Gunness, for which he earns our gratitude. He was also thoughtful enough to insure his life for $4,000, which Belle reluctantly allowed to be pressed into her chubby hands. And he wasn't fully acclimatized to his new surroundings in the grave when Belle discovered that she was heavy laden with child, as they used to say. "Son of a bitch," Belle hissed between her teeth when she discovered the dirty trick Peter had pulled on her from the grave. The object of her dilemma popped into the world in 1903, and was named Philip for no particular reason.

After the birth of her son Belle settled down to farming, and occasionally hired a transient hand to help her. Most stayed for a short time and moved on. There was something strange and sinister about working for the quiet, puffing butterball, who could not only pitch hay with the best of men, but who also seemed to take a delight in butchering her own hogs. Rough and tough as these men were, Belle's actions didn't appear natural to them.

Belle worked hard, but a chubby nymphomaniac needs a man around the house. Like so many men and women in similar circumstances Belle gravitated to advertising in matrimonial journals. This direct approach has produced many good husbands and wives, so we cannot completely condemn the practice of selecting a partner by mail order. But it would be as well to warn the lovesick advertiser that a certain risk is involved in communicating with a total stranger. Belle reduced the risk factor, but unfortunately her male partners weren't quite as cautious. She refined the ads and eliminated a lot of the riffraff with her no-nonsense approach.

For example—"Comely widow who owns a large farm in one of the finest districts in La Porte County, Indiana, desires to make acquaintance of a gentleman equally well provided, with view of joining fortunes. No replies by letter considered unless sender is willing to follow answer with personal visit. No triflers please."

The number of men attracted to ads of this nature is uncertain. For one thing, we will never know how many men showed up at the widow's doorstep, took one look at Belle's 230 pounds, and said thanks, but no thanks. Conversely, we have no way of knowing how many prospective suitors didn't measure up to Belle's standards. She obviously preferred men of Scandinavian extraction who had accumulated some cold, hard cash.

In answer to one of her ads, a Norwegian named John Moo arrived from Minnesota in 1906. John must be placed in the missing, presumed dead category, for he was seen and met by neighbours as the bridegroom apparent, and just as suddenly as he appeared on the scene, he vanished. During the inquiries that followed, not a trace of him could be found, and Belle claimed she had no idea where he went when he left the farm.

Another native of Norway, George Anderson, travelled from a small village in Missouri to meet Belle. By now she had developed a line that could charm the birds out of the trees. Mr. Anderson had taken the precaution of not bringing his nest-egg with him, but admitted later to being completely captivated by his hostess. She wined and dined him in the grand manner. Visions of the good life on the farm danced before his eyes, giving a rosy tinge to her obvious shortcomings. One night at the farmhouse, Anderson was startled out of a deep sleep. There, towering over him by candlelight, was the huge form of Mrs. Gunness with a strange, wild look in her eyes. As he awoke she ran from the room, and Anderson, scared half out of his wits, made the wisest move of his life. He got out of bed, put on his pants, ran all the way to the station in La Porte, and went back to Missouri on the next train.

Not quite as fortunate was Bud Budsberg, another native of Norway, who arrived at Belle's door in 1907. Mr. Budsberg had travelled from Iola, Wisconsin, with $2,000 in his poke. Despite extensive inquiries conducted by relatives back in Wisconsin, Bud was never heard from again. He simply crossed Belle's threshold and disappeared.

Nothing seemed very permanent on the Gunness farm. But there was one exception; Belle had finally found a hired hand who didn't move on like the rest. He was a French Canadian named Ray Lamphere, who was not only able to tolerate Belle as an employer, but actually fell in love with her. Ray, who had the personality of a born follower, was of average height and had a handlebar moustache and bulging eyes that made him look as if he was always afraid of something, as well he might have been. It is pretty certain that Belle kept Ray around the farm for a variety of reasons, not the least of which was instant sex. Her other gentlemen friends had developed the annoying habit of disappearing, but steady, if not heady, Ray was always available. Jealous though he was of the other men who were continually coming to the farm, Ray was secure in the knowledge that he would outlast them all.

At about this time neighbours noticed that a large eight-foot-high fence had been put up around the farmhouse. The shutters on the windows were closed for weeks on end, and it was well-known that the basement was equipped as a slaughterhouse for Belle's hogs. She had a large table down there, as well as a pulley system for raising the carcasses of slaughtered animals. Along one wall hung a top quality set of butchers' knives and cleavers.

The parade of suitors continued. Andrew K. Helgelein arrived from Aberdeen, South Dakota, with $3,000 in a bulging wallet. This gentleman differed from those who had come before in that he got under Ray Lamphere's skin. For some reason, Ray, who had become accustomed to seeing his beloved being courted by other men, couldn't take it when Helgelein and Belle were together. Ray and Belle argued bitterly about this, and Ray packed up his belongings and left the farm in a tantrum.

He went to La Porte and started gossiping about his former lover and employer. Nothing serious, mind you, but enough so that when word of his loose tongue got back to Belle she had him arrested and tried to have him judged insane and committed to an institution. A sanity hearing actually took place, and Lamphere was declared sane. He made up with Belle, and returned to the farm. He commenced to pick another fight; this time Belle had him arrested for trespassing. Lamphere was found guilty of this offense and paid a fine.

Still in La Porte, the French Canadian continued to bad-mouth Belle, even mentioning to a farmer, Bill Slater, "Helgelein won't bother me no more. We fixed him for keeps."

By coincidence Helgelein had disappeared the day before this conversation took place. Then something happened that was even more vexing than Ray Lamphere shooting off his mouth in town. For the first time in all her years on the farm, Belle was the recipient of a serious threat, in the form of inquiring letters from Mr. Asle Helgelein of Mansfield, South Dakota, who was the brother of the missing Andrew. Belle met his pointed questions with the claim that Andrew had gone back to Norway, to which Asle replied, "Rubbish."

With the heat definitely on, Belle hitched up the team, drove into La Porte and paid a visit to her lawyer, M. E. Leliter. On April 27, 1908, Belle asked the lawyer to draw up her will, leaving her estate to her three children, with the proviso that should she outlive her children, the money would go to a Norwegian orphanage in Chicago. She said the reason for this sudden urge to put her affairs in order was because Ray

Lamphere was threatening to kill her and burn down her farmhouse. She told Leliter that she was in mortal fear of the insanely jealous Lamphere. The whole thing took a matter of minutes, and was drawn up and signed before she left the lawyer's office.

That very night the new hired hand, Joe Maxon, said goodnight to the family and went to bed. In the middle of the night he was awakened by the loud crackling of a fire. Shaking the cobwebs from his mind, he rose slowly, then realized that the entire house was engulfed in flames. He shouted at the top of his lungs to wake Belle and the children, then staggered toward the window, and jumped from the second storey, wearing only his underwear.

The next morning, as the charred rubble cooled, the remains of Belle's three children, Lucy, Myrtle, and Philip, together with the headless body of a woman, were found in the cellar, having fallen through the floor.

Because of the veiled threats made by Lamphere, and the well-known feud that existed between him and Mrs. Gunness, he immediately came under suspicion. A youngster swore he had not only seen Lamphere near the farmhouse on the night of the fire, but had actually spoken to him. Ray was arrested, and Belle's lawyer came forward and told of her accusations against the accused man. In due course Lamphere was charged with the murder of Belle Gunness.

Neighbours who had known Belle for years were asked to identify the headless corpse. At the time of the fire Belle was estimated to weigh 280 pounds; not an easy figure to mistake. All her neighbours said the burnt corpse was too short and far too light to be Mrs. Gunness. This rather startling development threw an entirely new light on the macabre affair. For starters, who was the burned, headless corpse? If the corpse wasn't Mrs. Gunness, then where was she? To further confuse an already confusing situation, Mr. Antone Olson heard about the fire and rushed down to the farm to find his Jennie. She too was nowhere to be found, although neighbours said that some time previously Belle had mentioned that she had gone to California to continue her schooling.

The authorities searched everywhere for the missing head, but try as they might, they couldn't find it. Then Mr. Asle Helgelein showed up, looking for his brother. He didn't even know there had been a fire, but he had a deep suspicion that his brother had met with foul play at the hands of the woman he had come to Indiana to marry. Asle noticed that the Gunness' yard was uneven, and that patches of earth in the yard were of different colours. Maxon, the hired hand, volunteered that there had been slight depressions in the ground, and Mrs. Gunness had told him to bring earth from an adjoining field to even it off. Asle wasn't taking any offhanded answers, and urged the police to dig in these areas. The very first hole they dug uncovered the corpse of Andrew Helgelein, whose brother had the unfortunate experience of staring down at it as it was unearthed. He positively identified the body, and the digging started in earnest.

The next hole produced the body of Jennie Olson, who hadn't gone to California at all. Three more bodies were uncovered before darkness fell on the eerie scene and the diggers had to stop for the night. The next day, May 4, 1908, four more bodies were dug out of the farmyard, and on the third day one further body was uncovered. The bodies were in various stages of decomposition, and some were never to be identified. Others were positively identified as Andrew Helgelein, Jennie Olson, John Moo, and Bud Budsberg. Over and above these complete corpses police uncovered bits and pieces of other bodies that had no matching parts, leading them to believe that many more suitors had been put to death on the farm. With the discovery of these parts of human bodies, the police had to consider Belle's private abattoir in the basement. The implication was obvious—had Belle been butchering more than hogs?

Gossip comes a narrow second to farming as the principal occupation in the Hoosier State, and the murder farm was soon on everyone's lips. Crops lay unattended as men gathered to discuss the case, with the more curious driving out to the farm to peer at the now excavated farmyard. All the while they talked, exchanging information, telling stories, until one bit of gossip became so prominent that it took on the status of a distinct possibility.

The night the house burned Belle had been seen heading for her farm in her buggy with a stout lady. Joe Maxon, who was in the house that night, said that he didn't see any stout lady, but added that it would have been possible for a woman to be in the house without his knowledge. The local speculation was that Belle had somehow arranged to bring a strange woman out to the farm, kill and decapitate her, set the house on fire, and take off, thinking that everyone would believe she had perished in the fire. She had come up with a stout lady, but she couldn't quite duplicate her own massive poundage.

By now the weird case was on the front page of every newspaper in the U.S., and because of its doubtful aspects it gave rise to theory and speculation. Everyone had a story to tell about Belle or one of the victims. Dr. Ira P. Norton read about the case and volunteered the information that he had once done dental work for Belle, and could identify his own work if the authorities could produce it. This appeared to be a hopeless task, as the police felt that a fire hot enough to destroy a head would certainly melt gold caps and change porcelain beyond recognition. The doctor explained that this was not so, and that if his dental work could be found, it would be easy to identify. The police looked at the rubble of the burned farmhouse and realized they had a mammoth task before them.

Into a case already loaded down with strange and interesting characters came the most colourful of all, Louis Schultz. He had heard about the missing gold dental work in the rubble of the fire. Louis was an experienced gold miner just back from the Yukon, and told the police that if they would build him a sluice box he would sluice the entire farmhouse and if there was any gold in the rubble he would find it, using the same methods he had used in the Yukon.

The scheme seemed practical enough. In due course the sluice box was set up in the farmyard with running water piped over from the barn, and Louis set to work.

The sluice box manned by Louis in the yard received almost as much publicity as the crimes themselves. Crowds poured out to the farm to take in the spectacle of a sourdough mining gold on an Indiana farm. They cheered Louis on, and rising to the occasion, he waved and joked with the crowd. Christened Klondike Louis by the press, he was always good for a colourful quote, and because of him and the eeriness of the scene, on a good day the crowd surrounding the farm swelled to 5,000. You could even place a friendly wager as to whether Louis would strike gold or not.

Then it happened. After four days on the job, and after washing tons of mud and debris through his sluice box, Schultz came up with a bridgework containing two lower bicuspids capped with gold and four porcelain teeth. Louis was proclaimed a hero, and the teeth were rushed to Dr. Norton for examination. He positively identified the work as his own, and the teeth as belonging to Belle Gunness.

This lent considerable weight to the assumption that Belle's head had been completely burned by the fire and only her dental work had survived, and Ray Lamphere stood trial for Belle's murder. The evidence against him was strong; he had argued bitterly with Belle and had been seen near the house on the night of the fire. There was just one thing—the jury didn't believe that Mrs. Gunness was dead. Lamphere was acquitted, but was tried for arson and convicted. After hearing all the evidence, the jurors came to the conclusion that Belle was alive but that Lamphere had burned down the farmhouse. Lamphere was suffering from tuberculosis, and died in Michigan City Prison in December, 1909.

Before he died he told two different versions of his life with Belle and particularly what happened on the night the house burned down. The first version was told to a friend in prison who came forward after Ray's death. Ray told him that the whole thing was a setup—Belle did not die in the fire. She had advertised for a housekeeper and had culled the applicants, trying to find one as large as herself. With pressure mounting from Andrew Helgelein, she had to settle for the stoutest woman she could find, but one still far short of her massive structure. After drugging her, Belle cut off her head, and Ray and Belle buried it in quicklime in the nearby swamp. Belle had dressed the stranger in some of her own clothing to further aid in the identification; then she had killed her three children, leaving Ray to light the fire. Ray claimed that he never actually killed anyone himself, but had aided Belle in any way she asked in getting rid of her bothersome bodies. She had killed her own children because they knew too much of the strange goings on. He said there had been twenty-eight more murders committed on the farm that were never uncovered. Belle butchered the bodies in her basement, feeding the smaller parts to the hogs and burying the larger pieces in quicklime in the swamp.

Upon hearing the story of the hogs' unorthodox eating habits the man who purchased them in La Porte was reported to have remarked, "They were still the best damn hogs in the county."

Lamphere said that Belle had sneaked up behind Mr. Gunness and split open his head with an axe. She then placed his body under the shelf that held the sausage grinder and dropped it on his head. A little girl in La Porte remembered a conversation she had with Belle's daughter Myrtle who told her, "Mama brained Papa with an axe. Don't tell a soul."

Lamphere died shortly after telling his friend these details about the crime. After he had passed away Reverend E. A. Schnell, the prison minister, told of Lamphere's confession of his part in the crimes. This version differs in many details from that given to his friend. Lamphere told the minister that on the night of the fire he had chloroformed the three Gunness children and set fire to the house. He said he was completely captivated by Belle and would comply with anything she desired. But whatever the major variations, the two stories were the same in one important detail—he swore that Belle had not died in the fire.

Readers can pick their own version of what took place that last night on the farm, but whichever they choose they must consider Belle's bridgework found in the debris of the burned out farmhouse. Is it within the realm of possibility that Belle, operating in a mad frenzy, with her three children dead beside her, could have taken a pair of pliers and torn the permanent bridgework from her own mouth? Dentists have recorded instances where lumberjacks and others working in isolation have suffered from terrible toothaches and pulled out several of their own teeth. A 280-pound woman who had disposed of a possible forty-two human beings might not find the act as appalling as it appears to us.

Belle Gunness has not been seen or heard of since the night of April 27, 1908, when her house burned to the ground.

Perverted Killer

rnold and Mary Corll were both twenty-three years old when their first son, Dean, was born on Christmas Eve, 1939. The Corlls almost immediately started to disagree on the way the child should be brought up. Arnold was a strict disciplinarian who thought that young Dean should be taught to obey his parents almost before he learned to walk. This proved to be a bone of contention, and when Arnold was drafted in the Air Force and stationed in Memphis, Tennessee, it became apparent that the marriage had a limited lifespan. Sure enough an amicable divorce took place and the couple separated, but not before another child, Stephen, was born.

Mary, who still loved Arnold, sold her comfortable little home, bought a trailer and headed for Memphis, where she put Dean in school. She and Arnold took up where they had left off, fighting and arguing, and eventually, despite bickering, they decided to give marriage another try. When Arnold received his discharge from the Air Force, Mary, Arnold and the two children headed for Houston, Texas. At first they lived in a trailer, but later they bought a house. Their attempts to salvage their marriage proved futile, and they agreed to their second amicable divorce. Mary and her two sons moved again, this time to an apartment.

Dean and Stephen were again enrolled in a strange school, and it was here that doctors discovered that Dean suffered from a congenital heart defect. Dean had his first taste of being different from other boys; while they played energetic games he watched from the sidelines; while they ran, he walked.

In 1953, when Dean was an impressionable fourteen years old, his mother married a salesman named West. The entire family moved to Vidor, Texas, where Dean attended Vidor High School. Because of his heart trouble he took up music, and played the trombone as a member of the school band. Dean was an average trombone player, an average student, and was so inconspicuous that many of his teachers don't remember him.

In his spare time he helped his mother sell pecans from her garage. When he graduated from high school in 1958, he saved his money and bought a car. His mother started to manufacture pecan candies and he worked for her for two years, delivering candies to stores which had placed orders.

In 1962 Mary West had a flourishing little candy business going at 721 East 6 ½ Street. She had set up a kitchen and turned the garage into a candy store, and Dean's workload grew steadily as the family business prospered.

In 1964 Dean was drafted into the army and sent to Fort Polk, Louisiana. He was later transferred to Fort Hood in Texas, but received a hardship discharge on July 11, 1965, as he was needed at home to keep the candy factory going. By this time the factory was relocated at 505 West 22nd Street, and the West family moved to an apartment at 1845 Airport Boulevard, with the exception of Dean who lived by himself in an apartment a block away at 444 West 21st Street.

Across the street from the Corll Candy Company was the Helms Elementary School, and quite naturally the children were constantly dropping into the store section of the candy factory. Dean built a games room at the back of the factory and installed a pool table for the use of his customers. At the time the family thought the room was an astute business move, but in hindsight Dean's motives appear more sinister. The nature of his mother's business was enough to attract young boys, and the poolroom made the bait doubly alluring. If Dean had homosexual tendencies at this period in his life, he had managed, by accident or design, to place himself in an ideal position to indulge his sexual appetite.

Dean's mother went through another divorce, and then met and married a seaman, who took an immediate dislike to Dean and his habit of entertaining young boys in the candy factory. The marriage only lasted a matter of months, ending in divorce in 1968. Then the Corll family started to break up. Mrs. Corll dissolved the business and moved to Manitou Springs, where she set up another thriving candy factory, Stephen took a job as a machinist in Houston, and Dean went to work for the Houston Lighting and Power Company as an electrician.

By 1969 it is certain that Dean Corll was a confirmed homosexual who regularly enticed young boys to his residence at 2020 Lamar Street. No physical harm was done to the youngsters, and either fear or shame prevented them from ever talking about their experiences. One youngster, fourteen-year-old David Brooks, came under Corll's spell so completely that he dropped out of high school in order to spend all his time with his older friend. Later, Brooks was to state that their relationship started with Corll paying him for sexual favours. Brooks was a tall, slender, good-looking boy, with long hair falling to his shoulders. His parents were divorced, and he spent time with each parent, travelling from Houston to Beaumont.

In 1970 David Brooks introduced Dean to Wayne Henley. A relationship grew between Wayne and Dean, until gradually the boy fell completely under the spell of the older man's dominant personality. Wayne was a carbon copy of Brooks in appearance—lean, good-looking, with long hair. The three of them, all the products of broken

271

homes, were inseparable. The two younger boys were so subservient to Corll that they would carry out his every desire without question.

The world heard for the first time of Dean Corll, David Brooks and Wayne Henley on Wednesday, August 8, 1973. The police received a telephone call reporting a shooting at 2020 Lamar Street. When they arrived at the scene they were stopped by three youths, two boys and a girl, standing in front of a white frame house. Wayne Henley gave his name to the police, and handed them a .22 calibre pistol. The gun held six spent shells. Then Henley introduced five-foot-two-inch Rhonda Louise Williams, a fifteen-year-old with the knowing look of someone twice her age. She hung on Henley's arm while he told the officers that the other youth's name was Tim Kerley.

The three teenagers told of shooting a man named Corll, and were hustled into a patrol car. As the officers entered the hall of 2020 Lamar Street they could see the naked body of Dean Corll spread out on the floor. Tiny holes dotted the dead man's back, and his legs were entangled in telephone wire. The police went on to a bedroom, where they carefully opened the door and stood amazed at the strange paraphernalia which lay before them. The floor was covered with beige carpeting, which in turn was covered by a sheet of clear plastic. The room contained a long pine board with holes in each corner. These holes had chains running through them, and at each corner of the board was fastened a pair of handcuffs. On the floor the police also spotted a long knife.

Detective Sergeant Dave Mullican, a huge, 220-pound, six-foot-two career cop, had investigated many homicides, and he knew instinctively that he was now involved in something beyond a routine killing.

An examination of the body showed that Corll had been shot six times, the full capacity of the .22 calibre revolver which Henley had turned over to the police. He had been shot once in the shoulder, once in the head, and four times in the back. The board found in the bedroom measured two and a half feet wide by eight feet long, obviously designed to accommodate a human being. A total of eight sets of handcuffs were found in the house, as well as a gas mask. In the garage attached to the house, the police found traces of dehydrated lime on the floor.

Henley told the story of what went on at 2020 Lamar on the night Dean Corll met his death. It all started when Corll asked Henley to a party at his house. Henley had brought Kerley, and the three men sat around smoking pot and drinking beer, when Henley thought it would be a good idea to bring his girlfriend Rhonda Williams over to the party. He called Rhonda, who managed to sneak out of her home to meet them. The two boys picked her up in Kerley's Volkswagen and drove back to the house. Corll was furious that they had brought a girl to the party, but was soon pacified. The three youngsters started inhaling the fumes from acrylic paint sprayed in a bag. All the while Corll smoked pot and drank beer, the three youngsters "bagged" the fumes. Eventually, they passed out.

When Henley came round he found that Corll had handcuffed him. He looked about the room and saw that Rhonda and Kerley were both handcuffed and had masking tape over their mouths. Corll was acting like a madman, waving a knife and brandishing a pistol. When Kerley and Rhonda regained consciousness he threatened to torture them all and then kill them. Henley realized that somehow he had to reason with Dean, for he was the only one who could talk. He started to get on Corll's good side by promising him that he would assist him in torturing Kerley. Slowly he gained Corll's confidence, convincing him that he would help him to kill his two friends. Corll and he devised a further plan; Corll would assault Kerley and Henley would rape Rhonda, after which they would kill them both. On this understanding, Corll unlocked Henley's handcuffs.

With a great deal of difficulty Corll proceeded to handcuff his two captives to the board. He then undressed the pair and started to assault

Kerley, who despite being handcuffed, tried to fight him off. In the meantime Henley tried to have intercourse with Rhonda, but found that he couldn't.

While all this was going on Henley noticed a pistol on a small table, the one piece of furniture in the room. On the pretence of going to the bathroom, he managed to leave the room. When he returned he picked up the pistol and pointed it at Corll, who was still fighting with the desperate Kerley. The moment Corll saw the gun, he rushed Henley, who started pressing the trigger and didn't stop until all six bullets were discharged. Corll fell to the floor and died instantly. Henley unlocked Kerley's and Rhonda's handcuffs. The three got dressed and called the police; and not wanting to stay with the dead man, they waited outside for the police to arrive.

Had Henley stopped talking it is in the realm of possibility that the police would have wound up the case. It was a weird sex dope killing, but Henley's story had a ring of truth to it, and was corroborated by all the physical evidence.

But Henley didn't stop. For some reason he thought the police didn't believe him, and he figured the only way out of his dilemma was to paint Corll as a sex-crazed monster. He requested another interview with the police and this time he added that Corll had once boasted that he had killed some boys. He remembered the names Cobble and Jones, and thought Dean had mentioned that he had buried them in a boathouse. Detectives checked the names, and sure enough, Charles Cobble, seventeen, and Marty Jones, eighteen, who had lived together, had disappeared on July 27, about two weeks prior to the shooting of Corll. The backgrounds of these two boys had already been checked, and had been found to be normal in every way. They were achieving good marks at school and both got along well with their parents. They had disappeared without any warning and no trace of them had been found since they were reported missing.

Henley told the police he thought he could direct them to the boathouse. The police took him up on his offer, and equipped with shovels and ropes, they proceeded out of the city. The handcuffed Henley directed them to a field adjoining Silver Bell Street, where there stood a lone corrugated steel structure. "That's the boathouse," said Henley. Inside were twenty stalls measuring twelve feet wide and thirty feet deep. Each stall had six-foot-wide double doors, which were securely locked. Henley pointed out Stall 11 as Dean's, and volunteered that the owner of the boathouse lived just a minute or so away.

The police explained their mission to Mrs. Mayme Meynier, the owner of Southwest Boat Storage. She confirmed that Stall 11 had been rented to Dean Corll, but stated that only he had the key. The police broke the lock and entered. The first thing that came into sight was a bicycle leaning against the righthand wall. As their eyes became accustomed to the semi-darkness they discovered two bags of dehydrated lime and a plastic bag containing a pair of new red shoes and other clothing. The police cleaned out the stall and commenced digging. Only six inches below the surface their shovels struck something harder than earth. The heat inside the corrugated boathouse was intense, and the men soon became soaked in perspiration, except Henley, who sat handcuffed on the ground beside the patrol car.

The men were now being hampered by the fading early evening light, but they carried on, gently parting the earth with their hands. Finally the object of their efforts became all too visible; the body of a young boy wrapped in a clear plastic sheet. The body was removed from the hole with great care and placed outside the boathouse. The men returned to their distasteful task. A second corpse, which had been buried for a longer period of time, was uncovered and removed from the boathouse.

By this time the unmistakable stench of death was permeating the entire area surrounding the boathouse. The police installed fans and lights to aid the diggers, who were now reinforced by eight trusties from a nearby jail. The entire floor of the stall was being excavated in six-inch levels. As the night wore on, the fans whirred and the lights cast strange shadows on the eerie scene; and the diggers found a third body, then a fourth, then a fifth and a sixth. Some were recent victims, wrapped in clear plastic, while others had been in the earth longer and were decomposed beyond recognition. By the time the diggers stopped at 1 a.m., two further bodies had been dragged from the boathouse.

By now the case was receiving nationwide and even worldwide attention. On Thursday morning, August 9, 1973, newspapers, radio broadcasts and early morning television news carried the sensational story of the eight bodies found in the boathouse. One ghostly presence held sway over the eerie events, and that presence belonged to Dean Corll. His name was on everyone's lips, but he was dead and it was left to others to explain his strange impulses and passions.

Wayne Henley told of an association with Corll which went back several years. It all started when Dean offered him $200 to procure young boys. Henley said he did nothing about the offer for a full year, but then, when he badly needed money, he took Corll up on the proposition. And so it began; sometimes he would just pick up a lad who was hitchhiking, and on one pretense or another deliver him to Corll. Dean was a sadistic homosexual, and often he would use the boys, then kill them in front of Henley. Henley claimed that although he had been present, he had never taken part in torturing or killing anyone.

Typical of the many stories Henley told of picking up boys for Dean was the one about the youngster who was reported missing only six days before Dean himself was killed. Fourteen-year-old James Stanton Dreymala was riding his bike when Henley and Corll, who were parked in Corll's van, called him over. Dean told the boy he could have some empty Coke bottles he had found in his van and take them in the store to get the deposit, which he could keep for himself. When James came out of the store he strolled over to the van and thanked Dean. Corll then told the boy to throw his bicycle into the van, explaining that he had more bottles at home. James jumped at the chance to earn some extra money, and after putting his bike in the van, he clambered in beside Henley and Corll. They drove out to 2020 Lamar Street where Corll assaulted the boy, tortured him, and then strangled him to death. It was his bicycle which was found in the boathouse. Henley kept up his nonstop stories of horror, but the strange case was to take another bizarre twist.

A Mr. Brooks arrived at the Houston police station with his son, David, who gave the police a statement about his relationship with Henley and Corll. He implicated Henley far more than Henley had admitted, but predictably stated emphatically that he himself was only a witness to all the unnatural sex acts and murders. When Henley was told that David Brooks was making a formal statement he immediately said, "That's good, now I can tell the whole story."

Henley told of meeting Brooks, who in turn had lured him to Corll. He now described in detail how he had actively participated in killing some of the boys, and he offered the startling information that there were a lot more bodies than those found at the boathouse. Henley was blossoming in the glare of publicity, and once started he didn't want to stop. He said one burial site was near Lake Sam Rayburn in San Augustine County and another was on High Island Beach in Jefferson County.

Hardened detectives winced; they believed the boy and believed they would find more bodies at these locations. How was it possible for a man and two youngsters to kill in wholesale lots and remain undetected? Henley explained that Corll moved a lot so that any suspicious action would be an isolated case and not one of a series of incidents that might be reported to the police. His van was ideal for transporting bodies. It could be backed up to a door, so that no one could see what was being put in or taken out. There were a lot of hitchhikers who didn't hesitate to accept a ride, and were susceptible to being invited to a party. Dean had developed these parties to a fine art, and always had some beer and grass available for the youngsters. Nothing untoward happened at many of the parties; sometimes they were over early and the boys left with a promise that they would be asked to the next one. Some of them felt secure because they knew either Henley or Brooks personally.

Brooks and Henley both felt that Corll was growing more demanding in his desire for young boys, and was in fact going mad. As matters now stood, Henley admitted to active participation in the murders, but Brooks claimed he was only a bystander.

Digging at the boathouse continued the next day, and more bodies were uncovered. Four further bodies were lifted from Stall 11 before the diggers broke for lunch. In the afternoon and early evening five more bodies were brought to the surface, making an unbelievable total of seventeen excavated from the boathouse in two days. The diggers then hit solid rock, and the authorities knew that here at least their work was done.

The ever co-operative Henley led police to where he and Dean had buried more boys on the shores of Lake Sam Rayburn. He even gave the police the name of one of the youngsters before they started digging. Sure enough, only a few minutes later the body of a young boy was uncovered. He pointed to another site, where he said Corll and Brooks had buried another boy. In a matter of minutes another body was uncovered. In all, four bodies were removed from the shores of the lake, making a total of twenty-one victims.

Brooks and Henley then directed the police to High Island where six additional bodies were found, bringing the final total to twenty-seven. The two boys couldn't remember any more names or grave sites, so the search was stopped. At the outset they had estimated that there had been between twenty and thirty victims. No one will ever know for sure if twenty-seven is the correct total.

Tim Kerley and Rhonda Louise Williams, the two youngsters who witnessed the shooting of Dean Corll, were released. Wayne Henley was charged with the murder of eight boys, and David Brooks was charged with two. Both received lengthy prison sentences designed to keep them behind bars for the rest of their lives. The authorities ruled that Henley's killing of Corll was an act of self-defense, and Henley was not charged with Corll's murder.

At the height of the investigation, a small fifteen-minute service was held at Pasadena's Grand View Memorial Park. About thirty-five friends and the immediate family of the deceased wept as the Reverend Robert D. Joiner of the Sunset United Methodist Church said a few kind words. The flag of the United States draped the casket. Just before it was lowered into the ground forever, the flag was presented to Dean Corll's father.

The Corpse Travelled by Train

Winnie Ruth McKinnell was born on January 29, 1905, in Oxford, Indiana, the daughter of a clergyman. She was an eighteen-year-old student nurse at Southern Indiana Hospital for the Insane in Evansville, Indiana, when she met Dr. William C. Judd, who was on the staff of the hospital. When the doctor left the hospital to take a position in Lafayette, Indiana, Winnie followed him, obtaining a job as a telephone operator so that she could be close to him. The doctor, who was Winnie's senior by twenty-two years, had previously been married to a seventeen-year-old, Lillian Colwell, in 1920, but his young bride had died of natural causes about a month after they were married. Winnie fell hard for the older man, and he seemingly was attracted to younger women. They were married in Lafayette in April 1924.

In 1925 Mrs. Judd became pregnant. She started to lose strength and her health deteriorated rapidly. She was almost continually nauseous, and as a result she eventually became so weak that Dr. Judd brought in another physician for a second opinion. He felt that Winnie's condition was serious enough to warrant an abortion, and her pregnancy was terminated in her third month.

Although the doctor led a rather nomadic life, practising medicine in several different cities, the constant moving didn't seem to have a detrimental effect on the couple's marriage, which appeared to be a happy one. They ended up living in a duplex at 2929 North 2nd Street in Phoenix, Arizona. Here they made the acquaintance of two neighbours, Agnes Anne LeRoi and Hedvig Samuelson.

In 1925 Anne had been training to become a nurse in Portland, Oregon, when she met and married Walter Monroe. The marriage lasted only eighteen months, ending in an amicable divorce. Anne later married again, this time to LeRoi James, but this marriage also ended in divorce. In 1929 Anne accepted the position of superintendent of a hospital at Wrangler, Alaska, where she met Hedvig Samuelson, who was a schoolteacher. Sammy, as she was called by everyone, was an outgoing personality who was extremely well-liked. Everyone was saddened when she took ill and her condition was diagnosed as tuberculosis.

The two girls had become such close friends that when it became imperative for Sammy to live in a drier climate, Anne would not hear of her making the move alone. The two good friends moved to Phoenix, Arizona, where Anne worked as an X-ray technician at the Grunow Clinic. In the course of her work she met Winnie Ruth Judd, now working as secretary and assistant to Dr. William Curtis. Sammy, who was convalescing at home, was unable to work.

The main characters in the drama had wandered the length of North America. Now, assembled in Phoenix, Arizona, they were ready to play their parts.

Winnie became friendly with Anne at the clinic, and often she and her husband would drop over to the girls' duplex and play bridge. On other occasions Anne and Sammy would visit with the Judds. Everyone seemed to get along extremely well.

In August 1931, the itchy-footed doctor left Phoenix to seek a position in Los Angeles, California. When this happened Winnie moved in with Anne and Sammy, and became as close to the two girls as they were to each other. She took care of Sammy, and was particularly kind to her on a few occasions when Anne had to leave Phoenix for a few days at a time.

In early October Winnie suddenly moved out of the girls' duplex and took an apartment at 1130 East Brill Street, telling them that Brill Street was closer to the Grunow Clinic where she worked.

On Saturday morning, October 17, Winnie Ruth Judd called her office at about nine o'clock and told the receptionist that she would be a little late arriving for work. At 9:45 a.m. the office received another call. This time the caller identified herself as Mrs. LeRoi, and advised them that she wouldn't be coming to work that day. The receiver of the call, Beverly Fox, thought that the caller was really Mrs. Judd trying to disguise her voice to sound like that of Mrs. LeRoi. A few minutes after ten o'clock a shaking and nervous Mrs. Judd showed up for work.

That night Winnie called the Lightning Delivery Company, who dispatched driver John W. Pritchett and a helper to 2929 North 2nd Street. Winnie Judd wanted to have a trunk moved, and explained to the men that the darkened condition of the house was due to her having the power turned off because she was vacating the premises. To help the men see their way about the darkened house, she lit some matches and explained that she wanted the trunk taken to the station so that she could check it out on a train leaving at 10:40.

Pritchett gave Winnie one portion of a claim check and fastened the other half to one of the handles of the trunk. Then the two men bent down and heaved. It hardly budged, and the men inquired as to its contents. Winnie told them that it held books, which satisfied Pritchett. He voiced the opinion that he thought the trunk weighed over 400 pounds, and felt it was too heavy to be checked on a ticket, but would have to remain overnight and go by express in the morning. If that was the case, Winnie said, she would have the trunk removed to 1130 East Brill

Street. With the aid of a handcart the men lifted the trunk on its end and placed it on their truck. Winnie joined them in the cab of the truck and all three drove to 1130 East Brill Street. The men placed the trunk in the front room, and Mrs. Judd waved to them from her doorway as they drove away.

The next morning, Sunday, October 18, Winnie asked her landlord, M. G. Koller, to take some baggage to the Union Depot, as she was leaving for Los Angeles. Koller showed up with his son to gather up the luggage. He noticed Winnie's hand was bandaged, and she mentioned to him that she had burned it on an electric iron. From the bedroom the father and son took one large trunk and one smaller one, while Mrs. Judd carried an old suitcase, a little leather grip and a large hatbox. The whole kit and caboodle, including Winnie, left for the station in Koller's car. When they arrived they received some help with the larger trunk from the baggage agent. Then, at 8:05, the baggage messenger placed the two trunks aboard the Golden State Limited bound for Los Angeles. He noticed a dark liquid dripping from the larger trunk.

In the meantime Mrs. Judd boarded the train and a porter placed her personal luggage by her side. At 7:45 a.m. on Monday the train arrived in Los Angeles. The two trunks were unloaded from the train and placed on a baggage rack. Winnie gave her personal luggage to a porter and left to get her brother, Jason. At noon she returned with Jason and went directly to the baggage rack containing the two trunks. Winnie didn't know that an unpleasant smell had started to emanate from the larger, leaking trunk. The district baggage agent had been notified and he was waiting for the trunks to be claimed. He demanded that Winnie and her brother open the trunk in his presence. Winnie stuttered a bit and finally said she didn't have the key, but would phone her husband, who would bring the key down to the station. She went through the motions of trying to contact him, but claimed she couldn't reach him. Finally, Winnie left the station with her brother, promising to return with the key.

Winnie never returned to the station, and later it was learned that Jason had loaned her five dollars and dropped her off at Sixth Street and Broadway. Back at the station the two trunks lay on the baggage rack, waiting for someone to claim them, but the afternoon wore on and no one showed up. The baggage agent grew increasingly suspicious and finally called the Los Angeles Police, who arrived on the scene and opened the larger trunk.

The officer who opened the trunks later testified:

"There were a number of books and papers, also some bloody clothing and a quilt. I pulled the quilt down at the corner where the blood appeared to be coming from until I uncovered a woman's head.

"Then I returned back out to the platform and, using the same key, opened the smaller of the two trunks. There were several sheets of blank paper, some of these bloodstained, and a light a statement—what you would call a sheet—blanket. This, when I pulled it apart, I discovered was a bundle wrapped up in a piece of woman's clothing. When I unwrapped it, it proved to be a foot and a leg, from the knee down, of a human being. I opened down a little further through the blanket and discovered a woman's head. That was as far as the examination went at that time."

At no time had Winnie made any attempt to conceal her identity, so she was immediately suspected of murder. Detectives took apart her apartment at 1130 East Brill Street, finding a set of surgical instruments and men's clothing. They also found a spent shell from a small-calibre weapon. At 2929 North 2nd Street police discovered several bloodstains on the carpet, and they noted that one piece of the carpet had been cut away. From the appearance of the two residences and the apparent physical strength that was required to dissect the bodies and place them in the trunks, the police surmised that more than one individual had been involved.

The police picked up Jason, and he frankly told them that he knew the trunk contained the bodies of Agnes Anne LeRoi and Hedvig

Samuelson because Winnie had confessed to him that she had killed them. He had accompanied his sister to the station hoping to pick up the trunks and dump them in the ocean. He told the authorities he had dropped his sister off at the street corner, and went on to say that she was a bit unstable, liable to go into fits of rage. Winnie's husband was also questioned, and while Dr. Judd readily admitted knowing the two girls, he could shed no light on Winnie's whereabouts. He pointed out that in his opinion his wife was mentally ill.

Where was the elusive Mrs. Judd? With each passing day her absence seemed to make the already strange case even more sensational. She was reported sighted in twelve different states, as well as Canada. Rewards were posted by the major newspapers for information leading to her apprehension. Through the newspapers Dr. Judd pleaded with Winnie to give herself up, and on October 23, six days after the murders were committed, she responded to this plea by telephoning her husband's lawyer. They agreed that they would meet in, of all places, the Alvarez and Moore Funeral Parlor. Dr. Judd and Jason were present when Winnie showed up. She looked terrible; her clothes were wrinkled and filthy, a stained rag was wrapped around her hand and wrist, and she complained of excruciating pain from her injured hand. The authorities sent her to the George Street Receiving Hospital, and so widespread was the interest in her case that a crowd of over 500 people had gathered, trying to catch a glimpse of the suspect. A twenty-five calibre bullet was removed from between Ruth's middle and index fingers, and she was taken to the Los Angeles County Jail and booked on suspicion of murder.

The day after Winnie gave herself up, a plumber in the Broadway Department Store in Los Angeles came forward with the interesting bit of news that he had found a scrap of paper in the ladies' restroom of the store with the name Judd on it. The police descended on the ladies' room. In the toilet drain they found ten handwritten telegraph pages directed to Dr. Judd in Mrs. Judd's handwriting. This letter was much the worse for wear, but only small parts were completely illegible. There was little doubt that the letter was genuine. Its contents are tantamount to a confession of murder; but more than that, it gives us some idea of what one human being felt on killing and dissecting another.

Darling:

A confession I've kept from you for life because I was so happy with you and loved you so why tell you. I am crazy only when I am very angry or too tired physically my brain goes wrong. One obsession I've always had is wanted or saying I had a baby. 1st when I was seven years old I wanted a baby at our house so bad I told at school that mother had one and for days told the neighbours we had one and such cute anticks it did far beyond an infants ability. Then when I was 16 on my birthday a fellow I was going with and I had a split up. I was furious my girl friend was the cause curiously I liked her just as well we chummed together, but this boys cousin antagonized me by crowing that some one could take him from me. I had taken her boy friend months before from her. The man's name was Fred Jensen he wished to be friends but liked my chum Laura Walters. It was O K until j-y Burns I hate her always will crowed (I had taken a fellow Ronald Carpenter from her later they married) I told Fred Jensen about it and asked him not to go with Laura. I loved Laura, but I hated Joy her crowing Fred thought I was doing it for meanness etc. and so finally as so many unmarried girls in that part of the woods were having babys I conceived of stating I was and would make Fred marry me if necessary. I was 16. He was 26. Fred Jensen never touched me. I had never had intercourse with him or with any man until I met you. Fred I believe is honest. He cried and cried and told daddy he'd never touch

me. He used to tell me I was crazy. I said well quit going with
Laura or I'll send you to the Pen. I won't be tormented by Joy
Burns. I was going pretty good at school then my teachers loved
me. I was good in English class my stories were published in the
school paper and in the city paper I made up in my 90 Botany
zoology. The teachers all like me and I did splendid in Modern
History my class mates like me and I them but I got so worked
up I quit school and said I was pregnant and swore out warrants
against Fred made darling dresses all kinds of dainty things I
later gave for little girls dolls. Fred would walk home from
church with me and tell me I was crazy. I said I knew it, but if I
started this thing I would finish it. I wanted him to go away until
I went back to college then go with Laura, but please not then
that I had an insane temper. So finally after about ten months I
decided I'd have to confess a lie or do something drastic so I
preceeded to hop out of my window one night in cold October
in my gown and I grabbed a few gunny sacks and overshoes and
run away and say I'd been kidnapped. First I wrote a letter that I
had a baby girl (Why I don't know) then I ran away was going
to get some clothes at my home sixteen miles from there and be
gone awhile and my Fred had had me kidnapped and I got away.
I brought suits against him and assumed a (as soon as) Joy
moved I dropped charges and that was the end. This is the first
time I have ever told this my parents believe Fred wicked. I did
it all myself and never have told it to anyone until now. I've
always wanted to tell Fred I was sorry He was a good boy He
thought it was funny until I had him arrested for rape and kidnapping etc. I'm sorry to tell you this doctor. Here is a
confession I should have carried to my death if I had been intimate with any man I would have told you but I didn't tell you
anything to hurt you I've wanted your respect confidence and

love. There in Mazatlan or rather Tyoltita I was sick a couple of days so as Mrs. Heinz had been so thrilled over being pregnant I decided Id say I was. I had hoped for three weeks I might be until I came unwell so when you moved I wrote I had had a miscarriage. Then again I told Mrs. . . . and Mrs. Aster I was where you saw I was menstruating the very week we left there. I don't know what possessed me to tell that I had a little boy. I even showed pictures of you with a baby and showed Dyers baby pictures as my baby who was with Mama so I'm crazy on that line. And aside from that and occasionally a rage I get into I seem quite bright. I was working so hard at Phoenix when you went to Bisbee then something went wrong in my head and I registered under an assumed name and called you up gave a fictitious address just to hear your voice and see you then cried all night for doing it. Got a car next morning to sooth my nerves at the garage below the Hotel and drove to Warren. Then finally wanted you to soothe me and told you I was there. You know how I cried and cried. I was crazy You said I was at the time, I came back and Mr. H. came out the next evening he had been on the coast and he said what's the matter you look terrible you look crazy. My two doctors said I looked terrible. I've written you for a month how my nerves were doing. Then Thursday Mr. H. bought the girls a new radio Mr. Adams had let them have his but they didn't like him so hated to use his radio. Mr. H. wanted me to get some other girl and go with him out to the house I knew a pretty little nurse who is taking Salvarsan but she has nothing contagious now. I certainly am not expecting them to do wrong, anyhow, so saw no harm she's pretty and can be interesting so we went out to the girls house. Dr. Brinckerhoff and a couple Mr. H. friends were there. The girls didn't like to it so Mr. H. asked us to have dinner with them I refused so he got dinner and came over to the house. The first time he has ever done it but it was a nice clean evening I truly didn't even take a drink you can ask. The remains of their drinks are in the ice box. Next day Ann came over and we had lunch together the remains of the dinner the night before. She wanted me to go home with her that night. Denise Reynolds was going. I had some histories to do and couldn't, I said if I get through in time I'll come over and play bridge, but I stayed all night. The next morning all three of us were yet in our pajamas when the quarrel began I was going hunting. They said if I did they would tell Mr. H. I had introduced him to a nurse who had syphillis. I said Ann you've no right to tell things from the office you know that only because you saw me get distilled water and syringes ready and she hasn't it contageoush the doctor lets her work nursing. Well Ann said I asked Denise and she thinks I should tell Mr. H. too. And he certainly won't think much of you for doing such a thing. You've been trying to make him like you and Mr. D. too getting him to move you and when I tell them you associated with and introduce them to girls who have syphillis they won't have a thing to do with you. And when we tell Mr. P. about it he won't take you hunting either. I said Sammy I'll shoot you if tell that we were in the kitchen just starting breakfast she came in with my gun and said she would shoot me if I went hunting with this friend. I threw my hand over the mouth of the gun and grabbed the bread knife she shot I jumped on her with all my weight and knocked her down in the dining room Ann yelled at us I fired twice I think and since Ann was going to blackmail me too if I went hunting by telling them this patient of Dr. Curtis' was syphillitic and would hand me over to the police I fired at her. There was no harm introducing this nurse who is very pretty to the men. One doesn't get it from contact but they were going to kill me for introducing this her initials are D. E. St. Josephs to their men friends Ann said before Sammy got the gun Ruth I could kill you for introducing that girl to...and if you go hunting I will tell them and they won't think your so darn nice anymore. I don't want to bring Mr. H. into this he has been kind to me when I was lonesome at the 1st place I worked and has trusted me with many secrets of all he did for the girls such as caring for Ann giving her extra money and the radio and he's been a decent fellow. It would separate he and his wife and he's been too decent. Mr. D. kept Ann in an apartment here in L.A. for several days then got her state room to Ph and she was mad enough to kill me when he helped me move me over. Part of my things are still the girls 3 hats, thermos bottle, black dress cook book, green scarf you got me in Mexico and a number of things. Doctor dear Im so sorry Sammy shot me whether it was the pain or what I got the gun and killed her. It was horrible to pack things as I did. I kept saying I've got to I've got to or I'll be hung I've got to or I'll be hung. I'm wild with cold hunger pain and fear now. Doctor darling if I hadn't got the gun from Sammy she would have shot me again. Forgive me not forget me. Live to take care of...sick. Doctor, but I'm true to you... The thots of being away from...it me crazy. Shall I give up to...don't think so the police will hang me. It was as much a battle as Germany and the U.S. I killed in defense. Love me yet doctor.

Blonde, blue-eyed Winnie, who at this time weighed only 109 pounds, was extradited to Phoenix, Arizona, and on November 3 she was charged with the murder of Agnes Anne LeRoi. If for any reason she should be acquitted on this charge, the second murder charge awaited her.

The trial of Winnie Ruth Judd began on January 19, 1932. The first four days were taken up with the selection of a jury, then the police who actually removed the contents of Mrs. Judd's luggage commenced to give their gory evidence. The large trunk held the intact body of Mrs. LeRoi, as well as two ladies' purses. Inside the purses were found two empty shells and one lead bullet. The smaller trunk contained the dissected body of Miss Samuelson; the feet and legs up to the knees were wrapped in ladies' clothing, while the head, arms, and upper part of the torso had been tossed in without any protective covering. The torso had been separated, with the lower portion being found in the brown leather suitcase which had accompanied Winnie on the train. Examination of the parts of the body revealed a gaping bullet wound in the head. The hatbox carried by Winnie on her lap for part of her trip to L.A. contained a set of surgical instruments and a .25 Colt automatic pistol.

Ballistics experts stated that the spent shells, the bullet from the victim's head and the one taken from the accused's hand all came from the same weapon; the gun which was found in Winnie's hatbox.

The jury found Winnie guilty of murder in the first degree, and she was sentenced to death by hanging. She was sent to the Arizona State Prison in Florence, where she was placed on death row. Throughout her ordeal her father, Reverend McKinnell, stood by her side, and was the first person to visit her in the death cell.

Winnie's case captured the imagination of the country, and indeed of the entire world. Every sentence she uttered, every bit of food she consumed, was reported in the press. If she was newsworthy during her trial, she was even more notorious now she had the added dimension of death hanging over her head. Her slender five-foot-seven-inch frame, together with her pale, pleasant face, belied the enormity of the dreadful deed of which she had been proven guilty. Legal manoeuvres by her lawyers continued to keep her case before the public, and she received hundreds of fan letters every week. Whenever things slackened, Winnie would provide the press with enough to keep them going.

The months dragged by, and she received many reviews and stays of execution. On one occasion she came within three days of being executed. Through it all, she acted calmly one minute and hysterically the next. Finally, in 1933, Winnie was judged insane and transferred to the Arizona State Hospital for the Insane.

Normally this would mark the end to a remarkable crime committed by a demented woman. But such was not to be the case with Mrs. Judd. She was to make headline news off and on for the next forty years.

Once Winnie acclimatized herself to the less restrictive routine of a hospital, she started to care for the very ill. She had training as a nurse, and now she applied this training to the benefit of her fellow inmates. Soon she won the sympathy and affection of all who met her.

On October 24, 1939, almost eight years after the double murder, Winnie made a model of herself asleep in bed, fooled her attendants and walked away from the institution. Before leaving she wrote a letter to the governor of Arizona, saying she was going to see her ailing father and then surrender. True to her word, she rapped on the hospital door a few days later and turned herself in. One month later, Winnie again fled the institution. The hospital came under attack for allowing its most illustrious inmate to leave almost at will. It is believed she had assistance in her escapes, for over the next twenty-four years she was to escape a further four times. On each occasion she was apprehended by the authorities, or gave herself up after a few days of freedom.

Then on the night of October 8, 1962, she escaped from the hospital for the seventh time, and completely disappeared for six and a half years. She changed her name to Susan Leigh Clark, studied practical nursing, and then obtained a job as a housekeeper to an elderly lady in a small central California town. She loved children and babysat for the wealthy families in the immediate area. When her elderly employer had a heart attack and died, Susan was so well-liked that one of the lady's daughters retained her to run her home.

During the routine investigation of a murder in the suburb where Susan worked, her parked car was dusted for fingerprints, and the prints were discovered to be those of Winnie Ruth Judd. She was quickly traced and identified. Again she was caught up in a series of legal manoeuvres in an attempt to gain her freedom. A few more years dragged by, and the once beautiful Winnie became a grey-haired, sixty-six-year-old woman. Finally, in December 1971, the governor of the State of Arizona paroled Mrs. Judd. She went back to live with the people who had known and loved her for six long years as Susan Leigh Clark.

The Worst Monster of All

Ed Gein lived with his brother Henry and his mother on a sixty-acre farm near Plainfield, Wisconsin. Ed's father passed away in 1940, and the two brothers fell under the sole influence of their mother, who completely dominated them. This bible-thumping matriarch seemed to dote on Ed more than she did on his brother Henry. Ed was deeply affected when Henry died while fighting a forest fire, just two years after the death of his father. That same year his mother, Augusta, suffered a crippling stroke. Now alone on the farm with his mother, Ed nursed her and took care of her every wish, but despite his sincere efforts to comfort her, her health deteriorated and she died within a year.

In the space of three years Ed had lost his entire family. In spite of this, people who knew him described him as being a cheerful, pleasant man of thirty-eight, with a winning smile and an even disposition. Left alone in the big farmhouse, he boarded off the upstairs, his mother's bedroom and the parlour. For his living quarters he used only a bedroom, the kitchen and a small shed.

Ed received a small soil conservation subsidy, and as a result stopped farming his land. Instead he became a handyman around Plainfield, and was sometimes called upon to babysit for people he had known all his life. He always brought the children bubble gum, and they all loved him.

From 1947 to 1957, Ed Gein came and went among the seven hundred citizens of Plainfield. He lived alone, and while he may have been considered a bit odd, he was certainly thought of as a harmless, soft-spoken guy who wouldn't hurt a fly.

Then one blustery November day in 1957 Ed walked into a hardware store in Plainfield, took a .22 rifle out of a display case, loaded it, then shot and killed the owner, Mrs. Bernice Worden. He loaded the body and the cash register into the store's pickup truck. Then he locked up and drove home.

When Mrs. Worden's son Frank returned from deer hunting that Saturday afternoon, he found his mother missing. Nothing like this had ever happened to Worden before. His mother had always been reliable, and he knew she would never leave the store without notifying someone of her whereabouts. Then he noticed a small pool of blood on the floor. Now beside himself with worry, he had the presence of mind to check the last sales slip of the morning, and found it was for half a gallon of antifreeze. He remembered that on the previous night Ed Gein had said that he would be around to pick up some antifreeze the next morning. Frank called the police and told them of his mother's disappearance and his suspicions of Gein.

Sheriff Art Schley and Captain Lloyd Schoephoester drove over to Ed's farmhouse and knocked on the front door. After repeated knocking it became apparent that Ed was not at home. The Sheriff and the Captain entered the unlocked house, and moved about the musty neglected rooms by the light of an oil lamp and a flashlight.

As they groped in the semi-darkness the beam of their flashlight fell upon a bloodcurdling sight. There, mounted upon the wall, was a woman's death mask made of human skin. The Sheriff's hand shook as he played the shaft of light along the wall, revealing three more grisly masks. Lying in the debris of the rooms were ten female skulls cut off at the eyebrows; these had obviously been used as pots and pans. An adult pair of leotards made of human skin was found, and even some of the chairs in the house had been repaired with skin. A human heart sat gently simmering in a pot on the stove; and in the shed the butchered body of a headless woman was hanging by the heels. The officers felt as if the earth had swallowed them up and they were probing the depths of hell.

While the Sheriff and the Captain were being revolted by their discoveries, other officers went to a grocery store in West Plainfield where Ed sometimes shopped. Sure enough, he was leisurely eating supper with the couple who owned the store. Ed was taken into custody and immediately started to talk.

It appeared that Ed Gein operated on two levels; one was the little fifty-one-year-old handyman who bought bubble gum for children, while the other was a cannibal, necrophile, ghoul, murderer and transvestite. Seldom if ever has the world had the misfortune to have several of the most revolting characteristics known to man wrapped up in one individual.

Ed started out relatively normal, and it wasn't until he was alone on the farm that he began to fantasize about sex. His late mother's influence made him suspicious of all women, and shy and afraid in their presence. His sexual drive had no healthy outlet, so when he read in the newspaper of a woman who had just been buried, his tortured mind hit upon the idea of robbing the grave. That night he went to the cemetery and carefully removed the fresh corpse from the grave, meticulously replacing everything at the gravesite so that his theft would not be discovered. He placed the corpse in his truck and returned to the farm. The perverted mind of Ed Gein now reasoned that he had his own private woman, as indeed he did. Ed's perversions grew in intensity, driving him to eat parts of the bodies and to make garments of their skin.

When the officers searched the house of horror they carried away the grisly artifacts of murder and perversion. One of the items they removed was the head of Mary Hogan, who had been a tavern keeper in the small town of Bancroft, and had disappeared in 1953. In all, eleven heads were taken from the Gein farm. Only two, Mrs. Worden and Mary Hogan, had actually been killed by Gein. The other nine heads belonged to bodies which had been stolen from the local graveyard.

Ballistics experts proved that the .22 calibre bullets which had killed Mrs. Worden were fired from the gun Ed had taken from the hardware store. When Ed was confronted with this evidence, he readily admitted killing Mrs. Worden. He claimed that when the urge for a woman came over him, he operated like someone in a trance and had no control over his own actions. Each time, he suffered from enormous guilt feelings, swearing he would never do it again.

Ed Gein was judged insane, and in 1957 he was committed to the Waupan State Hospital for life.

Mother in the Lake

Wayne Ford and his mother Minnie lived together in a red brick bungalow in the middle-class area of the Toronto suburb of Willowdale. Lorne Ford, his father, had died of natural causes when Wayne was fourteen. He left his wife and only child rather well-off financially; his estate amounted to over $100,000.

Minnie almost immediately had to cope with the arduous task of bringing up a strapping teenager without a man around the house. To neighbours and relatives, the short, pleasant widow seemed to be succeeding in raising her son, but they didn't know that all was not as it appeared to be at the Ford residence. Wayne was now a six-footer weighing 180 pounds, struggling through his teenage years without the benefit of the steadying influence of a father. He felt that he was being smothered by his mother, who doled out money to him and sometimes even curtailed his freedom by denying him the use of the family Cadillac. Like many middle-aged widows left with one teenaged son, Minnie doted on her only boy. Or at least friends and neighbours called it doting; Wayne called it picking on him.

The reasons for Wayne's resentment of his mother are not as important as the fact that he started answering her back, until the pair were often shouting at each other. They seemed to argue incessantly about everything, including Wayne's friends, his long hair and his schoolwork.

By 1963 Wayne was a Grade 10 student at Earl Haig Collegiate, and his sporadic attendance was a cause of great concern to Minnie. She also worried when she gave him the Cadillac, watching anxiously as he and his friends roared out of the driveway. In the early spring of 1963 Wayne smashed up the car, incurring over $1,000 in damage, which was covered by insurance. Minnie was furious, not only because it deprived her of the car while it was being repaired, but because the accident confirmed that Wayne wasn't to be trusted with the vehicle.

The shouting and bickering erupted into a full-fledged battle the day Wayne came home from school and found the repaired car parked in the driveway. When Wayne asked for the car keys, Minnie refused. The pair started to argue violently. Wayne told his mother to go to hell; she retaliated by slapping his face. He returned the blow. Wayne later claimed that his mother then grabbed an ice pick, forcing him to retreat to his bedroom, where he picked up a small baseball bat. The argument moved out of the bedroom, down a hall, and into the kitchen. In the kitchen Wayne struck his mother several blows to the head with the bat, one blow in particular landing squarely on her left temple, causing Minnie to stagger and finally sink slowly to the floor.

Wayne sat down on a kitchen chair and stared at the body of his mother. He was later to state that he assumed she was dead. He thought of calling a hospital, except, he reasoned, there wasn't anything they could do. He even thought of calling the police, but he knew that if he did that he would be in a great deal of trouble. Finally he got up off the chair, placed a plastic bag over his mother's head and threw a sheet over her body. Then he jumped into the Cadillac and drove over to see his friend, Ron Walli. A fellow student at Earl Haig Collegiate, Ron stood six feet tall, and like Wayne, was sixteen years old. Wayne confided to his friend that he had killed his mother.

From this point our narrative differs in detail and in insinuation, depending on whose version we wish to accept, Walli's or Ford's. We do know that Walli agreed to go back to the Ford house and help his friend. Walli claimed that he was influenced by a .38 calibre revolver which was lying at Ford's feet on the floor of the Cadillac. The facts do not change materially—we still have two sixteen-year-old boys from good homes matter-of-factly discussing the murder of the mother of one of them.

The two youngsters entered the brick bungalow and were confronted by the body. Wayne removed the gory sheet and noticed that there was now blood on the floor as well. Wayne grasped his mother's arms while Ron took hold of the legs, and the boys carried the 140-pound body down into the basement. The head clunked on each step as they made their way slowly down the stairs. Blood splattered the steps and walls, until finally they were all the way down. Then Wayne took hold of the arms and dragged his mother's body across the floor to the rear room of the basement. A ten-inch-wide smear of blood showed where the body had been dragged, so the two friends took a mop and pail and cleaned up the kitchen, stairs, and basement floor. Then they stuffed Minnie's body into a box about three feet square, tied up their package with a green plastic garden hose, and went upstairs to make plans to dispose of the body. Ron Walli went home and told his parents that he would be sleeping over at the Fords' the following night so that Mrs. Ford, Wayne and himself could get away early on Saturday morning to go to their cottage at Lake Couchiching, where they would be spending the weekend. On Friday morning the boys went to school, returning to Wayne's house at lunchtime. They didn't go back in the afternoon; instead, they sandpapered and repainted the stairs. They then had a few drinks and took in a movie at a drive-in. After the movie they returned to Ford's house, and with much huffing and puffing, they managed to lug the box containing Minnie Ford's body up the stairs and placed it in the trunk of the Cadillac.

300

Then Wayne and Ron took off for the Ford cottage. A mile or so from their destination they tried to dig a grave with a shovel they had borrowed from a garage, but the ground was too hard and they gave up. After placing the box containing the body in a small garage beside the Ford cottage, they drove back to Toronto.

On Saturday morning they invited another boy, Larry Metcalfe, to join them for the weekend at Lake Couchiching. The three took in a Saturday afternoon movie, then headed for the lake. They started drinking on Saturday and continued to drink steadily until Sunday morning. They were tired and hung over until Sunday night, when Ford and Walli had a strange conversation. Ford confided to Walli that his mother hadn't died easily—she had continued to struggle even after she had received the blows with the baseball bat. It had been necessary to stick an ice pick in her head. Ford told Walli the handle had broken off and the pick was still in his mother's head. He asked his friend to get a pair of pliers and pull the spike out of his mother's skull. Walli flatly refused. Later Ford went out of the cottage, returning with a foot and a half of railway track. He asked Walli to take it out to the garage and knock his mother's teeth out with the heavy piece of metal. Walli agreed to this, but when he opened the box he became terrified and left, placing the piece of railway track in the garage. When Ford asked if the job was done, Walli lied and said it was.

That same Sunday evening Wayne and Ron decided to tell Metcalfe that Minnie Ford's body was in a box in the garage. Ford explained to Metcalfe that he had killed his mother, and Metcalfe claims that he was threatened into going along with disposing of the body. Ford's version is that Metcalfe was a willing partner, doing a friend a favour.

The three boys found a child's cart and wheeled the box containing the body down to the dock. They placed the box in an old rowboat and rowed about three hundred yards into the lake. When they started to push the box overboard, the boat capsized, plunging the three boys into the water.

Wayne pushed the box and it sank. Ron swam to shore, got another boat, rowed back to the overturned boat and picked up his two friends.

The boys dried their clothing, had a few drinks and decided to go to a dance in Orillia. On the way Wayne smashed the car into a telephone pole and ended up in the Orillia police station explaining the accident. They managed to give satisfactory answers, then walked to the dance where they got a lift back to the Ford cottage. Here they started to drink again, sleeping until Monday afternoon. On Tuesday they discussed the murder, agreeing that if they all kept their mouths shut no one would ever be the wiser. Ron hitchhiked to Toronto and he and his father returned to Lake Couchiching to pick up the other two boys.

By Thursday some of Minnie Ford's friends started to wonder why they couldn't reach her. Becoming suspicious, they called the police, who made a routine inquiry at the Ford residence. Wayne showed the police into the house, explaining that he and two friends had gone to the family cottage on Saturday morning, expecting his mother to join them sometime during the weekend, but she hadn't arrived nor had he seen her since. Walli and Metcalfe were also interrogated, but stuck to their story of expecting Mrs. Ford to join them at the cottage. Wayne insisted that his mother just took off and left without any warning.

The days became weeks, then months. Wayne started to miss school, then quit altogether to try his hand at a series of odd jobs, but he stuck to none. At first his mother's disappearance was actively investigated as a missing persons case, but gradually the investigation wound down, and the police appeared only sporadically at the Ford home.

As the months passed, Wayne started to get into scrapes with the law. He was charged with carrying a concealed weapon, then was caught in possession of stolen goods. A year after his mother's disappearance he was sentenced to a year in jail for possession of stolen goods and petty theft. When he got out he was charged with theft again, and drew two years in the reformatory. On May 17, 1966, three years after his mother's disappearance, he escaped from the reformatory but was quickly recaptured, receiving an additional six months in the Kingston Penitentiary for his escapade.

While he was serving his time in Kingston Pen, the box containing what was left of his mother's body bobbed to the surface of Lake Couchiching. On November 23, 1966, two Toronto detective sergeants went to Kingston Penitentiary to formally charge Wayne with the murder of his mother. Later, during Ford's trial, the detective who had broken the news to Ford told of the conversation which had taken place between them on that day.

"At 10:50 a.m. I was at the Kingston Penitentiary and I was ushered into a small room adjacent to what is known as the board reception room, and there for the first time I saw the male accused, Wayne Ford. He was standing alone in this room. I introduced myself and Sergeant Alexander to Ford, saying, 'I am Sergeant Crawford. This is Sergeant Alexander. We are from the Metropolitan homicide squad. We have a warrant for your arrest on a charge of murder. Do you wish to say anything in answer to the charge? You are not obliged to say anything unless you wish to do so, but whatever you say will be taken down in writing and may be given in evidence.' Now there was a pause of a few moments, and then I said, 'Do you want to talk to me now or in Toronto?' and the accused replied, 'I will talk to you in Toronto'."

In the days following his arrest Wayne became very depressed. It was as if a great burden had been partially lifted from his shoulders. Now that his mother's body had been found, he was anxious to have the entire matter cleared up without delay. He wrote to the arresting officers. The letter was edited before being admitted into evidence at his trial; it is presented here in the same form as it was placed before the jury:

> Dear Sirs:
> This letter is to inform you that I intend to plead guilty to the charge of Capital Murder. I wish to wave (sic) all evidence in this matter in court also, and ask that this case be pushed through court as quickly as possible.
> I am not receiving any visits or mail as of today. There is no need for anyone to visit me now.
> I remain, Wayne L. Ford.

In the middle of May 1967, four years after his mother disappeared, Wayne Ford stood trial for her murder. His two friends, Larry Metcalfe and Ron Walli, testified to helping him get rid of his mother's body. Their versions of the details differed from those stated by Wayne. They both claimed to have been forced and coerced by Wayne into disposing of the body.

Psychiatrist Dr. Robert Turner testified that Ford was a psychopathic personality. He was unable to cope with stress, had no sense of responsibility and was unable to control violent impulses. The jury brought in a verdict of non-capital murder. The now towering six-foot-three-inch Wayne Ford sat impassively as the judge said, "It is the sentence of this court that you be imprisoned for the balance of your natural life." Wayne Ford is still in prison serving his sentence.

The Savage Clan

Rumours drifted back to Edinburgh that travellers in the south-west part of Scotland were disappearing. People would start out from one town and drop out of sight before reaching their destination. Not a trace of a violent act was ever uncovered. Alarmed by the frequency of the disappearances, the King took a personal interest in the strange happenings, finally sending his own officers to investigate. They picked up a few tramps in the Galloway area and hanged them, but the mystery still wasn't solved.

But then one fine day, a man and his wife were returning from a fair in a neighbouring village, both riding the same horse. Suddenly, without warning, a group of sub-human savages surrounded the terrified pair. The woman was pulled from the horse to the ground, where one of the savages cut her throat from ear to ear and disembowelled her. Her husband fought with all the strength he could muster, slashing at the frenzied tribe with his sword, to little avail. Meanwhile, some of the savages were tearing at the dead woman's body, ripping off pieces of flesh and eating it raw.

A group of about thirty citizens, returning from the same fair as the man and woman, came upon this gruesome scene. As quickly as they had appeared, the cannibals vanished into the surrounding countryside, and the newly-widowed traveller was rescued.

Now all the disappearances that had taken place over the past twenty-five years took on a new aspect. Could this band of savages have been practising cannibalism for a quarter of a century without anyone surviving their attacks? Even in those distant times the horror of the possibility brought King James himself and four hundred men from Edinburgh to investigate.

They started off where the most recent attack had taken place. The posse proceeded across the moors to the sea, where dark tunnels cut into the steep, rocky shore. They were not going to bother searching these narrow openings, thinking they were too small for any appreciable number of fugitives to hide, when suddenly one of their dogs started barking at the entrance to one of the cracks in the rocks, and finally several dogs entered the tunnel. Lighting torches, the men squeezed into the narrow openings one by one. The odour emanating from the warren almost sent them back. Abruptly the hole in the rocks opened into a huge cave.

There, lurking on shelves and in corners, crouching and shielding their eyes from the light, were the figures of human beings. Though they put up a fierce struggle they were outnumbered and quickly overpowered by the King's men. In all, forty-eight people were taken from the cave. Inside their lair the soldiers found assorted arms, legs, heads, and torsos of victims, some hanging from the ceiling and others preserved in pickle. The soldiers buried the human remains and took their prisoners to Edinburgh.

Who were these wild, inhuman savages, and who was their leader? Little by little the King's men pieced the story together. Sawney Beane was born in East Lothian, a few miles from Edinburgh, and was, as they used to say, a ne'er-do-well. His parents were hardworking ditchdiggers, but Sawney was lazy and tried to get out of performing any manual labour that was thrust upon him. He played around with loose women and eventually took up with a permanent mate without benefit of clergy. They ran away and lived together in a big cave near the sea, which not only provided them with shelter but also gave them a head-quarters from which to strike out at travellers and rob them of their money and goods. Soon they began to fear detection, and commenced to murder their victims, dragging the bodies into their cave.

We can imagine Sawney and his mate during one of the frequent famines which swept the country in those days. He now had several off-spring; food was scarce and there were few travellers to rob. The family attacks and kills one lone stranger, dragging the body to their lair only to find that the victim has no money or food. The thought occurs to Sawney that to eat the human flesh means life to him and his family. At the beginning the meat was probably cooked over a flame, and from there it was only a small step to eating it raw.

The children born to Sawney and his mate, and other offspring born incestuously later, were brought up eating human flesh, and to them this practice was most natural. In all, Sawney is reported to have had eight sons and six daughters. Various other combinations went to make up the total of forty-eight tribe members.

As the family grew, their ability to make successful attacks on groups of five or six foot-travellers increased, and they became a still bigger terror in the countryside. They always avoided molesting more than two men on horseback, for the cunning Sawney knew that he could ill afford to let one victim get away. For twenty-five years no one did escape, until that day when the traveller and his wife were returning from the fair.

There was some speculation as to how many innocent souls fell vic-tim to Sawney and his family during the twenty-five years they terrorized southwest Scotland. Estimates range from a minimum of one hundred up to one thousand, making them one of the highest-scoring families of mass murderers in recorded history.

The whole family was immured in the Tolbooth Prison in Edinburgh. It was thought that a trial was unnecessary, and every last one of them was executed. The men had their hands and legs cut off and were allowed to bleed to death. The women were made to watch this gruesome sight and were then burned alive in three large fires. It is reported that not one showed any remorse, and all cursed their tormentors until the end.

In Cold Storage

D avid Wilfred Todd was born on May 3, 1934, in Hamilton, Ontario. From the outset he wasn't interested in school and only continued until he had completed grade six. Dave was something of a loner, a born watcher rather than a doer. After his brief academic career he started on a variety of labouring jobs not designed to tax his mental abilities nor make him a fortune, and by the time he was twenty-five he had held over thirty different menial jobs which he quit for one reason or another. Sometimes his reasons were not all that good—he loved to skip work and wander the streets of Hamilton, just bumming around looking in the shop windows.

Todd stood five feet eight inches, with receding curly hair, a rather weak voice, and the limp handshake of the introvert. When you spoke to him he had the annoying habit of staring blankly back at you, and it was difficult to know what he was thinking about.

Grace Filmore was somewhat taller than Dave, but she didn't seem to mind, and dated him throughout the spring and summer of 1959. Though some of Grace's friends made no secret of the fact that they thought Dave wasn't good enough for her, she married him on August 17, 1959.

After their marriage the young couple (Dave was twenty-five and Grace twenty) lived in Hamilton, where Dave held a job as desk clerk at the Windsor Hotel for three years, which was something of a record for him. When the manager of the hotel left to open his own restaurant, Dave went to work for him. The new job didn't work out because Grace objected to the long night hours, and after three months he left to join Hamilton Cotton Company, where he stayed one full year.

Like many young couples, the Todds felt that Toronto had more opportunities for them, and in 1965 they moved to Ontario's capital. They had just moved into 1 Deauville Lane, when Dave got a steady job at Dunlop Rubber. He remained gainfully employed at Dunlop until the company closed its plant in 1970. Grace, who worked for the North American Life Insurance Company in Hamilton, managed to get a transfer to the Toronto office of the same company.

When Dunlop closed its plant, putting Dave out of work, the Todd marriage started to go steeply downhill. Instead of actively trying to find a job, Dave became paranoically suspicious of his wife's actions, and entirely without justification began to suspect Grace of being unfaithful to him. He kept phoning her office to make sure she was there. It got so bad that he made a point of picking her up at work so that she wouldn't have the opportunity to go with anyone else.

Occasionally Grace's company had a party and she and Dave would attend. Grace was charming and mixed easily with her fellow employees, but Dave would sulk in a corner, watching his wife. If any man put his arms around her or gave her a playful peck on the cheek, he seethed with silent rage. At home they started to argue incessantly, and Dave accused Grace of taking birth control pills to prevent her becoming pregnant by another man, though she explained that the pills were to relieve her pains when she menstruated.

Dave later claimed that at this time Grace would have nothing more to do with him in bed. She had never refused him before, but now she turned her back on him. He retaliated, truthfully or not, by bragging to her that he had slept with another woman. Grace, who knew her husband, probably didn't believe him, but the bickering went on. All their small differences, which hadn't seemed to matter earlier, came to the surface and festered, causing irreparable chasms in what had been a relatively happy marriage.

At the North American Life parties Grace loved to dance, while Dave sulked on the sidelines. Later his comment was, "I would be lucky to see her for about an hour without some other guy getting her on the floor." The scuttlebutt at the office affairs often revolved around salaries, while the unemployed Dave, hands deep in his pockets, became red-faced at what he considered the bragging conversation of the insurance people.

And so it went. Sometimes Dave would console himself by consuming twenty-four beers in one evening. After so much beer he occasionally fell asleep on the chesterfield, and finally he ended up sleeping there alone while Grace had the bed to herself. This became more or less the permanent arrangement. Throughout all the arguing Grace worked, earning the money on which they both lived. She took care of all the bills and even accompanied her husband when he bought a new pair of pants. Grace saw to it that Dave always had a few dollars in his pocket, but she often quarrelled with him for spending his allowance on liquor. When they went out in the evening for a few drinks at the nearby Mississippi Belle it was Grace who picked up the bar bills.

The few acquaintances they used to meet at the well-known club later remarked that even here Grace came off as being far more socially accomplished than her husband. He again took up the wallflower stance, and peered in from the perimeters of conversations. In fact, poor Dave Todd began to believe that now he was steadily unemployed he was losing his wife's love and respect, yet he continued to do nothing about it. He became obsessed with hovering over her—keeping his eye on her, ever watchful to catch her in one of the unfaithful acts which were taking place only in his mind. Everyone who ever knew Grace stated that she was a respectable woman in every way.

Sometimes Dave, in his shy, introverted fashion, would try to initiate some activity he knew they both enjoyed. On Thursday night, July 29, 1971, he had talked Grace into going on a camping trip to one of Ontario's parks the next morning. She agreed, and things were looking bright for the Todds when they rose on Friday.

Just before Christmas 1971, Charles Cassidy, a twenty-one-year-old acquaintance of Todd's, told him that he could move in with his family at 4 Vendôme Place. Cassidy's family included his sister Catherine, who was fifteen, and his mother. Todd had been having trouble getting up the rent at his previous residence at Deauville Lane, and was going around mumbling something about his wife leaving him. Cassidy knew that Todd had recently got a job as a truck driver, and felt that if given a break he would straighten out.

The whole Cassidy family thought it strange that Todd had brought along an electric freezer. Not only was it an unusual piece of furniture to have near the dining area, but it was locked, sealed and never used. It just sat there, humming away.

On the night of January 12, 1972, Charles Cassidy, his sister Catherine, their mother and two friends, John Moore and Layne Jackson, were spending an evening at home watching television. The program they were viewing was a thriller, One Step Beyond. The young people joked about the story because of the weird plot which at one point revealed a body in a trunk. Right in their dining area they had a mysterious freezer humming away, while its owner slept peacefully in an upstairs bedroom. Well, they thought, it is quite one thing for a piece of fiction to have bodies in trunks, but in real life those things just don't happen. Still, the thought of something sinister in the freezer was too fascinating to resist. A screwdriver was produced; the screws holding down the hinges came out easily. Laughing and joking, the young people peered into the freezer. There, among the turkey pies and vegetables, was the tanned, solidly frozen body of Grace Todd.

Placid, timid David Todd readily confessed to killing his wife, but steadfastly maintained that he never meant any harm to come to her. He was charged with non-capital murder. A jury heard the psychiatric evidence in a report given by Dr. Peter Watts Rousell at the trial. The doctor had many interviews with Todd, and related in his own words what had taken place that Friday morning of July 30, 1971.

"She had taken a shower the next morning and they were having another verbal fight. She had made the quip about his being an old man and he quoted her, in addition to these remarks, as saying further 'You couldn't satisfy any of the whores around town. We are not man and wife. I tolerate you; I don't love you.' He quotes her as going on—he, of course, accusing her of walking out on him, which he went on to say was exactly what she was going to do after she had had an hour's sleep following her shower. She lay down on the chesterfield; she went on, 'By the time I am back to work, I will be under a new roof and when I get out today I am going to walk into the first man's bed I can get into.' He says 'I took it that she had another man because she had been mixing all of a sudden this two years.' It was very evident as he described it, that this was in his mind because of his telephoning her so frequently, always asking her, as he described to me himself, who was in the office with her at any given time, and he says frankly 'I was at the point of watching everybody, even my brother-in-law and my brothers.' Concerning his brothers also, he disliked their putting their hands on her when talking to her or holding her arm. He said he was becoming rather depressed, wanting to avoid large crowds; just wanting to be with Grace where they would be alone; where he could have her all to himself. This was one of the chief reasons for camping as a vacation, to be alone with her then he didn't have to worry about anybody else putting their hands on her. He indicated to me that they had planned to go to Simcoe. As this morning argument, Friday July 30th, occurring about 11:00 a.m. had built up and she had told him she was going to walk out, that she was going on no camping trip with him, he said 'I accused her of running out on me with another man and she laughed in my face.' She again referred to his being a watch-dog and she was referring, of course, to his picking her up at work and the constant telephone calls. He had not been sleeping during that year prior to the tragedy, staying on the chesterfield to satisfy his wife but occasionally putting away a case of 24 beer, almost, while he was on that chesterfield in one night. This would bring a further rebuke from his wife that he was being a drunk and if he had not finished all the beer, to go back and finish what was left. His appetite was not so good. One year ago he says he weighed 200 pounds and, as one can observe Mr. Todd now, he gives his present weight as 150 pounds and is certainly no 200. Most of the weight has been lost since his wife's death. Apparently she criticized his weight, too, calling him 'hippo,' 'pear-shaped,' and telling him he was a disgrace to be seen in the street with being so fat. She told him to go on a diet. Apparently most of this weight had in fact gone on during the last two years prior to the tragedy.

"Meantime, returning to the fateful morning of July 30th with his wife's bitter statement, he said he was burning inside, wanting to scream, get something out of his system, a feeling going up into his chest and his head but somehow couldn't just let go. When she allegedly further taunted him that Friday July morning that he was pussy-footing and screaming about women and he couldn't satisfy any of them anyway, at this point he had been telling her, while she lay not looking at him on the chesterfield, he being behind her, 'Won't you look at me while I am talking?' He indicated to me that he asked her three times and Grace had turned her back to him as she lay on the chesterfield. Having just said she was going to leave him after an hour's sleep, at this point he reached over and got the gun which was loaded, as he knew, and cocked. He says, 'I walked across and picked it up and I pointed it at her. Then she turned; I guess she was scared. She twisted and put her arm up and somehow I flipped it and it went off.' As he described this to me, he made this gesture. She—imitating her lying on the chesterfield, raising the right arm, head turning and as I understand it from his description, he was standing I think behind her, but this is the gesture that he imitated for me as he quoted those words; the turning to the right and looking back, bringing up the right arm. His wife, of course, fell back on the chesterfield. He said, 'I tried to talk up to her to say I was sorry and then I felt her pulse, her stomach and I got some towels to try and stop the bleeding.' He also indicated to me that he was crying at this point. He thought of an ambulance but just sat, scared, for an hour, wondering what to do. For the time being, he says, 'I put her in the freezer. I was going to call Bob Rowe who I respect; he is a man's man to get his advice but I didn't. I was in the house for an hour. The car was full of things. I brought some of them up. I was talking to Larry Hough while I was unloading the car. I went to the bar but Bob was not at the bar and tomorrow never

came when I would do something.' In June 1971 he indicated
that he had told Larry Hough that when they returned from
vacation, that is, he and Grace, that Larry could move in with
them. Then it seems that Larry and friends came up and then of
course with the freezer present, he had to start telling stories to
'cover up.' I was particularly struck by the cover-up stories so
frequently alluding to Grace running off with another man, of
course it became his preoccupation all the way along. He himself slept on the chesterfield and regarding his state at that time,
bearing in mind that the freezer with his wife's body was so
close to him, he said, 'I felt my wife was with me. I dreamt
good dreams, all the good times we had had together in the past.
I was going to look at her twice, but somehow I couldn't.
Someone was coming in.' At this point, when he was retreating
into the happy and comfortable past, into what might be called
his world of fantasy, of course the intrusion of the harsh reality
of that freezer was always in front of him; the reality of keeping
the secret of the body kept intruding on him. He invented more
and more stories to cover her disappearance. The cash was running out. He was no manager of money. He admitted to feeling
hopeless, as he has felt all the way along, drifting along, letting
things happen. He has never thought of suicide during all this
time. He felt very tired, he complains, after that. He lost a lot of
weight, 50 pounds, he quoted in all and is uptight. It is notable
at this point of my examination he is giving a fairly straight,
apparently, description of his actions and that is over this long
period of time."

J. Crossland, Q.C., acting for the Crown, wanted to know what
caused mild-mannered David Todd to kill his wife. Dr. Rousell gave the
opinion that after examining Todd, he felt that the accused didn't have

the capacity at the time of the killing to form the intention. Crossland asked for the doctor's reasons for his opinion.

Dr. Rousell continued:

"This accused man, Mr. Todd, in my opinion first of all can be labelled under a true psychiatric diagnosis as an inadequate personality. Now although this is a true diagnosis, it does not imply that such a person is in any way insane within the legal meaning...

"The man himself, a wallflower, a quiet, always pleasant, easy-to-get-on-with individual, yet so inadequate in so many ways, could function and in fact, as his work record bears out, did function very well provided that he had that strong woman on whom he depended so much. She—it was in a sense very much like a mother-child relationship that really lay between them, so he is basically a clinging person, who when he has got somebody strong behind him, can function and function very adequately in a job so long as he doesn't have to take too much of the responsibilities. That is his basic personality diagnosis: inadequate personality."

The doctor then traced Todd's escalating possessiveness up to the morning of Friday July 30, 1971:

"...when there was the same set of accusations and recriminations, as he described it, on both sides but with one difference and the difference was that this time she said, as he quoted, 'I am leaving you; I am not going camping with you. I will be under another roof when I come back from vacation,' so in the situation we have his description of his pointing the gun at her, trying to force her, in my opinion, as he expressed it to me, to make her stay and her subsequent actions as he described them which led to the gun going off and the subsequent tragedy that followed... after all, his basic motive was to keep his wife. Following her death the only way he could, in his mind, keep her was to go into what is called a psychosis and this is a different matter because this does fall within the legal definition of insanity and a psychosis, by definition, is a disorder of thinking, feeling and behaviour accompanied by what is called a break with reality... Following Grace's death, David Todd, in my opinion, became, so to speak, split into two different states of consciousness and behaviour. First, the harsh reality of everyday living and having a roof over one's head, the presence of his wife's body in a freezer a few yards from him, knowing that money had to be obtained, knowing that he felt he had to conceal what he had done, this is the level of reality which is impossible to get away from. It was there. On the other hand, there is the seemingly incomprehensible behaviour of this person who sleeps only a few yards—and makes a point of it—from the freezer containing the body of his loved one and his fantasy life, as he quotes from reality, dreams and indulges in all his happy memories, if you like, almost denying inside himself that she was dead, so in one way he keeps her alive through his happy memories and hangs onto the body and yet, in another way, he has to cover up and make up stories so he is forced into reality by the harsh things of life one moment and retreating from reality into his happy fantasies the next, and the mind in such chaos as a person—occurs in a person who is under extreme tension. He started to change his behaviour. He went around with the young people far more and of course had to cover up with his stories about the refrigerator to them, and he lost 50 pounds in weight which, of course, is a leading symptom of... a major nervous breakdown in the way I have defined it. An instance of his communication over the happiness aspect of it was his remark to, I think it was, Mr. Moore that she had come in one night and kissed him on the cheek. This is a fairly good example of the type of fantasy, wishful thinking, removed from the harsh reality of the situation which he appears to have been going through."

David Wilfred Todd changed his plea to guilty of manslaughter and was sentenced to ten years in Kingston prison with the stipulation that he receive psychiatric treatment.

The Long Arm of the Law

D r. Hawley Harvey Crippen was born in Clearwater, Michigan, in 1863, and from the very beginning of his academic career he was considered to be a good student. He was singleminded in his desire to become a doctor, and to this end he studied medicine in Cleveland and New York. After he qualified, he did post-graduate work, becoming an eye and ear specialist. Then he completed his education with further studies in London, England, before returning to the United States, where, between 1885 and 1893, he moved frequently, practising in Detroit, Salt Lake City, New York, St. Louis, Toronto, and Philadelphia.

In 1887 the doctor married one Charlotte Bell, who died, presumably of natural causes, in 1890. After his wife's death Crippen returned to New York, where he again set up his practice. Dr. Crippen was now a mature thirty-one years old. He was five feet seven inches tall, with a decidedly receding hairline, protruding eyes that stared out from behind thick-lensed spectacles, and a small, well-kept moustache. While not altogether a ladies' man, Crippen was neat in appearance and a pleasant, intelligent conversationalist. When he was practising in New York he met a seventeen-year-old medical secretary called Kunigunde Mackamotzki, who had had the good sense to change her name to Cora

Turner. The doctor took one look at Cora's substantial bust, slim waist and well-turned ankle and said, "That's for me." The love-stricken pair were married almost immediately.

By 1899 the Crippens were living in Philadelphia, and it was here that Cora let the mild Hawley in on a little secret—she wanted to be an opera star. Now, Crippen was no student of voice, but he had heard his wife sing and knew she had a pleasant soprano warble. On occasion at parties he would become rather proud when she rendered a tune or two, but an operatic career—that was something else. The little doctor looked quizzically at his wife. Yes, she said, she seriously wanted to study music. Hawley suggested that they relax in the bedroom and continue the discussion about singing another day. No, said Cora, there would be no sex in the Crippen household until she was promised that he would finance her singing lessons. She received a firm promise that very night.

Soon Crippen found that every cent he made was going for singing lessons for his wife. Cora was extremely serious when it came to her career, even to the point of taking the professional name of Belle Elmore. A few years passed, and Cora's singing lessons had practically bankrupted the distraught Crippen. Besides the financial difficulties her singing had brought him, deep down in his heart he didn't think she was all that good.

By 1900 the couple had been man and wife for eleven years. Like all of us, they had grown older; the doctor was now a worry-racked forty-two, and his once receding hairline was in full flight, while Cora, at twenty-eight, had begun to put on weight and was becoming slovenly in her appearance. More than that, as the months went by, she started to find fault with Hawley. Little by little she had become an overweight nag; and to make matters worse, she had failed to make a name for herself in the singing world. As she became more frustrated with her career, she more and more frequently denied Crippen that which every husband figures is his right. At the Crippen residence, conjugal bliss had given way to continual bickering.

Then the doctor decided to do something about his dilemma. He was offered, and accepted, the position of manager at Munyon's Patent Remedies in London, England. He figured the move would keep him one step ahead of his creditors, as well as providing him and Cora with a welcome change which might improve the climate of their marriage. Cora had other ideas; she felt that at last she would get an opportunity to appear on the stage of the British Music Hall.

The Crippens arrived in London and took furnished rooms in Bloomsbury. Even before they were comfortably settled, Cora started making the rounds of booking agents, trying to get a high-class singing position. She soon lowered her sights, and was satisfied to accept any singing job she could get. But she had one major drawback. While she made placid Hawley buy her expensive clothing to enhance her appearance when auditioning, she simply couldn't sing. She managed to obtain a few engagements in provincial halls, reaching the pinnacle of her career when she appeared on the same bill as George Formby, Sr., at the Dudley New Empire. A short time after this appearance, she was booed off the stage during another performance. Cora was finding out that the road to fame and fortune was a rocky one.

In 1905 the couple moved from Bloomsbury to 39 Hilldrop Crescent in the Holloway district. It was around this time that twenty-two year old Ethel Le Neve became Dr. Crippen's private secretary. The doctor, now in his forties, fell hard for the winsome Ethel, and she for her part was not averse to the positive vibes coming her way from the little doctor. By 1907 Ethel and Hawley were lovers, and not only in the physical sense, for it is a fact that they sincerely loved and cared for each other. Crippen was charmed by the passive, unassuming Ethel who gave so willingly of herself, in sharp contrast to the domineering, aggressive

Cora. And that closed bedroom door in the Crippen residence had to be an additional factor.

Further aggravating an already explosive situation, Cora started to invite her theatrical acquaintances over to Hilldrop Crescent. Cora and her friends hardly missed a day whooping it up, while the mild-mannered doctor would shrug and pay the bills. One day after the gang had left the house, Hawley meekly mentioned to Cora that maybe she should cut down on the expensive food and drink she was serving her friends. Crippen received a blast that could be heard as far away as Stonehenge on a clear day for even suggesting such a thing. On occasion Cora would do more than party; some evenings she stayed out until the early morning hours, and Crippen knew full well she was having affairs with her broken-down thespian buddies. On the other hand, Cora was aware that her meek husband was playing around, and if his infidelity managed to keep him out of her hair, so much the better. And so life went on at Hilldrop Crescent, both husband and wife leading separate lives, each tolerating the other's indiscretions.

On January 17, 1910, Dr. Crippen strolled in to Lewis and Burrowes, Chemists, on Oxford Street. He purchased five grains of hyoscin hydrobromide, which, in small doses, is used as a sedative. The clerk had Crippen sign the poisons register—taken in large doses hyoscin hydrobromide is a deadly poison—and remembered the transaction because he could not recall ever having sold such a large amount of the drug before. It can be administered in tea or coffee, and is tasteless. Its effects in massive doses are loss of consciousness, paralysis, and death in a matter of hours.

Two weeks later, on the night of January 31, Cora and Hawley had another couple over for an intimate little dinner party followed by a game of cards. Clara and Paul Martinetti were retired entertainers, who were really friends of Cora's. They had a pleasant enough evening, and left at about one thirty in the morning. The Martinettis were the last people to see Cora alive.

The first sign that all was not normal at the Crippen household came when an organization Cora belonged to—the Music Hall Ladies' Guild—received a letter of resignation advising them that she had to rush to America to take care of a seriously ill relative. The letter was signed by Crippen using his wife's professional name, Belle Elmore, per H.H.C. By word of mouth the news spread that Cora was away in America. Some of her close friends remarked that it was strange that she didn't call someone with an explanation. Still, serious illnesses do strike suddenly and the entertainment set seemed satisfied for the time being.

Then Dr. Crippen commenced to make moves which were not designed to enhance our opinion of his intelligence. He pawned some of Cora's jewellery for £200. On February 12, Ethel Le Neve moved into the house on Hilldrop Crescent, causing tongues to wag. As if that wasn't enough to raise an eyebrow or two, Hawley showed up at a Music Hall Ladies' Ball with Ethel. Only a blind man could have failed to notice that the brooch Ethel was sporting over her left breast was the property of Cora Crippen. Cora's friends didn't like the look of things, and started to ask the doctor embarrassing questions. They simply couldn't get over the idea of Cora leaving without so much as a good-bye. Crippen told the ladies that a relative of his who lived in San Francisco was seriously ill. He had been told that this relative had mentioned him in his will, and as the sum involved was substantial, Cora and he thought that one of them should go to California to protect their interests. He couldn't go due to his workload, so Cora had made the trip. That story pacified the ladies for a few more weeks.

Then the Music Hall Ladies' Guild received a telegram from Dr. Crippen advising them that dear Cora herself was seriously ill in California. An official of the Guild, a Miss Hawthorne, visited Hilldrop Crescent, and found the mild little doctor half crazy with worry. She left the house with tears in her eyes, feeling guilty that suspicious thoughts about Crippen should ever have entered her mind.

A few days later Miss Hawthorne received another telegram from Crippen, this time advising her that the worst had happened—Cora had passed away from pneumonia. The ladies of the Guild inquired as to where the funeral would be held; they wanted to send flowers. Dr. Crippen told them that the body was to be cremated and the ashes would be sent back to London. He then inserted a memorial notice in *The Era*, a theatrical newspaper. Immediately after he placed the notice, he left for a short trip to Dieppe, France. When Cora's friends dropped around to his office, they noticed that Ethel wasn't at her desk. The ladies talked about Ethel's absence for a moment or two, but the consensus of opinion was that it was most natural for Crippen to have given his secretary some time off while he was away.

Ethel, however, had accompanied her lover to France, and was continually at his side, consoling and comforting him. She couldn't help but notice that the doctor carried a large leather hatbox with him when he boarded the boat for the English Channel crossing. When she inquired about the box while in Dieppe, the doctor replied that he had misplaced it during the crossing, and it never entered her mind again.

When the pair returned to London, Crippen found that the suspicions concerning his wife's disappearance had grown. It seems that Mr. Nash, a friend of Cora's, had just returned to London from New York. He had been there while Cora had supposedly passed through that city on her way to California. Nash knew Cora well, and knew how she felt about their mutual friends in New York. He found it incredible that she had never once contacted them. When he told Miss Hawthorne of his suspicions, they decided to contact Scotland Yard.

It was over four months since Cora had last been seen when Chief Inspector Walter Dew and Sergeant Arthur Miller knocked on the door of 39 Hilldrop Crescent. Dr. Crippen amicably invited the officers in for a cup of tea. In a somewhat hesitant manner Inspector Dew broached the reason for their visit. It seems some friends had become suspicious when they noticed Miss Le Neve wearing a piece of jewellery belonging to his wife. Dr. Crippen cleared his throat—there was something he had to explain to the officers—you see, his wife wasn't dead at all; she had run off with a music hall performer named Bruce Miller. She had been "carrying on" with him for some time, and had finally picked up and left without a word to any of her friends. He had been too ashamed and embarrassed to tell anyone the truth, so he had made up the story of his wife's death. In reality he thought the two lovers had headed for Chicago.

"Now, doctor, about Miss Le Neve and the jewellery?" Crippen didn't bat an eyelash. He explained that his wife had left in such a hurry she had left her jewellery behind. With a knowing wink Crippen admitted that he had taken up with Ethel Le Neve after his wife ran away, and he was now her lover.

The Inspector looked at the Sergeant and the Sergeant looked at the Inspector. The whole story had a ring of truth to it. The two men conducted a cursory examination of the entire premises and found nothing suspicious. They advised Crippen to place an advertisement in a Chicago paper to assist in finding his wife and still the gossip once and for all. Crippen assured them that he would take their advice. The policemen apologized to Dr. Crippen for the disturbance and returned to the station satisfied that no crime had been committed.

On July 11, 1910, three days after the police visit to Crippen's house, Miss Hawthorne called Inspector Dew for a progress report on the Crippen affair. Dew told Miss Hawthorne that Cora had run away with another man, and that the whole matter was not of concern to the police. Miss Hawthorne informed Dew that something was wrong. Crippen and Le Neve had disappeared. Dew was forced to look into the case again. This time he found out that shortly after his meeting with Crippen on the previous Saturday, July 8, the doctor had written notes to his business associates resigning his position, cleaned out his office, and together with Ethel Le Neve had dropped from sight.

The doctor, who had appeared cool as a cucumber from the first day his wife was noticed to be missing, had finally panicked. Dew questioned Crippen's fellow employees and found a young man who had performed an unusual errand for him. The doctor had asked his colleague to purchase an entire outfit of clothing to fit a boy of sixteen. The young man gave a detailed description of the articles he had purchased for Crippen—brown tweed suit, boots, a hat and an overcoat. After some reflection, Dew came to the conclusion that the clothing had been purchased to disguise Ethel Le Neve in her flight with Crippen. On Tuesday, July 12, Scotland Yard decided to make a thorough search of 39 Hilldrop Crescent. For three days the police peered into and poked at the house while the garden was being dug up. On the third day some loose bricks were discovered under the coal bin in the cellar. The remainder of the floor had mortar between the bricks. The loose bricks were removed, and under a few inches of clay, the police found the remains of Mrs. Crippen—really just "a mass of flesh" wrapped in a pyjama jacket. The body had been dissected and the head was missing.

Inspector Dew checked back on Crippen's actions and found the chemist where he had purchased the hyoscin hydrobromide. Chemical analysis of Cora's remains confirmed that she had met her death as the result of the administration of this drug. On July 16 a warrant was issued for the arrest of Crippen and Le Neve for murder and mutilation. The story was a sensation, and became even more newsworthy because no one seemed to know where to look for the two fugitives. In England during the time Crippen and Le Neve were at large, little else was discussed. Everyone had a theory about the missing pair, and they were constantly being spotted throughout England and the continent by both the police and the public.

In reality Dew was on the right track. Crippen had dressed his lover as a boy, and the two of them had left the country, heading for Rotterdam, Holland. The doctor used the alias of John Philo Robinson, and Ethel took on the identity of his son George. They made their way to Antwerp, Belgium, where on July 20 they booked passage for Quebec City, Canada, on the SS *Montrose*.

It is quite possible that the fugitives would have made good their escape had it not been for the captain of the *Montrose*. Almost from the first hour the pair boarded his ship, the captain noticed the unnatural actions of the Robinsons. He watched the way they held hands, which seemed decidedly odd for a father and son. The second day out of Antwerp he noticed how feminine young Robinson's movements were when he caught a tennis ball on deck. By July 22, the captain was sure that he had Crippen and Le Neve on his ship. Captain Kendall radioed his suspicions to the managing director of the Canadian Pacific Shipping Company in Liverpool, who passed the message along to Scotland Yard. Several messages went back and forth, and Scotland Yard became convinced that they had located the wanted pair. On July 23, Inspector Dew boarded the *Laurentic*, a much faster ship than the *Montrose*, at Liverpool. It was calculated that Dew would overtake his quarry just before the *Montrose* docked in Canada. The case now took on the aspect of a race. Each day the press carried the relative positions of both ships, vividly illustrating the relentless pursuit of the *Montrose* by the *Laurentic*. The distance between the two ships diminished steadily as the *Montrose* approached Canada.

It is well to remember that the passing of radio messages was relatively new to the public. Guglielmo Marconi had established wireless communication across the Atlantic in 1901. This added feature of the chase captured the imagination, not only of England, but of the entire world. At the time of Crippen's flight for freedom, only about one hundred ships were equipped with radios. Within six months over six hundred ships were so equipped, and it is believed the Crippen case was instrumental in making radios a legal requirement for oceangoing vessels.

While all this was going on Crippen and Le Neve thought they had succeeded in evading the authorities, and didn't even know that Cora's body had been discovered. Finally, on July 31 the *Laurentic* caught up with the *Montrose* off Father Point, Quebec. Dew boarded the ship and arranged with Captain Kendall to meet Crippen in the Captain's quarters.

"Good morning, Dr. Crippen, I am Chief Inspector Dew."

"Good morning, Mr. Dew," replied Crippen.

"You will be arrested for the murder and mutilation of your wife, Cora Crippen," stated Dew.

"I am not sorry, the anxiety has been too much."

The dramatic confrontation between detective and murderer was over. Extradition proceedings were dispensed with speedily, and the couple were returned to England to stand trial. Crippen's trial took place in October 1910, and took four days to complete. Public interest in the Crippen trial was greater than in any other heard in London's famous Old Bailey. Huge crowds spilled out onto the street. People stood waiting for hours to catch a glimpse of the accused. The proceedings had all the right ingredients—a love triangle, promiscuous relations, poison, a mutilated body, a missing head, drama on the high seas, a beautiful young girl, and a man of medicine gone wrong.

When it was all over Dr. Crippen was found guilty of the murder of his wife. He was executed on the gallows at Pentonville on November 23, 1910. His last request was that a photograph of Ethel be buried with him, and this request was granted and carried out. Crippen went to his death proclaiming Ethel's innocence.

Two weeks after Crippen's trial, Ethel Le Neve stood trial as an accessory after the fact at the Old Bailey. The evidence against her was flimsy, and it is doubtful if she ever realized that she was doing anything more than running away with her lover. Ethel steadfastly professed that she did not even know of Mrs. Crippen's death. She was acquitted, and left for Canada on the day Dr. Crippen was executed.

After five years she returned to England using an assumed name, Ethel Nelson. She married a clerk called Stanley Smith, and lived a quiet life in Croydon, South London. Only her husband and one other close friend ever knew her real identity. In 1967, fifty-seven years after the Crippen-Le Neve trials, a gentle, grey-haired grandmother, lying close to death in Dulwich hospital, made a last request; that a locket containing a picture of Dr. Hawley Crippen be placed in her casket. So Ethel Le Neve passed from this earth.